PROPHECY

Truth for Today
Light for Tomorrow

Pat Collins C.M.

First published in 2018 by
New Life Publishing, Luton
Bedfordshire LU4 9HG

*Imprimatur: Most Reverend Peter Doyle,
Bishop of Northampton, 31st March 2018.
Nihil obstat: Monsignor Kevin McGinnell Censor Liborum*

The Imprimatur and Nihil obstat are declarations that this work is considered to be free from doctrinal or moral error. It is not implied that those who granted the same agree with the contents, opinion, or statements expressed.

British Library Cataloguing in Publication Data
A catalogue record for this book is available
from the British Library

ISBN 978 1 903623 09 1

Typesetting by Goodnews Books,
Luton, UK www.goodnewsbooks..co.uk
Printed and bound in Great Britain

PROPHECY

TRUTH FOR TODAY
LIGHT FOR TOMORROW

PAT COLLINS C.M.

'Be eager to prophecy' 1 Cor 14:39

New Life Publishing

CONTENTS

continued......

CONTENTS

......continued

FOREWORD

Fr. Pat Collins has written a well-informed and insightful book on the contemporary exercise of the gift of prophecy.

In the past 40 years there has been an explosion of scholarly interest in Christian prophecy. Prior to the mid-1970s almost no one was interested in or wrote about prophecy as a gift available to the church today. The recent interest is due primarily to the Pentecostal and charismatic movements which claim that the gift of prophecy is alive and well, and active in our midst.

In this context, Fr. Collins has done his homework, familiarising himself with recent scholarly works as well as much in the long tradition of the church. But he also writes as a practitioner of prophecy, and one who believes the church needs to hear from God in a direct and convincing manner.

There are, of course, a myriad of issues that one could address, and anyone writing on the subject has to decide which ones are worth pursuing and which not. The flow of the book is helpful in that regard. In the first few chapters, Fr Collins quickly and clearly sketches out the main lines of his understanding of prophecy without involving the reader unnecessarily in the details of competing views. He then does Catholics a great service by rooting his views of prophecy in Catholic Church teaching and tradition.

The next few chapters bring the discussion down to the untidy realities – that prophecy is both divine and human, and always has been. In the immediate, prophecy appears to be very human, and that was as much true for the great prophets of the Old Testament as it is for the Pentecostals and charismatics of today. Nevertheless, Fr. Collins upholds that the prophetic gifts are real, and that when they are exercised well they can be life changing for those to whom the Lord speaks.

I said above that Fr. Collins writes as a practitioner of prophecy. He believes – as I do, as well – that the very exercise of the prophetic gifts and the experience of its hearers open the way for a fuller understanding of what we read about the gift in the scriptures.

> 'Many people, including myself, claim to have had charismatic experiences, including experience of the charism of prophecy. From an interpretive point of view, this is an important point, because first-hand experience of the charism can enable the graced person to interpret what is recounted in the scriptures in a more understanding way.'

In this helpful book, Fr. Collins shares with us the fruits of his experience and in doing so contributes significantly to our understanding of the use and usefulness of prophecy in the church today.

Bruce Yocum, 2017
(Member of the International Executive Council of the Sword of the Spirit Community, and author of *Prophecy: Exercising the Prophectic Gifts of the Spirts in the Church today* (Ann Arbor: Word of Life, 1976)

INTRODUCTION

Back in the 1960s I wrote an article for a student magazine. Having referred to Bob Dylan's song, 'The times they are a-changing,' I went on to talk about the rapid growth in human knowledge and its practical applications. I remember quoting from an American professor who said that human knowledge about the world had doubled between the time of Christ and 1760, between 1760 and 1900, between 1900 and 1950 and again between 1950 and 1960. In other words, knowledge is growing exponentially at an ever accelerating rate.

As this knowledge accumulates in tens of thousands of academic journals and books it is being applied in practical ways by means of such things as engineering, science and technology. As a result, our world is being transformed. The rate and pressure of change caused what futurologist Alvin Toffler referred to in a 1965 magazine article as 'future shock.' Rapid change not only calls into question the assumptions and certainties of bygone years, it also creates all kinds of instability, political, financial and ideological. One has only to recall the financial crash of 2008 and the current long drawn out political and military crisis in the Middle East to see how this is true. During times of crisis when the future is uncertain, people look for some sense of reassurance about what might be about to take place. Some turn to occult forms of divination, others to scientific extrapolations and probabilities for answers, while a minority look to the prophets for intimations of God's providential purposes (Cf. par 2115 *Catechism of the Catholic Church).* Christian prophecy of different kinds is the fascinating subject matter of this book.

Moses (1393-1273 BC) was the great man of prayer in the Old Testament. We are informed that, 'As Moses entered the tent [of meeting] the column of cloud, [a symbol of God's presence], would come down and stand at its entrance' (Ex 33:9). Presumably, he used to pour out his heart to the Lord and tell him about his struggle to lead the Jewish people. Then we are told that, 'The Lord used to speak to Moses face to face, as a person speaks to a friend' (Ex 33:11). The Lord commented on the unique relationship Moses enjoyed with the divine by saying, 'When a prophet of the Lord is among you, I reveal myself to him in visions, I speak to him in dreams. But this is not true of my servant Moses; he is most faithful in all my house. With him I speak face to face, clearly and not in riddles' (Num 12:6-8). One might wonder why Moses was chosen to enjoy such unprecedented intimacy with God. In 1 Pt 5:5 we are told that, 'God opposes the proud but gives grace to the humble,' and Num 12:3 says that, 'Moses was a very humble man, more humble than anyone else on the face of the earth.' The fact that Moses received revelation from God meant that he was equipped to speak to the people as a prophet, someone who was communicating on God's behalf.

In Num 11:24-25 we are told that Moses, 'brought together seventy of their elders and had them stand around the tent. Then the Lord came down in the cloud and spoke with him, and he took of the Spirit that was on him and put the Spirit on the seventy elders. When the Spirit rested on them, they prophesied, but they did not do so again.' It is clear that Moses imparted the prophetic spirit he had received on the seventy elders who helped him to lead the people. As a result they prophesied, but only on that unique occasion. It is thought that what was in question was something like resting in the Spirit. The men went into a trance, and acknowledged the glory of the Lord, but without giving any spoken message. Then we are told in Num 11:26-30 that, 'two men, whose names were Eldad and Medad, had remained in the camp. They were listed among the elders, but did not go out to the Tent of meeting, but prophesied like the others . Then Num 11:7-29 tells us that, 'A young man ran and told Moses, 'Eldad and Medad are prophesying in the camp.' Joshua son of Nun, who had been Moses' aide since youth, spoke up and said, 'Moses, my lord, stop them!' But Moses replied in this magnanimous way, 'Are you jealous for my sake? I wish that all the Lord's people were prophets and that the Lord would put his Spirit on them!'

In the Old Testament prophecy was the prerogative of only a few outstanding men and women. The universal desire of Moses was echoed when the Lord said through the prophet Joel, 'afterwards, I will pour out my Spirit on all people. Your sons and daughters will prophesy, your old men will dream dreams, your young men will see visions. Even on my servants, both men and women, I will pour out my Spirit in those days' (Joel 2:28). You will remember how, on Pentecost morning, St. Peter declared that Joel's promise had been fulfilled through the outpouring of the Spirit (cf. Acts 2:28-29). We are all potential prophets. That is why St Paul says in 1 Cor 14:39, 'my brothers, be eager to prophesy.'

The word prophecy is often misunderstood by religious and non-religious people. I'd like to begin by saying what it is not. It is not a form of clairvoyance, futurology, prediction, extrapolation, soothsaying or divination that enables a person to anticipate what will happen in the future. It is not necessarily a matter of doing something innovative, which is ahead of its time, and much admired by others, such as initiating a social justice project to help the poor and oppressed, or founding a new community, etc. Prophecy is neither a matter of having profound spiritual or theological insight, nor of preaching or teaching in an inspired and inspiring way. Protestant theologian, Eugene Boring has written, 'Modern religious leaders who are suspicious of charismatic phenomena but want to claim the biblical prophets as their heroes can consider the essence of 'prophetic' ministry to be championing the cause of the oppressed in the name of social justice, as in Protestant liberalism, or simply identify 'prophecy' and 'preaching with authority,' so that 'every real preacher is a prophet,' as in some conservative streams of Protestantism.'[1]

Although many of the aforementioned activities are indeed graced by God, that does not mean that they are necessarily prophetic in the way that the scriptures understand the word. The gift of prophecy is the special ability that God gives some members of the Body of Christ to receive and communicate a message that has been revealed by God to a person, as a result of a private revelation from God. It can be pointed out, however, that reception of a message from God is supernatural and transcends the person's intelligence, learning, experience and natural efforts.

Sad to say, although the gift of prophecy is highly esteemed in the Bible, it is widely misunderstood and neglected in the contemporary church. It is my hope that this book will help to explain such things as:

- what prophecy is
- how prophetic revelation is experienced
- how to discern true from false prophecies
- how to minister in a prophetic way
- prophetic intercession
- prophetic leadership
- prophetic ministry, especially when seeking to evangelise those who do not yet know the Lord and his saving mercy and love.

The Nicean Creed professes, 'I believe in the Holy Spirit . . . who spoke through the prophets.' Not surprisingly, therefore, the gift of prophecy can have many good effects. As Paul says in 1 Cor 14:3, 'everyone who prophesies speaks to men for their strengthening, exhortation and comfort.' Those descriptive words are interrelated in so far as they all seek to edify the hearers. Prophecy is rooted in love, expresses love, and helps to build up love in the community. It urges the members to do what they can to be united and to express love to outsiders. No wonder Paul says in 1 Cor 14:1, 'Follow the way of love and eagerly desire spiritual gifts, especially the gift of prophecy.' The reason for this, as Prov 29:18 explains, is because, 'Where there is no prophecy, the people cast off restraint.'

Prophecy: Truth for Today, Light for Tomorrow is a follow up to my *Guided By God: Ordinary and Charismatic Ways of Discovering God's Will* (2015).[2] Inevitably, there is a certain degree of overlap between the two books because both of them explore ways in which God communicates more directly with believers. For example, the subject of prophecy as private revelation is an important one. But because that topic was dealt with in *Guided by God,* it is only mentioned in passing in this book. *Guided by God* also contained a chapter entitled, 'The apparent silence of God,' which argued that believers need to reject many aspects of the prevailing rationalistic, and reductionist, post-Enlightenment world view, in order to be open to the supernatural realm and the possibility of receiving revelations from God. I think that Dr Alice Von Hildebrand was correct when she wrote, 'let us abolish the terms 'conservative' or 'liberal,' the terms 'left' and 'right' which are secularistic. I suggest that we say from now on, 'those who have kept the sense of the supernatural and those who have lost it. That is the great divide, that is the essence.'[3] That topic is not dealt with here at any length, not because it is unimportant, but because it has been done already in *Guided by God.* Although apocalyptic is related to the subject of prophecy it will not be dealt with here. It is my intention to complete a trilogy on how God communicates with us in supernatural ways by writing a book about the end-times.

I have only mentioned one or two of the many reported apparitions and messages of Our Lady. It seems to me that there is a common theme in many of them, i.e., 'repent, pray and fast.' Although I do believe that God's prophetic word has been spoken during some of those Marian apparitions, the messages are mainly beyond the scope of this book. Suffice it to say that commenting on those approved by the Church, David Connolly says, 'When the apparitions are considered from a different angle, the messages foretell increasingly dark days coming upon the Church and there is a very clear link with the Apocalypse. Not only is the theme a recurring one but the intensity of the messages also increases. The 'buzz words' generated by these apparitions include 'Apostasy,' 'the end times,' 'Freemasonry in the Catholic Church,' and 'the arrival of the Antichrist.' If you are interested in the state or fate of the Church, it would be hard to ignore the apparitions as being simply nice, pious additions to the faith. The messages in fact, become rather frightening.'[4]

I want to stress that I do not write as a professional theologian with any particular expertise in this subject. Rather, I write as someone who, through contact with the Charismatic Renewal, has been interested in the nature and practice of prophecy for a long time. While I do quote what some eminent scripture scholars say about particular Biblical texts it is not my intention to use the historical critical method to assess contentious interpretative issues. For example, although the writers of some texts in the Old Testament may not have been consciously aware of the Messianic implications of what they were writing, I believe that those implications were not only implicit in the verses they wrote under the inspiration of the Holy Spirit, they were recognised retrospectively by inspired New Testament writers. As the New Testament scriptures are the revealed word of God, I'm inclined to accept the validity of such interpretations at their face value. Writing about this approach to scripture interpretation, Pope Benedict XVI referred in the 'Foreword' of his *Jesus of Nazareth*, to 'canonical exegesis,' i.e., 'reading the individual texts of the Bible in the context of the whole.' He says that this holistic, Christ centered approach, 'is an essential dimension of exegesis.'[5]

Many people, including myself, claim to have had charismatic experiences, including experience of the charism of prophecy. From an interpretive point of view, this is an important point, because first-hand experience of the charism, can enable the graced person to interpret what is recounted in the scriptures in a more understanding way. For example, in the early Church many of the post apostolic fathers had charismatic experience, and were consequently self-assured in their interpretation of 1 Cor 12:8-9. But once the charisms began to die out, the later fathers were not nearly so self-assured in their exegesis of that passage. For example, St. John Chrysostom (347-407) admitted, 'This whole passage 1 Cor 12:8-12, is very obscure; but the obscurity is produced by our ignorance of the facts referred to, (i.e. experiential knowledge) and by their cessation, being such as when they used to occur, but now no longer take place.'[6]

This interpretive point will have to be kept in mind when looking at what people like St Thomas Aquinas and Prospero Lambertini had to say about the charism of prophecy. There is no compelling evidence that either of them exercised the gift. Conversely, while contemporary scholars who exercise the charisms are more likely to have an experiential understanding of scriptural references to prophecy, exegete Raymond Brown has cautioned, 'No person reared in the 21st century has a world view of a person reared in the 1st century, and therefore it is impossible today to know or duplicate exactly what Paul describes, no matter how genuine the self-assurance of the charismatic.'[7] Jerome Murphy O' Connor echoed that point when he wrote, 'The list of gifts in 1 Cor 12:1-11, is not exhaustive and precise definitions are impossible. Many of the meanings assumed by charismatic groups are arbitrary.'[8] This book will presume, rather than seek to prove, that contemporary religious experiences and those recounted in the New Testament are governed by a principle of continuity and discontinuity.

There is continuity because the same Holy Spirit, who was at work in the New Testament community, is presumably at work today. There is discontinuity because contemporary religious experiences occur within a different cultural milieu and are consequently understood in a slightly different way.

Although, I refer to many public and personal prophecies, I do so merely to give examples of what I am talking about. I do not want to assert however, that, because of that fact, any of them are necessarily true. I believe that all such private revelations are subject to church approval. Even when they are considered to be of supernatural origin and free of doctrinal or moral error, the faithful are not bound to believe them. As Pope Benedict XIV wrote, 'What is to be said of those private revelations which the Apostolic See has approved of?... We have already said that those revelations, although approved of, ought not to, and cannot receive from us any assent of Catholic, but only of human faith, according to the rules of prudence, according to which the aforesaid revelations are probable, and piously to be believed.'[9]
It is my hope that this study, in spite of the fact that it has some of the characteristics of a theological textbook, will help its readers to understand and exercise the neglected but important spiritual gift of prophecy. I have included footnotes and an index to aid those who wish to check references and do further study. If ever the Church needed to hear the prophetic voice of God, it is in these troubled times as we confront the formidable challenges posed by post-modernity. As for myself I'd have to say that I'm fed up listening to merely human opinions about what is needed. I long to hear the voice of the living God. I want to cry out with Samuel, 'Speak Lord, your servant is listening' (1 Sam 3:1)

Finally, I want to express my gratitude to Bruce Yocum for writing the foreword. He was one of the two people who contributed to the well-known prophecy which was delivered in St. Peter's Basilica, Rome, on Easter Monday 1975. The following year he published an influential book entitled *Prophecy*. I also owe a big debt of gratitude to Gerard and Toni Pomfret for all their gracious, conscientious, and professional help in publishing this book which is dedicated to Fr. Bonaventure of the Archdiocese of Moscow together with the Vincentians and Daughters of Charity in Israel who were so kind to me when I visited the land of the prophets in October 2016.

NOTES

1. *The Continuing Voice of Jesus: Christian Prophecy and the Gospel Tradition* (Louisville: John Knox Press, 1991), 35.
2. (Luton: New Life, 2015).
3. *'The Secular War on the Supernatural,'* a talk given at the Faith of Our Fathers conference held in London on 13th June 1998.
4. *One Message One Truth: The Prophecies of the Blessed Virgin at Fatima, Lourdes, Akita and Other Approved Apparitions,* (CreateSpace Independent Publishing, 2012), 1.
5. *Jesus of Nazareth: From the Baptism in the Jordan to the Transfiguration* (London: Bloomsbury, 2007), xix.
6. *Homily , XXIX on 1 Cor, NFP 1st. Series 12:168.*
7. *An Introduction to the New Testament* (New York: Doubleday, 1997), 532.
8. *New Jerome Biblical Commentary,* ed. Brown, Fitzmyer, (London: Geoffrey Chapman, 1990), 810.
9. Prospero Lambertini (Benedict XIV), *Heroic Virtue, vol. 3,* (London: Thomas Richardson and Son, 1852), 395.

ONE

The Nature of Biblical Prophecy

A little girl was drawing a picture. Her mother asked her, 'what are you drawing?' The girl responded, 'it is a picture of God.' The mother said, 'but no one knows what God looks like.' 'They will when they see my picture,' replied her daughter with assurance. Since the dawn of history there have been men and women who have asked, 'Does God exist?' 'If so, what is God like? 'What does God want me to do?' and 'what is going to happen in the future?' Male and female prophets have repeatedly answered those questions on God's behalf. We know from historical records that they tried to do so in pagan as well as Jewish culture.[1]

The Biblical writers were well aware of the many ways in which the pagans had engaged in divination in order to prophesy. For example the philosopher Plato (c. 427-347 BC) was fascinated by inspired diviners such as the Sybil, the Pythia and the priestesses of Dodona. In one of his writings, *Ion* 534d he said, 'And for this reason God takes away the mind of these people and uses them as his ministers, just as he does soothsayers and godly seers, in order that we who hear them may know that it is not they who utter these words of great price, when they are not out of their wits, but that it is God himself who speaks and addresses us through them.'[2] However, in Deut 18:9-14 pagan practices of this kind were roundly condemned in these words, 'When you come into the land that the Lord your God is giving you, you shall not learn to follow the abominable practices of those nations. There shall not be found among you anyone who passes his son or his daughter through the fire, anyone who practices divination or tells fortunes or interprets omens, or makes potions from herbs or a spell binder, or one who consults a non-human spirit that has knowledge, or who inquires of the human dead, for whoever does these things is an abomination to the Lord. And because of these abominations the Lord your God is driving them out before you. You shall be blameless before the Lord your God, for these nations, which you are about to dispossess, listen to fortune-tellers and to those who practice divination. But as for you, the Lord your God has not allowed you to do this.'

In the New Testament St. Paul said in 1 Cor 10:20 that, 'the sacrifices of pagans are offered to demons, not to God.' In 2 Cor 4:4 Paul went so far as to say about the devil that, 'the god of this age has blinded the minds of unbelievers.' This implied that when pagans consulted their gods for prophetic revelation and guidance, the responses they received were likely to be demonic in origin. There is an example of this in Acts 16:16-18, where we are told that, 'Once when we [Paul and Silas] were going to the place of prayer, we were met by a slave girl who had a spirit by which she predicted the future. She earned a great deal of money for her owners by fortune-telling... Finally Paul became so annoyed that he turned around and said to the spirit, 'In the name of Jesus Christ I command you to come out of her!' At that moment the spirit left her.' As a result, St. Augustine wrote, 'All arts [occult] of this sort, therefore, are either nullities, or are part of a guilty superstition, springing out of a baleful fellowship between men and devils, and are to be utterly repudiated and avoided by the Christian.'[3]

AN ARCHETYPAL EXAMPLE OF BIBLICAL PROPHECY

Arguably, there is an archetypal example of the supernatural nature of authentic prophecy, in Daniel chapter two which describes the way in which, in marked contrast to the pagan astrologers, magicians and wise men, Daniel was graced with divine revelation in two interrelated ways. Firstly, when King Nebuchadnezzar had a disturbing dream he asked his advisers to tell him what he had dreamt and then to interpret its meaning and significance. His advisers said to him, 'There is not a man on earth who can do what the king asks! No king, however great and mighty, has ever asked such a thing of any magician or enchanter or astrologer. What the king asks is too difficult. No one can reveal it to the king except the gods, and they do not live among men' (Dan 2:10-11). Because they didn't know what the king had dreamt, they couldn't interpret the dream and were subsequently executed. In contrast, Daniel and his three friends prayed that God would reveal the unknowable to them. We are told how God responded, 'During the night the mystery was revealed to Daniel in a vision' (Dan 2:19). Having described what the king had dreamt, Daniel went on to interpret the dream in an inspired way. Among other things Daniel spoke these remarkably prescient words about the coming kingdom of God, 'the God of heaven will set up a kingdom that will never be destroyed, nor will it be left to another people. It will crush all those kingdoms and bring them to an end, but it will itself endure forever' (Dan 2:44).

Commenting on what he had been able to do, Daniel testified, 'As you were lying there, O king, your mind turned to things to come, and the revealer of mysteries showed you what is going to happen. As for me, this mystery has been revealed to me, not because I have greater wisdom than other living men, but so that you, O king, may know the interpretation and that you may understand what went through your mind' (Dan 2:29-30). By way of response king Nebuchadnezzar declared, 'Surely your God is the God of gods and the Lord of kings and a revealer of mysteries, for you were able to reveal this mystery' (Dan 2:47). What was striking about this incident was the fact that Daniel's ability to know and interpret the king's dream had nothing to do with his natural knowledge, intelligence, or experience. Rather, it was the fruit of pure, unmerited revelation from God. That incident not only pointed to the true nature of prophecy, it also demonstrated the difference between the pagan and Jewish understanding and exercise of the gift. The Old Testament seemed to talk about the nature of prophetic revelation in Is 42:9 were the Lord said, 'new things I now declare; before they spring forth I tell you of them,' and again in Is 48:6-8, 'From now on I will tell you of new things, of hidden things unknown to you. They are created now, and not long ago; you have not heard of them before today. So you cannot say, 'Yes, I knew of them.' You have neither heard nor understood.'

Word meanings

The Old and New Testaments of the Bible contain many references to prophets, seers and prophecies. According to 1 Sam 9:9, in earlier Israel the prophet was commonly referred to as a person who perceives that which does not lie in the realm of natural sight or hearing. Another similar designation, was of a person who sees in a supernatural way (cf. 2 Sam 24:11). Later, in Hebrew, *naba* was the word for the verb 'to Prophecy.' It was mentioned 115 times in the Hebrew text. The related noun *nabi* referred to a person, male or female, who prophesied. It occurred about 309 times in Biblical Hebrew.

The meaning of this essential word can be seen in Exod 7:1 where the Lord said to Moses, 'See, I have made you like God to Pharaoh, and your brother Aaron will be your prophet.' In other words, a prophet speaks on behalf of another.[4] So in the Old Testament, a prophet had a vocation to announce a revealed message, on God's behalf. Several texts make this explicit. God promised Moses, 'Now go; I will help you speak and will teach you what to say' (Ex 4:12). The Lord said to Jeremiah, 'I have put my words in your mouth' (Jer 1:9). God commissioned Ezekiel by saying, 'You must speak my words to them' (Ezek 2:7). And many of the OT prophetic books begin with the words, 'The word of the Lord that came to so and so.' (Hos 1:2; Joel 1:1; Mic 1:1; Zeph 1:1). In the New Testament the Greek for prophecy refers to elevating or asserting one idea over another, especially through the spoken word. A prophet then, was someone inspired by God to tell-forth or to fore-tell by the word of God.[5] That said, it would probably be true to say that in everyday parlance, to prophesy referred to the prediction of future events.[6]

THE ESSENTIAL NATURE OF PROPHECY

Protestant scripture scholar Wayne Grudem wrote his doctoral thesis on biblical prophecy and subsequently examined the subject in a number of his books, notably in *The Gift of Prophecy in the New Testament and Today*[7] and *The Gift of Prophecy in 1 Corinthians*.[8] In an article entitled, 'Why Christians Can Still Prophesy,' he stated,

> 'An examination of the New Testament teaching on this gift will show that it should be defined not as 'predicting the future,' or 'proclaiming a word from the Lord,' or 'powerful preaching' - but rather as *'telling something that God has spontaneously brought to mind* (my italics).'[9]

David Aune, another scholar who has written about prophecy, defines the activity as follows,

> 'The Christian who functions in the prophetic role (whether regularly, occasionally or temporarily) believes that he or she receives divine revelations in propositional form which he or she customarily delivers in oral or written form to Christian individuals and / or groups.'[10]

James Dunne, another well known Protestant New Testament scholar has stated that,

> 'For Paul prophecy is a word of revelation. It does not denote the delivery of a previously prepared sermon; it is not a word that can be summarised up to order, or a skill that can be learned; *it is a spontaneous utterance, a revelation given in words to the prophet to be delivered as it is given* (my italics).'[11]

Catholic scripture scholar Paul Kariuki Njiru writes,

> 'Generally the NT understands the prophet as a person who has insight into the divine will and possesses the power of inspired utterance. Because of the revelation imparted to him by the Spirit, the NT prophet can have a special

knowledge of the future (cf. Acts 11:28) or past without prior information(cf. Jn 4:19); he is able to look into the hearts of those whom he meets (cf. Lk 7:39). However, essentially a prophet proclaims God's message.'[12]

It seems to me that the reference to revelation in the definitions of the scripture scholars is of central importance where a proper understanding of this gift is concerned. Prophecy is not the product of natural intelligence, academic knowledge, or human experience. As Jesus exclaimed, 'I praise you, Father, Lord of heaven and earth, because you have hidden these things [e.g. prophetic messages] from the wise and learned, and revealed them to little children' (Lk 10:21). Evidently, the gift is the result of a supernatural revelation, of a gratuitous nature, which discloses to those who are receptive, something about the mind and purposes of God. So Jer 33:3-4 says, 'Call to me and I will answer you, and will tell you great and hidden things that you have not known.' That is why one ancient writer could say paradoxically, but accurately, 'the prophet when he speaks, remains silent.'[13]

Prophecy as Revelation

As pure Spirit, God, or the mind of God, cannot be known by the power of the unaided human person. St Paul stated that God was incomprehensible when he wrote in 1 Tim 6:16, 'God lives in unapproachable light.' However, in his *Theology of the Body*, St. John Paul II explained how the person word and will of God can become accessible when he wrote, 'The body, in fact, and only the body, is capable of making visible what is invisible, namely the spiritual and the divine. It has been created to transfer into the visible reality of the world the mystery hidden from eternity in

God, and thus to be a sign of it.'[14] When Jesus became incarnate, the incomprehensible mystery of God finally became accessible. As Jn 1:14 says, 'The Word became flesh and made his dwelling among us. We have seen his glory, the glory of the One and Only, who came from the Father, full of grace and truth.' Later on, Jesus himself said, 'whoever sees me sees him who sent me' (Jn 12:45).

Speaking about his own personal experience in 1 Cor 9:1, Paul said that following his conversion experience on the road to Damascus (Acts 9:1-19) he had 'seen Jesus our Lord' when he appeared to him on more than one occasion. For example, in 1 Cor 15:3-8 he said, 'I received what I passed on to you as of first importance: Christ died for our sins according to the Scriptures, that he was buried, that he was raised on the third day according to the Scriptures, and that he appeared to Peter, and then to the Twelve. After that, he appeared to more than five hundred of the brothers at the same time, most of whom are still living, though some have fallen asleep. Then he appeared to James, then to all the apostles, and last of all he appeared to me also, as to one abnormally born.' Paul tells us in Gal 1:16-17 what he did following his conversion, 'I did not consult any man, nor did I go up to Jerusalem to see those who were apostles before I was, but I went immediately into Arabia and later returned to Damascus.' Despite the fact that he didn't seem to be taught anything about Christ and his teaching, Paul said, 'I want you to know, brothers, that the gospel I preached is not something that man made up. I did not receive it from any man, nor was I taught it; rather, *I received it by revelation from Jesus Christ*' (Gal 1:11-12). It sounds as if St Paul was saying that his knowledge of Jesus had been revealed to him in a supernatural, prophetic way. Having received divine revelation he tells us that after three years he visited Jerusalem and met Peter and James. Fourteen years later he visited Jerusalem again, 'this time with Barnabas. I took Titus along also. *I went in response to a revelation* (my italics) and set before them the gospel that I preach among the Gentiles' (Gal 2: 1-2), which apparently received the approval of the apostles. It is quite clear from these texts that the message and actions of Paul were the result of divine revelation rather than being the result of human learning.

In his letters Paul referred to the notion of revelation on a number of occasions. Here are a few examples. In 1 Cor 14:6-7 he said, 'Now, brothers, if I come to you and speak in tongues, what good will I be to you, unless I bring you some *revelation* or knowledge or *prophecy* or word of instruction?' Commenting on this reference to revelation, Gordon D. Fee says, 'Paul uses the word 'revelation' in a variety of ways, but only in the present argument to suggest some kind of utterance which is given by the Spirit for the benefit of the gathered community. Precisely what its content might be and how it would differ from... 'prophecy' is not at all clear.'[15] Later, in 1 Cor 14:26, Paul said, 'When you come together, everyone has a hymn, or a word of instruction, *a revelation,* a tongue or an interpretation.' Commenting on Paul's reference to 'a revelation,' in this verse Gordon D. Fee says that it could, 'very easily be a cover word for all other forms of intelligible inspired speech, including the 'prophecies.'[16] Yet again in 1 Cor 14:30-33, where Paul dealt with the subject of right order in prayer meetings, he said, 'if *a revelation* comes to someone who is sitting down, the first speaker should stop. For you can all *prophesy* in turn so that everyone may be instructed and encouraged. The spirits of prophets are subject to the control of prophets. For God is not a God of disorder but of peace.' Commenting on these verses, Gordon D. Fee says, 'Paul presupposes that while one is speaking, 'a revelation may come to someone who is sitting down.' The use of the verb 'reveal' in this context suggests that for Paul this was the essential character of what was spoken in a prophecy.'[17]

Relation of the Institutional and Prophetic

The author of Eph 2:19 referred to prophetic revelation in relationship to other gifts and ministries when he wrote, 'you are no longer foreigners and aliens, but fellow citizens with God's people and members of God's household, built *on the foundation of the apostles and prophets,* with Christ Jesus himself as the chief cornerstone.' The Apostles were those to whom the mystery of Christ had been revealed and who first preached the Gospel. The prophets referred to here were not those of the Old Testament but rather inspired people in the early Church. The Pauline author is saying that the Church is founded on the institutional role of the apostles, and the charismatic role of the prophets.[18]

Speaking about that relationship, Popes Paul VI and Pope John Paul II had interesting things to share. On September 17th 1973, Pope Paul said in the course of a teaching entitled, 'Spirit and Institution in the Church,' 'The Holy Spirit appointed the Apostles to govern the Church of God; charism [e.g. prophecy] cannot be contrasted with *munus* (i.e. offices of teaching, leading and worship) in the Church, because it is the same Spirit who works in the first place, in and by the *munus*... St Paul himself connects the exercise of charisms with the existing order of the Church' (cf. 1 Cor 14:37-40). John Paul II made a similar point when he spoke to the world congress of ecclesial communities and new movements which met in Rome in 1998, 'I have often had occasion to stress that there is no conflict or opposition in the Church between the institutional dimension and the charismatic dimension, of which movements are a significant expression. Both are co-essential to the divine constitution of the Church founded by Jesus, because they both help to make the mystery of Christ and his saving work present in the world. Together they aim at renewing in their own ways the self-awareness of the Church, which in a certain sense can be called a 'movement,' since she is the realisation in time and space of the Father's sending of his Son in the power of the Holy Spirit' (par. 5).

More recently, proposition 43 of the 2012, post Synodal document on *The New Evangelisation for the Transmission of the Christian Faith* echoed the teaching of Popes Paul and John Paul when it said, 'The hierarchical gifts and the charismatic gifts, flowing from the one Spirit of God, are not in competition but rather co-essential to the life of the Church and to the effectiveness of her missionary action.' As we will see in a later chapter, St. Thomas Aquinas maintained that prophecy is not only the most important charism, all the other charisms are related to it. So the institutional Church needs prophets and prophecies in order to remain true to its nature.

Conclusion

In the parable of the rich man and Lazarus, the latter was brought to Abraham's side when he died, while the former ended up in hell following his death. Abraham said to the rich man 'between us and you a great chasm has been fixed, so that those who want to go from here to you cannot, nor can anyone cross over from there to us' (Lk 16:26). How true. An unbridgeable gulf also separates the natural realm from the supernatural one. Only God can overcome that gulf. It happened in a primordial way when God became man in Jesus. But it also occurs every time human beings are granted prophetic revelation by God. On those precious occasions of grace, heaven touches earth; that which was hidden is made manifest, and that which was unknown is disclosed.

Not only is such a word a shard of divine truth; as God's divine word it contains the power to fulfill what it says. As Is 55:11 assures us, 'my word that goes out from my mouth: It will not return to me empty, but will accomplish what I desire and achieve the purpose for which I sent it.'

NOTES

1. See David E. Aune, *Prophecy in Early Christianity and the Ancient Mediterranean World* (Grand Rapids: Eerdmans, 1983), 24-77.
2. Ibid., 39.
3. St. Augustine, *'On Christian Doctrine,' Readings in Medieval History: The Early Middle Ages,* ed. Patrick J. Geary (Toronto: University of Toronto Press, 2010), 36.
4. 'To Prophesy' in *Expository Dictionary of the Old Testament,* ed. Merrill Unger & William White (Nashville: Thomas Nelson Publishers, 1980), 310-12.
5. Sam Storms, 'Prophets and Prophecy' in *NIV Zondevan Study Bible* (Grand Rapids: Zondervan, 2015), 2668-69.
6. *Chambers Dictionary of Etymology* (London: Chambers Harrap, 2012), 850.
7. (Wheaton: Crossway Books, 2000).
8. (Eugene Or: Wipf & Stock Publishers, 1999).
9. Wayne A Grudem, 'Why Christians Can Still Prophesy,' *Christianity Today* (Sept 16th 1988): 29.
10. David Hill, *New Testament Prophecy* (Atlanta: John Knox Press, 1979), 7.*11*. James D. G. Dunn, *Jesus and the Spirit* (London: SCM, 1975), 228.
12. *Charisms and the Holy Spirit's Activity in the Body of Christ* (Rome: Gregorian University Press, 2002), 157-8:
13. Philo of Alexandria, *Qui rerum, 266,* in *Les Oeuvres de Philon d' Alexandre,* vol. 15 (Paris: 1966), 300.
14· *Man and Woman he Created Them: A Theology of the Body* (Boston: Pauline Media, 2006), 203.
15. Gordon Fee, *The First Epistle to the Corinthians: The New International Commentary on the New Testament* (Grand Rapids: Eerdmans, 1987), 662.
16. Gordon Fee, *The First Epistle to the Corinthians,* op. cit., 691.
17. Gordon Fee, *The First Epistle to the Corinthians,* op. cit., 695.
18. Cf. Ruldolf Schnackenberg, *The Epistle to the Ephesians: A Commentary* (Edinburgh: T & T Clark, 1991), 122-3.

TWO

Types of Prophet and Prophecy

Early in 2015, twenty six year old Niamh Geaney from Dublin set out to find her look alike within 28 days. With the help of two friends she set up the Twin Strangers Facebook page, calling for anyone in the world who looked like her to get in touch. A young woman called Karen Branigan contacted Niamh. It turned out that she lived less than an hour away. The pair met up to see just how similar they were. Anyone who saw a photo of the two women, taken side by side, would think they were identical twins. In reality, there is no genetic relationship between them. I say this because in the Old and New Testaments a number of inspired forms of understanding are mentioned, such as wisdom and knowledge which are virtually inseparable. That said, they should not be confused with prophetic revelation.

In Is 11:2 we read, 'And the Spirit of the Lord shall rest upon him, the spirit of wisdom and understanding.' These are gifts of inspiration. In 1 Cor 12:8, St Paul says that they can find verbal expression as the utterance of wisdom and knowledge. Two questions arise. What is the nature of these revelatory gifts, and how are they different from the charism of prophecy? Scripture scholars and theologians alike seem to be agreed that it is hard to distinguish wisdom from knowledge. They seem to be inseparable like identical twins. However, I'd suggest that there are subtle differences between them.

A. The Gift of Wisdom

In Jm 3:17 we read 'the wisdom from above is first pure, then peaceable, gentle, open to reason, full of mercy and good fruits, impartial and sincere.' It is a practical, God given ability, to discern what is the will of God in specific circumstances. One could argue that James exercised that gift at the Council of Jerusalem, when he said that Gentiles did not need to be circumcised. 'It is my judgment, therefore, that we should not make it difficult for the Gentiles who are turning to God. Instead we should write to them, telling them to abstain from food polluted by idols, from sexual immorality, from the meat of strangled animals and from blood. For the law of Moses has been preached in every city from the earliest times and is read in the synagogues on every Sabbath' (Acts 15:19–21). In his letter James advised, 'if any of you lacks wisdom he should ask God, who gives generously to all without finding fault, and it will be given to him. But when he asks, he must believe and not doubt, because he who doubts is like a wave of the sea, blown and tossed by the wind. That man should not think he will receive anything from the Lord' (Jm 1:5-6).

B. The Gift of Knowledge

The gift of knowledge probably refers to a God given ability to comprehend something of the mystery of God. In Jn 16:13 Jesus said, 'When the Spirit of truth comes, he will guide you into all the truth, for he will not speak on his own authority, but whatever he hears he will speak.' In 1 Jn 2:27 we read, 'As for you, the anointing you received from him remains in you, and you do not need anyone to teach you. But as his anointing teaches you about all things.' Paul wrote in 1 Cor 2:10-16, 'The Spirit searches all things, even the deep things of God... We have not received the spirit of the world but the Spirit who is from God... 'For who has known the mind of the Lord that he may instruct him?' But we have the mind of Christ.'

C. Prophecy

Not surprisingly, the Old and New Testaments make it clear that, like wisdom and knowledge, prophecy is a revelatory gift of the Holy Spirit (cf. Num 24:2-3; 2 Sam 23:2; Neh 9:30; Is 59:21; Ex 11:5; Mic 3:8; Zec 7:12; 1 Cor 12:10). St. Thomas Aquinas observed in the *Summa Theologica*: 'In a broad sense the subject of prophecy is whatever man knows by God's revelation. It differs from other charisms such as wisdom and knowledge and understanding of speech, the subjects of which man can know by natural reason, though not as perfectly as by God's light... *Prophecy is knowledge imprinted on the prophet's mind by the teaching of God's revelation* (my italics).'[1] So although, wisdom and knowledge are first cousins of prophecy, they are distinct gifts.

Types of Prophet

Students of prophecy in the Old Testament discern two main types, ecstatic and verbal. It would seem that the earlier prophets sometimes went into a Spirit induced trance or rapture of a prophetic kind. To the modern ear it sounds something like what Charismatics refer to as 'resting in the Spirit,' or being 'slain in the Spirit.' For instance in 1 Sam 19:18-24, we are told that, 'When David had fled and made his escape, he went to Samuel at Ramah and told him all that Saul had done to him. Then he and Samuel went to Naioth and stayed there. Word came to Saul: 'David is in

Naioth at Ramah'; so he sent men to capture him. But when they saw a group of prophets prophesying, with Samuel standing there as their leader, the Spirit of God came upon Saul's men and they also prophesied. Saul was told about it, and he sent more men, and they prophesied too... So Saul went to Naioth at Ramah. But the Spirit of God came even upon him, and he walked along prophesying until he came to Naioth. He stripped off his robes and also prophesied in Samuel's presence. He lay that way all that day and night. This is why people say, 'Is Saul also among the prophets?' George Montague points out that it is significant that throughout this passage there is no indication of any intelligible word being uttered by the prophets. They simply experienced the Spirit of the Lord in a non-rational, non-verbal way.[2] That said, of course, prophets like Samuel did utter prophecies, e.g., the message he gave to Eli about the way he had mishandled his wayward sons. Indeed we are told in 1 Sam 3:19 that, 'As Samuel grew up, the Lord was with him and let none of his words fall to the ground,' i.e., all that he said was fulfilled, thereby entitling him to be referred to as a prophet (cf. Mt 12:36-37). Later in the Old Testament, the emphasis moved from trance like states to the prophetic message. When we look at the age of classical prophecy, the expression 'The Spirit of the Lord came to so-and-so,' was replaced by the phrase, 'the word of the Lord came to so-and-so.'

Although it would probably be true to say that the classical prophets did not act in the way their ecstatic predecessors did, nevertheless, there was a transcendental, mystical dimension to their spirituality. I will return to this topic in chapter eight. It enabled them to forget about themselves and to become absorbed in a contemplative way in the presence of God. Isaiah's encounter with the holiness of God in the temple is an outstanding instance of such a numinous experience (cf. Is 6:1-13). As prophets experienced that awesome, and fascinating mystery they became conscious of the nature, word and will of the Lord. As a result they were empowered to proclaim to the people what the Lord had revealed to them.

Scholars distinguish between different kinds of prophet. Firstly, there were Major Prophets who wrote, such as Isaiah, Jeremiah, Ezekiel, Daniel, and the so-called 'Minor Prophets' like Habakkuk and Zephaniah, who wrote shorter books . They are mentioned in Sir 49:10. Secondly, there were the speaking prophets, such as Nathan, who confronted David (2 Samuel 12), Micaiah, who saw the Lord sitting on His throne (1 Kings 22); and Ahijah, who condemned Jeroboam (1 Kings 14). Thirdly, there were those who acted in a prophetic way. For example, God told Isaiah to go barefoot and naked for three years (Isaiah 20:2). Jeremiah was told to wear a yoke on his neck to emphasise God's message that King Zedekiah should submit to Nebuchadnezzar (Jeremiah 27). Ezekiel was called, on one occasion, to pack all his bags and carry them around Jerusalem in the sight of the people as a sign that, if they did not repent, God would send them into exile (Ezekiel 12).

It is worth mentioning that, whereas we are familiar with the names of male prophets in the Old Testament, such as Samuel, Amos, Jeremiah, Isaiah, Ezekiel, and in the New Testament men such as John the Baptist and Agabus, we are not so familiar with female prophets who are also mentioned in both Testaments. For example, in the Old Testament there were women like, Miriam (cf. Mic 6:4), Deborah (cf. Jud 4:4), Huldah (cf. 2 Kings 22:14), Noadiah (cf. Neh 6:14) and Isaiah's wife (cf. Is 8:3), and in the New Testament, Anna (cf. Lk 2:36), and the four daughter's of

Philip (Acts 21:9). It is interesting to note that while women were not supposed to give teachings in public, they were permitted to prophesy. Finally, there is reason to think that at certain times there were bands or schools of prophets. Apparently, 'sons of prophets' lived together for instruction and worship under Samuel, Elijah, and Elisha (cf. 1 Sam. 10:11; 19:19–20; 2 Kings. 2:3, 5; 4:38; 6:1). Not all the 'sons of the prophets' claimed to have a supernatural gift; they were simply trained as religious teachers, while some inspired prophets had received no training in the schools.

TYPES OF PROPHECY

As has already been mentioned, the prophets were people who were chosen by God to speak on God's behalf. Describing them, the *Catechism of the Catholic Church* says in par. 64, 'Through the prophets, God forms his people in the hope of salvation, in the expectation of a new and everlasting Covenant intended for all, to be written on their hearts. The prophets proclaim a radical redemption of the People of God, purification from all their infidelities, a salvation which shall include all the nations. Above all, the poor and humble of the Lord will bear this hope.'

A. TRUTH FOR TODAY

The subtitle of this book, *Truth for Today, Light for Tomorrow*, is a succinct description of the purpose of prophecy. The first thing it does is to spell out the truth, as God sees it, and applies it to the social, political and religious circumstances of the time. The prophet's primary role was to make known the holiness of God and the obligation associated with the covenant agreement between God and the people, to denounce injustice, idolatry, empty ritualism, and to call God's people to repentance and faithfulness. In the pre-exilic period the prophets often denounced rampant injustice and the exploitation of the poor. In the post-exilic period they focused attention on the promise of national renewal and the spiritual blessings that would come from trusting God and doing God's will.

Prophets such as Amos, Micah, and Isaiah addressed the nature of true religion by stressing the link that should exist between genuine worship and social justice. For example, in Zech 7:5-10 the Lord asked, 'When you fasted and mourned in the fifth and seventh months for the past seventy years, was it really for me that you fasted?' Then the Lord stated, 'This is what the Lord Almighty says: 'Administer true justice; show mercy and compassion to one another. Do not oppress the widow or the fatherless, the alien or the poor. In your hearts do not think evil of each other.' Again in Is 1:13-17 we read, 'Stop bringing meaningless offerings! Your incense is detestable to me... Stop doing wrong, learn to do right! Seek justice, encourage the oppressed. Defend the cause of the fatherless, plead the case of the widow.' In similar vein the prophet Hosea says, 'For I desire mercy, not sacrifice, and acknowledgement of God rather than burnt offerings' (Hos 6:6). Amos warned, 'For three sins of Israel, even for four, I will not turn back. They sell the righteous for silver, and the needy for a pair of sandals. They trample on the heads of the poor as upon the dust of the ground and deny justice to the oppressed. Father and son use the same girl and so profane my holy name. They lie down beside every altar on garments taken in pledge. In the house of their god they drink wine taken as fines' (Am 2:6-8).

In the New Testament Jesus echoed those sentiments when he

said, ''These people honour me with their lips, but their hearts are far from me' (Mt 15:8). In other words there was a disconnect between what they said with their lips during times of worship, and what they did in their everyday lives such as the exploitation of, or neglect of the poor. Jesus displayed his righteous anger against this kind of social injustice when he, 'entered the temple and drove out all who sold and bought in the temple, and he overturned the tables of the money-changers and the seats of those who sold pigeons. He said to them, 'It is written, 'My house shall be called a house of prayer,' but you make it a den of robbers' (Mt 21:12). It would appear that the poor were being ripped off financially when they bought temple currency and sacrificial animals, without blemish, within the temple precincts. In all these cases, prophecy was not so much light for the future as truth for today.

B. Light for the future

While most prophecies shone the light of truth on the circumstances of the time, there were prophecies that did foretell things to come. As the Lord says in Is 46:10, 'I make known the end from the beginning, from ancient times, what is still to come.' Again in Amos 3:7 we read, 'Surely the Sovereign Lord does nothing without revealing his plan to his servants the prophets.' As chapters five and six of this book indicate, from Moses onwards, the prophets had been foretelling the coming of a future messiah. Prophets also made specific predictions of other events, e.g., Jeremiah saying that Jews would return from exile in Babylon, after seventy years. According to the Bible one of the ways of discerning true from false prophecy was the fact that true prophecies, the ones that came from the mind of God rather than the mind and will of man, were fulfilled. For example in Ezek 12:

27-28 the Lord says, 'Son of man, the house of Israel is saying, 'The vision he sees is for many years from now, and he prophesies about the distant future.' 'Therefore say to them, 'This is what the Sovereign Lord says: None of my words will be delayed any longer; whatever I say will be fulfilled, declares the Sovereign Lord.'' Again in Am 3:7 we read, 'Surely the Sovereign Lord does nothing without revealing his plan to his servants the prophets.' That verse finds an echo in the New Testament where John says, 'in the days when the seventh angel is about to sound his trumpet, the mystery of God will be accomplished, just as he announced to his servants the prophets' (Rev 10:7).

PROPHETIC TYPOLOGY

Scripture scholars distinguish between Old Testament prophecies which were fulfilled uniquely in Christ and those that were fulfilled typologically. For example, it is pretty obvious that Is 53:5-6 which reads, 'But he was pierced for our transgressions; he was crushed for our iniquities; upon him was the chastisement that brought us peace, and with his wounds we are healed. All we like sheep have gone astray; we have turned - every one - to his own way; and the Lord has laid on him the iniquity of us all' was fulfilled uniquely by Jesus on Good Friday. According to the *Merriam - Webster Dictionary* typology is a doctrine of theological types which maintains that things in Christian belief are prefigured or symbolised by things in the Old Testament. Speaking about typology, the *Catechism of the Catholic Church* says, in pars 128-9, 'The Church, as early as apostolic times, and then constantly in her Tradition, has illuminated the unity of the divine plan in the two Testaments through typology, which discerns in God's works of the Old Covenant pre-figurations of what he accomplished in the fullness of time in the person of his incarnate Son. Christians therefore read the Old Testament in the light of Christ crucified and risen.'

Let's look at an extended example which is taken from the writings of Scott Hahn. Having stated that the Gospel of Matthew is very Jewish, he says that the evangelist saw Jesus as the new Moses. In a brilliant passage he says, 'As Israel passed through the waters of the Red Sea as God's beloved son, Jesus too passes through water in his Baptism and is also called God's Son. As Israel left the waters to be tested in the desert for 40 years, following his Baptism Jesus was immediately driven into the wilderness to be tested for 40 days and 40 nights. When you hear the story of Jesus' testing by the devil on the First Sunday of Lent, be sure to notice how his temptations correspond to Israel's in the wilderness. Jesus is tempted by hunger, which had caused Israel to grumble against God. Then he is dared to put God to the test, to question God's care for him. This recalls the Israelites' testing of God at Meribah and Massah. Finally, he is tempted to worship a false god, which Israel actually did in creating the golden calf. Notice also that each time Jesus rebukes the devil, he quotes Moses. Each quote is carefully chosen from a key section in the Book of Deuteronomy in which Moses warns the people to learn a lesson from their unfaithfulness in the desert. As Moses climbed a mountain to bring the people the Law of God and the covenant, Jesus climbs a 'mount' and delivers a new Law and a new covenant. Moses commanded the Israelites to commemorate God's covenant in the Passover celebration. Jesus institutes a new Passover, the Eucharist. As Moses sealed the Old Covenant with the blood of sacrificial animals, Jesus seals the New Covenant with his own blood, and even quotes Moses' words: 'This is the blood of my covenant.' Matthew sees Jesus leading a new

Exodus: this time, not from a political tyrant whose armies are drowned in the sea, but from sin and death, which are destroyed in the waters of Baptism. It can't be stressed enough that, for Matthew, this is salvation history, not literary allusion. Matthew isn't writing a clever story designed to evoke memories of Moses and the Exodus. Matthew, like all devout Jews of the time, believed that God's saving words and deeds in the past formed a kind of template for what God would say and do to save Israel in the future. Moses himself had promised that a prophet like him would one day arise (Cf. Deut 18:15). And the prophets increasingly talked about a 'new exodus' that would return the scattered Israelites and bring them to Zion for a great festal gathering with all the nations.'[1] So in the Old Testament Scriptures the entire New Testament was foreshadowed. In the New Testament dispensation, all the Old Testament Scriptures were fulfilled. As Saint Augustine put it: 'The New Testament is concealed in the Old, and the Old Testament is revealed in the New.'[2] Only when the elegance of typology is comprehended can the mystery of Scriptural prophecy be fully appreciated.

THE GREATEST OLD TESTAMENT PROPHET

Who was the greatest of the Old Testament prophets? It is a debatable point. One could argue that it was Moses because God spoke to him face to face, or Elijah because he was expected to reappear before the coming of the Messiah (cf. Mt 11:14), and also because he appeared with Moses at the transfiguration of Jesus (cf. Mt 17:3). However, it seems to me that John the Baptist takes pride of place. In Lk 1:67-76 we are told that his father Zechariah was filled with the Holy Spirit and prophesied, 'And you, my child, will be called a prophet of the Most High; for you will go on before the Lord to prepare the way for him (i.e. the Messiah).

In Lk 3:2 we are told that, 'the word of God came to John son of Zechariah in the desert.' This is the Bible's typical way of referring to the reception of prophetic revelation. So after more than 400 years when there was a virtual absence of prophetic utterance (cf. 1 Macc 9:27), the gift was unexpectedly restored. Jesus spoke about John. Commenting on his cousin, he said on one occasion, 'But what did you go out to see? A prophet? Yes, I tell you, and more than a prophet. This is the one about whom it is written: 'I will send my messenger ahead of you, who will prepare your way before you.' I tell you, among those born of women there is no one greater than John' (Lk 11:26-27). It seems clear from these statements that Jesus thought that John as the new Elijah (cf. Lk 1:17), was even greater than any of the Old Testament prophets.[5] And then he added, 'yet the one who is least in the kingdom of God is greater than he' (Lk 7:28). It could be argued that Jesus was not saying that the least among the Christians, is greater than John as an Old Testament figure. Rather, the Christian who is least, i.e., in terms of humility and poverty of spirit, is greater than John.[6] As Jesus said, 'Whoever welcomes this little child in my name welcomes me; and whoever welcomes me welcomes the one who sent me. For he who is least among you all — *he is the greatest* (my italics)' (Lk 9:48).

JESUS AS THE PROPHET PAR EXCELLENCE

It goes without saying that Jesus, the new Moses, who was foretold in Deut 18:15; 18, was by far the greatest of the prophets. Commenting on this fact Joachim Jeremias said in his *New Testament Theology*, 'The unanimous verdict on him was that he was a prophet.'[7] More recently, Professor Paula Fredricksen has written, 'Jesus is... a prophet who preached the coming apocalyptic Kingdom of God. His message coheres both with that of his predecessor and mentor, John the Baptiser, and with that of the movement that sprang up in his name. This Jesus thus is *not* primarily a social reformer with a revolutionary message; nor is he a religious innovator radically redefining the traditional ideas and practices of his native religion. His urgent message had not the present so much as the near future in view.' The Jews of his day repeatedly endorsed this fact. For example, when people witnessed the feeding of the five thousand, they said, 'This is indeed the prophet who is come into the world' (Jn 6:4). When the Samaritan woman told Jesus she had no husband, 'Jesus said to her, 'You are right when you say you have no husband. The fact is, you have had five husbands, and the man you now have is not your husband. What you have just said is quite true.' 'Sir,' the woman said, *'I can see that you are a prophet'* (Jn 4:17-20). Jeremias says that, while Jesus did not reject the judgment that he was a prophet, the title was not a full description of who he was or the task for which he had been sent. Nevertheless, he included himself among the ranks of the prophets.[8]

While many people accepted that Jesus was a prophet, many did not. For example in Mk 6:4-we are told about an occasion when, Jesus said to his listeners, 'Only in his home town, among his relatives and in his own house is a prophet without honour.' He could not do any miracles there, except lay his hands on a few sick people and heal them. And he was amazed at their lack of faith.' It would appear that his legal brothers and sisters were among those who did not accept that he was a prophet. They are mentioned in Mt 13:55-56, 'Is not this the carpenter's son? Is not his mother called Mary? And are not his brothers James and Joseph and Simon and Judas? And are not all his sisters with us?' Presumably, these were the names of Jesus' legal siblings who were the children of Joseph by a previous marriage.[9] We are told that when, 'he went home, and the crowd gathered again, so that they could not even eat. And when his family heard it, they went out to seize him, for they were saying, 'He is out of his mind' (Mk 3:20-21). We are also told that on another occasion the crowd thought he was insane (cf. Jn 10:20).

As God, Jesus was completely at one with his Father, as man he was sinless and therefore there was no impediment in his heart to prevent him from receiving the word of the Father in all its pristine purity. Whenever Jesus prayed he did so in the context of a vivid awareness of the love that the Father had for him. Speaking about that love Pope Paul VI said in his apostolic exhortation *Gaudete in Domino,* 'He knows that He is loved by His Father... This certitude is inseparable from the consciousness of Jesus. It is a presence which never leaves Him all alone It is an intimate knowledge which fills Him:...' the Father knows me and I know the Father' (Cf. Jn. 16:32). It is an unceasing and total exchange: 'All I have is yours and all you have is mine' (Jn 10:15).' As a result, Jesus enjoyed the beatific vision in his human nature. Pius XII, wrote in par. 75 of his Encyclical *Mystici Corporis,* 'The knowledge and love of our Divine Redeemer, of which we were the object from the first moment of His Incarnation, exceed all that the human intellect can hope to grasp. For hardly was He conceived in the womb of the Mother of God when He began to enjoy the Beatific Vision.' Commenting on this point, Karl Rahner suggested that Jesus' human soul always enjoyed the direct vision of God and God's love. The knowledge implicit in that vision was not necessarily reflected upon or objectified in a conceptual way. As a man Jesus had to learn. Through his interaction with life he had to find out and conceptualise what he already knew in a non-thematic way as God.[10] It is significant that the scriptures clearly attest that, as a person with a human nature, he grew in knowledge like the rest of us (Cf. Lk 2:22; Heb 4:15).

No doubt Jesus poured out his love, thoughts, feelings and desires to the Father in his prayer. For example, on one occasion he prayed, 'I praise you, Father, Lord of heaven and earth, because you have hidden these things from the wise and learned, and revealed them to little children. Yes, Father, for this was your good pleasure' (Mt 11:25-26). In the course of his prayer, the Father poured out his love, thoughts and feelings to Jesus. In this way the Father's presence and desires were experienced directly by him. He testified, 'My teaching is not mine, but his who sent me' (Jn 7:16). On another occasion he said, 'What I speak, I speak just as the Father has told me' (Jn 12:50). In *Jesus of Nazareth: From the Baptism in the Jordan to the Transfiguration*, Pope Benedict XVI says that, 'Jesus' teaching is not the product of human learning, of whatever kind. It originated from immediate contact with the Father, from 'face-to-face' dialogue – from the vision of the one who rests close to the Father's heart. It is the Son's word. Without this inner grounding, his teaching would be pure presumption.'[11] Although the apostles acknowledged that Jesus was unusually close to the Father, e.g., when they asked him to teach them to pray, they did not quite grasp how intimate his union with God really was. You will recall how Jesus said to Philip, 'How can you say, 'Show us the Father'? Don't you believe that I am in the Father, and that the Father is in me? The words I say to you are not just my own. Rather, it is the Father, living in me, who is doing his work' (Jn 14:10-11). Surely, this is a description of unadulterated prophecy.

Jesus wanted to pass on his prophetic gift to the believers. Because they would be one with him, as he was one with his Father (cf. Jn 10:30; 15:4), he was able to declare, 'the things I do you will do' (Jn 14:12). There is a verse in Jn 16:13-14 where Jesus promised, 'when he, the Spirit of truth, comes, he will guide you into all truth. He will not speak on his own; he will speak only what he hears, and he will tell you *what is yet to come.*' In this verse Jesus seems to be saying that although the disciples did not fully understand all that he had revealed to them, in the future, with the Spirit's help, they would appropriate its true meaning and implications. That said, it would seem that his reference to 'what is yet to come' implied that public, biblical revelation, which is complete, would be augmented by private revelation which would spell out the implications of the former, both for the present and for the future. In Is 41:22-23 there are verses that throw light on what Jesus was getting at, 'Bring in [your idols] to tell us what is going to happen. Tell us what the former things were, so that we may consider them and know their final outcome. Or declare to us *the things to come*, tell us what the future holds, so we may know that you are gods.' The Lord was challenging the prophets of the pagan nations to ask, in vain of course, that their worthless idols would predict the future in the accurate way the Jewish prophets of the true God were able to do. So in Jn 16:14 Jesus seemed to be saying that the Holy Spirit would help the believers to have prophetic intimations of what is yet to come, just as he himself had. Quoting from Is 54:13, Jesus stated, 'It is written in the prophets: 'They shall all be taught by God' (Jn 6:45).

St Paul on Characteristics of New Testament Prophecy

St Paul wrote a good deal about the prophetic gift, especially in 1 Cor 12-14. It is worth mentioning that he says in 1 Cor 12:4-7 that, like the other charisms, the gift of prophecy has five characteristics.

- Firstly, he says, 'there are different kinds of gifts' (1 Cor 12:4). The Greek word for gifts is *charismata*. The charism of prophecy is not earned or merited in any way. Rather it is a gratuitous gift of God.
- Secondly, Paul describes the gifts as *pneumaticos*, i.e., supernatural (cf. 1 Cor 12:1). In other words, prophecy is not based on a natural ability of any kind. As St. Peter attested, 'prophecy never had its origin in the will of man, but men spoke from God as they were carried along by the Holy Spirit' (2 Pet 1:21).
- Thirdly, Paul said that, 'There are different kinds of service' (1 Cor 12:5). The Greek word used here is *diakoniai*, from which we get the English word deacon. The gift of prophecy is not a power whereby one person lords it over others, but rather it is a way of putting a towel around one's waist and serving the community in a humble and loving manner.
- Fourthly, Paul said, 'There are different kinds of working' (1 Cor 12:6). The Greek word used here is *energmata*, meaning energy or power. So prophecy is a Spirit empowered ability to act on God's behalf by speaking a word of revelation. In Eph 1:19-20 Paul said, 'That power is like the working of his mighty strength, which he exerted in Christ when he raised him from the dead.'
- Fifthly, Paul says, 'the manifestation of the Spirit is given

for the common good' (1 Cor 12:7). The Greek word that is used here is *phaneroisis*. So, when a prophecy is spoken, it is like an epiphany, a disclosure of the awesome presence and glory of the Lord. That is why Paul said in 1 Cor 14: 24-25 that, 'if an unbeliever or someone who does not understand comes in while everybody is prophesying, he will be convinced by all that he is a sinner and will be judged by all, and the secrets of his heart will be laid bare. So he will fall down and worship God, exclaiming, 'God is really among you!' While the gift of prophecy may be a real blessing for the person to whom it has been granted, it is given for the common good and the up-building of the Christian community.

Conclusion

Although a prophecy may be genuine, it doesn't necessarily mean that it will be fulfilled to the letter. It seems to me that when a prophecy is addressed to people who are free to choose how they will respond to the word of the Lord, they can influence the outcome. That principle was expressed by Jeremiah. Having predicted the destruction of Jerusalem he said, 'Now reform your ways and your actions and obey the Lord your God. Then the Lord will relent and not bring the disaster he has pronounced against you' (Jer 26:13-14). There are examples of how this principle was illustrated by events. For example, in Is 38:1-7, we are told that, when he was extremely ill, King Hezekiah asked the prophet Isaiah whether he was going to die. The prophet declared, 'Put your house in order, because you are going to die; you will not recover' (Is 38:1). Not surprisingly the king was distraught and poured out his heart to God asking for a reprieve.' Evidently, the Lord was touched by his prayer, and we are told,

'Then the word of the Lord came to Isaiah: 'Go and tell Hezekiah, 'This is what the Lord, the God of your father David, says: I have heard your prayer and seen your tears; I will add fifteen years to your life' (Is 38:4-5). On another occasion the prophet Jonah was commanded by God to go to the city of Nineveh and to prophesy against it, 'for their great wickedness is come up before me' (Jon 1:2). When Jonah arrived in the city he cried out, 'in forty days Nineveh shall be overthrown.' When he heard this prophecy the king of Nineveh put on sackcloth, sat in ashes, and proclaimed a time of fasting, prayer, and repentance. When God saw the repentant hearts of the people, God spared the city.' As it says in Jer 18:8, 'if that nation, concerning which I have spoken [in a prophecy], turns from its evil, I will relent of the disaster that I intended to do to it.'

It is clear in the New Testament that Jesus was aware of the impending disaster that threatened the very existence of Jerusalem and its temple. He felt that if the people responded to him and his message, the city and the temple could be spared. But in Mt 23:37-39 we read that, unlike the people of Nineveh, those of Jerusalem did not repent, so Jesus exclaimed, 'O Jerusalem, Jerusalem, you who kill the prophets and stone those sent to you, how often I have longed to gather your children together, as a hen gathers her chicks under her wings, but you were not willing. Look, your house is left to you desolate.' Jerusalem and its temple were in fact destroyed in 70 A.D. This point will be well worth remembering when various prophecies are mentioned in other chapters of this book. They are addressed to people who are free. If they respond in a positive manner they can have an influence upon the outcomes predicted by the Lord. If not, those outcomes kick-in as foretold.

NOTES

1. *Summa Theologiae: A Concise Translation,* ed., Timothy McDermott (London: Methuen, 1989), 446.
2. George Montague, S.M., *Riding the Wind: Learning the Ways of the Spirit* (Ann Arbor: Word of Life, 1977), 54.
3. *https://www.catholicfidelity.com/apologetics-topics/kingdom/matthew-gospel-of-fulfillment-by-scott-hahn/*
4. *Quaest. In Hept.* 2,73: PL34, 623 cited in the *Catechism of the Catholic Church.*
5. Cf. *The Catechism of the Catholic Church,* par. 719.
6. Cf. note on Mt 11:11 in *NIV Study Bible* (Grand Rapids: Zondervan, 2002), 1486.
7. (London: SCM, 1981), 77.
8. Ibid., 78.
9. See *Infancy Gospel of James,* par. 9, http://www.earlychristianwritings.com/text/infancyjames-roberts.html According to the historian Eusebius (263-339 AD) in chapter eleven of his Ecclesiastical History, mention of the brothers of Jesus may be a reference to his first cousins, the sons of Joseph's brother Clopas and his wife Mary.
10. Karl Rahner, S.J., *'Dogmatic Reflections on the Knowledge & Self-Consciousness of Christ,' in Dogmatic Versus Biblical Theology,* ed. Herbert Vorgrimler (Dublin: Helicon Press, 1964), 242-267.
11. (London: Bloomsbury, 2007), 7.

THREE

HOW BIBLICAL PROPHECY WAS RECEIVED

The prophets of the Old Testament were people of prayer, men and women who poured out what was in their hearts to the Lord and who listened carefully to what God had to say, no matter how challenging and disturbing it might be. The Bible has a good deal to say about the ways in which revelation was received. Moses, however, was one of the outstanding people in the Old Testament. In Num 12:6-8 we are told that, 'When a prophet of the Lord is among you, I reveal myself to him in visions, I speak to him in dreams'. Moses, however, was unique in so far as he received direct revelation from God.

A. PROPHETIC VISIONS

Balaam, who surprisingly was not Jewish, worked for king Balak, an enemy of the chosen people. However, on one occasion when the king asked Balaam to curse the Jews, he did not comply. Surprisingly, God gave him prophetic messages instead. In Num 24:2-4 we read, 'When Balaam looked out and saw Israel encamped tribe by tribe, the Spirit of God came upon him and he uttered his oracle: 'The oracle of Balaam son of Beor, the oracle of one whose eye sees clearly, the oracle of one who hears the words of God, who sees a vision from the Almighty, who falls prostrate, and whose eyes are opened.' In Amos 12:10 we read, 'I spoke to the prophets; it was I who multiplied visions, and through the prophets gave parables.' Anyone who reads the prophets Ezekiel and Daniel will see how they received many revelations in visions. For instance, in Dan 10:1 we read, 'In the third year of Cyrus king of Persia, a revelation was given to Daniel. Its message was true and it concerned a great war. The understanding of the message came to him in a vision.'

In the New Testament, there are many examples of prophetic visions, e.g., when the apostle Paul was in prison. Acts 23:11 says, 'That night the Lord appeared to Paul and said, 'Be encouraged, Paul. Just as you have been a witness to me here in Jerusalem, you must preach the Good News in Rome as well.' Admittedly, it is not clear whether Paul was describing an apparition or a vision. In any case there is reason to suspect they were virtually interchangeable terms. Those who receive and understand prophetic visions are sometimes known as seers in the Bible. For example, we read in 1 Sam 9:9, 'Formerly in Israel, when a man went to inquire of God, he said, 'Come, let us go to the seer.' In the second book of Kings we are told that Elisha and his servant were in the town of Dothan. When the servant got up in the morning he found that the area was surrounded by the soldiers of the army of an enemy king. Not surprisingly, the servant was scared. Then we are told that the prophet answered, 'Don't be afraid,' 'Those who are with us are more than those who are with them.' And Elisha prayed, 'O Lord, open his eyes so he may see.' Then the Lord opened the servant's eyes, and he looked and saw the hills full of horses and chariots of fire all around Elisha' (2 Kings 6:16-17). That God given ability to see things from a heavenly perspective is an aspect of prophecy. In Eph 1:18, Paul had the same kind of enlightenment in mind when he said, 'I pray that the eyes of your heart may be enlightened.'

B. Prophetic dreams

One of God's favourite ways of revealing the divine self and purposes was by means of prophetic dreams.[1] Quintus Septimius Florens Tertullian (155-240 AD) expressed a common view in the early Church when he wrote, 'Is it not known to all the people that the dream is the most usual way that God reveals himself to man?' I have dealt with this subject in *Guided by God: Ordinary and Charismatic Ways of Discovering God's Will.*[3] Suffice it to say, that while the Bible does not value natural dreams it does appreciate those which are prompted by God. Sir 34:6 said, 'Unless dreams are sent from the Most High as a visitation, do not give your mind to them.' On a more positive note, Job 33:14-16 says, 'For God does speak - now one way, now another - though man may not perceive it. In a dream, in a vision of the night, when deep sleep falls on men as they slumber in their beds, he may speak in their ears.' In the gospels, Joseph, the husband of Mary, repeatedly received prophetic guidance in dreams. They concerned his marriage to Mary (Mt 1:20), the exile of the Holy family in Egypt (Mt 2:13), their return (Mt 2:19) and the decision to settle in Galilee (Mt 2:22). Later in Matthew's gospel we are told how Pilate's wife said to her husband during the trial of Jesus, 'Have nothing to do with that innocent man because in a dream last night I suffered much on account of him' (Mt 27:19). Those dreams had a prophetic dimension.

C. Interpretation of dreams

More often than not, when Jewish people had religious dreams, sometimes of a prophetic nature, they could interpret them. But when pagans had similar dreams they often needed gifted Jews to discern their meaning on their behalf. For example, early in the Bible two men said, 'We both had dreams... but there is no one to interpret them.' Then Joseph said to them, 'Do not interpretations belong to God? Tell me your dreams' (Gen 40:8). Speaking about Daniel, another Jewish exile, we are told that 'Daniel could understand visions and dreams of all kinds' (Dan 1:17). Nebuchadnezzar's daughter in law said to the king that Daniel, 'has the spirit of the holy gods in him and... a keen mind and knowledge and understanding, and also the ability to interpret dreams, explain riddles and solve difficult problems' (Dan 5:11-12). Although the one who interpreted the dream, did not necessarily have the dream him or herself, it was thought that the God given ability to interpret its spiritual significance was in itself a prophetic gift.

D. Angelic visitations

The word angel in English is derived from the Greek *angelos,* meaning, 'a messenger.' So the angels are God's ambassadors who mediate between the Lord in heaven and his servants on earth. Not surprisingly, they can be instruments of God's prophetic purposes. Although they are pure spirits, God can cause them to assume human form in order to communicate with humans. St Thomas Aquinas wrote, 'the angels are not bodies, nor have they bodies naturally united with them, as is clear from what has been said, it follows that they sometimes assume bodies.' In Gen 18:1-2 we are told how 'the Lord appeared to Abraham near the great trees of Mamre while he was sitting at the entrance to his tent in the heat of the day. Abraham looked up and saw three men standing nearby. When he saw them, he hurried from the entrance of his tent to meet them and bowed low to the ground.' Two of the men were angels and the third was the Lord in disguise and they brought Abraham the prophetic news that, despite the fact that he and his wife Sarah were senior citizens, they would bear a child. In the book of Tobit we read how the angel Raphael appeared to Tobiah in human form (cf. Tob 5:4). Among other things he said to him, as he returned home to his blind father Tobit, 'I know that his eyes and the medicine will make the white scales shrink and peel off from his eyes; then your father will have sight again and will see the light of day.'

In the New Testament, we are familiar with the story which recounts how the angel Gabriel brought a message to Zechariah (cf. Lk 1:19). Around the same time, the angel Gabriel also appeared to Mary, to announce, in a prophetic way, that she was to be the mother of the promised Messiah (cf. Lk 1:26). In acts 8:26 we are told that an angel told Philip, a deacon, to, 'Go south to the road - the desert road - that goes down from Jerusalem to Gaza.' So is it any wonder that we read in Heb 13:2-3, 'Do not forget to entertain strangers, for by so doing some people have entertained angels without knowing it.' While that was literally true in the cases of Abraham and Tobiah, it can be metaphorically true when the Lord speaks a prophetic word to a person by means of another human being who is the Lord's angel or messenger.

E. Prophetic words

In *Guided by God,* I mentioned how one can receive a prophetic utterance. Spontaneously revelatory words bubble up in the person's mind, which did not originate in his or her own thinking, knowledge or imagination. As a word from God, it could be useful, 'for teaching, rebuking, correcting and training in righteousness' (cf. 2 Tim 3:16). It could also be useful for offering guidance or predicting future events. For example, St. Paul said to Timothy his young protégé, 'Do not neglect your gift, which was given you through *a prophetic message* when the body of elders laid their hands on you.' This verse implied that the elders received a revelatory word through which God spoke to Timothy about his calling and gifts. On an other occasion Agabus predicted that a severe famine would spread over the entire Roman world. This happened during the reign of Claudius' (Acts 11:27-29). Again in Acts 21:10-11, we read, 'a prophet named Agabus came down from Judea. Coming over to us, he took Paul's belt, tied his own hands and feet with it and said, 'The Holy Spirit says, 'In this way the Jews of Jerusalem will bind the owner of this belt and will hand him over to the Gentiles.'

Like Moses and Jesus, prophets listen to the word that God reveals to their hearts. As we read in Is 50:4-5, 'The Sovereign Lord has given me an instructed tongue, to know the word that sustains the weary. He wakens me morning by morning, wakens my ear to listen like one being taught. The Sovereign Lord has opened my ears, and I have not been rebellious; I have not drawn back.'

F. Ecstatic experiences

It was noted in chapter two that in the early days of Jewish prophecy it tended to be ecstatic and non-conceptual in nature. Philo Judaeus (25 BC – 50 AD), was a Jewish philosopher. On one occasion he wrote about the connection between ecstasy and prophetic utterance. 'A prophet being a spokesman has no utterance of his own, but all his utterance come from elsewhere, the echoes of another's voice... he has the vocal instrument of God, smitten and played by his hidden hand... This is what regularly befalls the fellowship of the prophets. The mind is evicted at the arrival of the divine Spirit, but when that departs the mind returns to its tenancy. Mortal and immortal may not share the same home. And therefore the setting of reason and the darkness which surrounds it produces ecstasy and inspired frenzy... The speech of the mouth and tongue, are wholly in the employ of Another, to show forth what he wills.'[4] The Jewish historian Josephus (37-100 AD) said of Balaam, who is referred to in Numbers chapters 22 - 24, 'He did speak by inspiration, as not being in his own power, but moved to say what he did by the Divine Spirit.' A little later Josephus tells us that Balaam said to the king, 'I had made to serve you; for those that take upon them to foretell the affairs of mankind, as from their own abilities, are entirely unable to do it, or to forbear to utter what God suggests to them, or to offer violence to his will; for when he prevents us and enters into us, nothing that we say is our own... canst thou suppose that it is in our power to be silent, or to say any thing, *when the Spirit of God seizes upon us*? - for he puts such words as he pleases in our mouths and such discourses as we are not ourselves conscious of.'[5] There have been Christian prophets who have also received their prophetic utterances when in rapture states.

Conclusion

Due to the fact that post-enlightenment culture is anti-supernatural, St Therese of Lisieux admitted that during her dark night of the soul, 'The reasoning of the worst materialists was imposed on my mind. Science which makes unceasing advances will eventually explain everything naturally. We shall have the absolute explanation for everything that exists and that still remains a problem, because very many things remain to be discovered yet.'[6] People who, unlike Therese, actually adopt such a rationalistic and naturalistic point of view, believe that the kinds of spiritual communication which are described in the Bible are mythological or naive in character, and no longer credible in contemporary society. However, anyone who is familiar with the mystical tradition, and those who are leading deeply prayerful lives know that many Christians in the past and present have received and continue to receive prophetic messages from God. It seems to me that prophecies which accurately foretell future events and miracles that cannot be explained by science are proof positive that the rationalistic worldview which predominates in our culture is both reductionist and sadly mistaken.

NOTES

1. See 'Dreams and Visions,' in *Guided by God: Ordinary and Charismatic Ways of Discovering God's Will* (Luton: New Life, 2015), 211-234.
2. *A Treatise on the Soul,* chapter XLVII.
3. Pat Collins, C.M. (Luton: New Life, 2015), 211-234
4. Quoted by James Dunn, in *Jesus and the Spirit* (London: SCM Press, 1975), 304.
5. *Antiquities of the Jews,* Book 4, chap. 6, par. 5.
6. Chris O Donnell, *Love in the Heart of the Church: The Mission of Therese of Lisieux* (Dublin: Veritas, 1997), 44.

FOUR

DISCERNMENT OF THE PROPHETIC GIFT AND MINISTRY

Are some people unmusical? There are two possible answers. The well known Irish musician, Professor Michael O'Sullivan, believes that musical ability has to do with our genes. Others say, it's not that people are naturally unmusical, it's simply that music has not attracted their interest enough to put in the long hours of practice that are needed to become proficient. So is musical ability a matter of nature or nurture? Surely, it is a matter of both.

Likewise it is hard to know whether everyone can prophecy. A later chapter dealing with prophecy in church teaching will point out that, in virtue of their baptism, all Christians share in the prophetic ministry of Christ. We noted in the introduction how Moses said, 'I wish that all the Lord's people were prophets and that the Lord would put his Spirit on them!' (Num 11:29). On Pentecost Sunday, St. Peter said those words were being fulfilled (cf. Acts 2:15-17). Speaking to the members of the Corinthian community St Paul said, 'For you can all prophesy in turn so that everyone may be instructed and encouraged' (1 Cor 14:31). That verse could be interpreted in two ways. Firstly, anyone can prophesy occasionally, but he or she should do so in turn so that good order is maintained at the meeting, or secondly, let those who have a prophetic gift, exercise it with due decorum. In Cor 12:7-10 Paul says, 'Now to each one the manifestation of the Spirit is given for the common good.' Having mentioned a number of gifts he added, 'to another prophecy' as if to say that only some members of the body of Christ are granted this particular gift. I suspect, that Paul believed that any individual could be granted a prophetic word, at least on an occasional basis, while there would be others who would have a more ongoing ability to prophesy.

THE GIFT AND MINISTRY OF PROPHECY

In the New Testament there are references not only to the charism of prophecy but also to the prophetic ministry. For instance, speaking about the latter in 1 Cor 12:28 we read, 'And in the church God has appointed first of all apostles, *second prophets,* third teachers,' and in Eph 4:11-13 Paul says, 'It was God who gave some to be apostles, *some to be prophets,* some to be evangelists, and some to be pastors and teachers, to prepare God's people for works of service, so that the body of Christ may be built up.' It would seem that besides the granting of occasional prophetic revelations to believers, there was a ministry of prophecy which was highly valued in the early Christian community. Writing about this distinction, German scripture scholar Arnold Bittlinger has said, 'Although many Christians have received the charismatic gift of prophecy, in some Christians this charism is so profound as to enable the congregation to recognise that God has entrusted the ministry of a prophet to one or another of its members.'[1] As was noted in the introduction, there is a good example of this distinction in Num 11:25-29. We are told that Moses imparted the spirit on seventy two elders which enabled them to prophesy on one occasion but not again.

That was the charism of prophecy. But as for Moses, he received revelations from God on a regular basis. As a result we could rightly say that he had a prophetic ministry. When Moses died the scriptures attested, 'But since then there has not arisen in Israel a prophet like Moses, whom the Lord knew face to face' (Deut 34:10).

It seems to me that it is important that the members of the Christian community identify what gifts and ministries its members have been granted. By doing so, not only can they affirm the gifts and/or ministries that various individuals have received, such as prophecy, they can also be responsive to the exercise of those charisms and ministries in the body of Christ. Sherry Weddell has written a helpful booklet on this subject entitled, *The Catholic Spiritual Gifts Inventory*.[2] She wisely points out that, 'Christians with a charism (or ministry) of prophecy require a great deal of emotional and spiritual maturity and disinterested discipline if they are to be fruitful and effective. It is possible to unintentionally offer our own ideas as a prophetic word, or to act in a prophetic manner out of anger or in order to meet unconscious personal needs. Those with this charism must communicate the message they have been given and leave the results to God and the discernment of the Christian community.'[3]

Prophetic preaching and teaching

Some non charismatic scripture scholars identify New Testament prophecy with what we today would refer to as anointed preaching or expounding the scripture. This was the viewpoint of Protestant reformers Martin Luther and John Calvin. Luther wrote, 'when Paul or the other apostles interpreted the Old Testament their interpretation was prophecy'.[4] He also believed that all, 'who can expound the Scriptures and ably interpret and teach the difficult books' were prophesying.[5] Calvin wrote in his *Commentary on Romans* (12:6) that, 'Prophecy... is simply the right understanding of scripture and the particular gift of understanding it.' What Calvin seems to be describing is inspired understanding rather than spontaneous revelation. It is interesting to see that commenting on Rom 12:6, contemporary Catholic scripture scholar, Joseph Fitzmyer, S.J., says, mistakenly perhaps, that the word prophecy refers to, 'inspired Christian preaching.'[6]

Scripture scholars who have been influenced by charismatic spirituality emphasise the revelatory nature of prophecy. Normally, a sermon or teaching is not the proclamation of content that has been revealed to the preacher in a supernatural way. Rather, it is the fruit of such things as reading, and prayerful reflection on the scriptures and the inspirations of the Holy Spirit.[7] As Paul says in Rom 15:4, 'everything that was written in the past was written to teach us,' and again in 2 Tim 3:16, 'all scripture is profitable for teaching.' Of course, a sermon or homily may be inspired and influenced by the gifts of wisdom and knowledge (cf. Is 11:2), and proclaimed effectively by means of the charisms of the utterance of wisdom and knowledge (cf. 1 Cor 12:8). But that would not necessarily mean a sermon or homily was prophetic in the sense that they were the expression of spontaneous, divinely originating revelation.

As has already been noted, Wayne Grudem could say in the light of this understanding of prophecy, that it should not be equated with 'powerful preaching.' It is possible of course, that there might be a section in a sermon or homily which was indeed the expression of a prophetic revelation. In his *The Theology of Paul the Apostle,* James D.G. Dunn says, 'The fact that Paul lists prophecy and teaching in close conjunction probably indicates that he saw the teaching function as an indispensable complement to prophecy... We should recall that he ranked prophecy above teaching. Teaching we may say preserves continuity; but prophecy gives life. With teaching a community will not die; but without prophecy it will not live because prophecy without teaching degenerates into fanaticism, and teaching without prophecy solidifies into law.'[8]

DISCERNMENT OF PROPHECY

From the beginning, the Bible was aware of the problem of false prophecy. For instance Jeremiah wrote, 'The Lord said to me, 'The prophets are prophesying lies in my name. I have not sent them or appointed them or spoken to them. They are prophesying to you false visions, divinations, idolatries and the delusions of their own minds. Therefore, this is what the Lord says about the prophets who are prophesying in my name: I did not send them, yet they are saying, 'No sword or famine will touch this land.' Those same prophets will perish by sword and famine' (Jer 14:14-16). Ezekiel said in like manner, 'Son of man, prophesy against the prophets of Israel who are now prophesying. Say to those who prophesy out of their own imagination: 'Hear the word of the Lord! This is what the Sovereign Lord says: Woe to the foolish prophets who follow their own spirit and have seen nothing!' In Mt 24:24 we read about a similar problem, 'For false Christs and false prophets will arise and will show great signs and wonders, so as to mislead, if possible, even the elect.'

A. Self serving prophecies

The false prophets were people pleasers. They told the Israelites what they wanted to hear. Instead of evaluating prevailing cultural values, attitudes and mores in the light of Divine truth and law, they were inclined to modify them in order to adapt them to prevailing cultural norms and expectations. In the New Testament St. Peter said, 'But there were also false prophets among the people, just as there will be false teachers among you. They will secretly introduce destructive heresies, even denying the sovereign Lord who bought them - bringing swift destruction on themselves. Many will follow their shameful ways and will bring the way of truth into disrepute. In their greed these teachers will exploit you with stories they have made up' (2 Pet 2:1-3). The reference to greed is interesting and relevant. Often the false prophets are secretly motivated by a love of money, 'a root of all kinds of evil' (1 Tim 6:10). That is one good reason why so many Christians are rightly wary of the prophetic statements of many televangelists who make repeated requests for financial donations. Not surprisingly therefore, problems like these give rise to the question, how can one distinguish between true and false prophecy? As Paul said in 1 Thess 5:20-22, 'do not treat prophecies with contempt. Test everything. Hold on to the good.' The Biblical writers came up with a number of answers.

B. Predictions unfulfilled

Frequently prophets made predictions about future events. So we read in Deut. 18:22, 'If what a prophet proclaims in the name of the Lord does not take place or come true, that is a message the Lord has not spoken. That prophet has spoken presumptuously. Do not be afraid of him.' Again in Is 41:22-23 we read in similar vein that, when those who believe in false gods are challenged with these words, 'Tell us what the former things were, so that we may consider them and know their final outcome. Or declare to us the things to come, tell us what the future holds so we may know that you are gods.' Like the false prophets in the Book of Daniel, who were unable to tell the king what dream he had, they will be unable to respond to this challenge. The first century historian Josephus tells us in his *Antiquities of the Jews* there were a number of men who promised their followers a prophetic sign succeeded by an uprising against the Romans. Among them were a prophet named Theudas who expected the waters of the Jordan to part for him, and a nameless Jew from Egypt who expected the walls of Jerusalem to fall when he commanded them to do so. Both men were sadly mistaken.

C. Non prophecy

Possibly, there is an interesting example of non-prophecy in Acts 21:3-5. Luke tells us that, 'When we had come in sight of Cyprus, leaving it on the left we sailed to Syria and landed at Tyre, for there the ship was to unload its cargo. And having sought out the disciples, we stayed there for seven days. And through the Spirit they were telling Paul not to go on to Jerusalem.' This seems to refer to a prophecy intended for Paul. He did not comply with it. Surely, he wouldn't have done this if he believed it was genuine. It seemed to be a non-prophecy as opposed to a false prophecy which, presumably, had been uttered in good faith. In reality it was wishful thinking of a loving kind which was expressed in a prophetic way. Instead of originating in a supernatural revelation it may have been motivated, in an unconscious way, by a human desire to save Paul from suffering in Jerusalem, just as Peter had wanted to save Jesus from suffering in Jerusalem. As Bruce Yocum has observed, 'Prophecy can be impure - our own thoughts or ideas can get mixed into the message we receive - whether we receive the words directly or only receive a sense of the message.'[9] Pope Benedict XIV said in the 18th century that there is a difference between a spirit of prophecy and a genuine prophetic revelation. Sometimes those who speak in the prophetic spirit, don't realise that they have not received a true revelation from God. Just as Jesus knew from his baptism onwards that he was destined to be the Suffering Servant who would die in Jerusalem, so Paul knew as a result of a prophetic word spoken to him by Jesus in a vision, that he had to witness to him in Rome (cf. Acts 23:11).

Perhaps Jesus had non prophecy in mind when he said, 'I tell you that men will have to give account on the day of judgment for every careless word they have spoken.' (Mt 12:36-3). Commenting on this verse Raniero Cantalamessa has observed that the words Jesus was referring to, 'are the empty, fruitless, purely human words spoken by those whose duty it is to proclaim the living, life-changing words of God... They are the idle words of false prophets, that is, the words of those who want us to believe that they speak to us in God's name, but in fact are simply putting forward their own ideas. They do not draw what they say from the heart of God, but merely think it up themselves.'[10] No wonder Jer 23:16 says, 'Do not listen to these prophets when they prophesy to you, filling you with futile hopes. They are making up everything they say. They do not speak for the Lord!'

D. False prophecy

In Deut 13:1-9 we read, 'If a prophet, or one who foretells by dreams, appears among you and announces to you a miraculous sign or wonder, and if the sign or wonder of which he has spoken takes place, and he says, 'Let us follow other gods' (gods you have not known) 'and let us worship them,' you must not listen to the words of that prophet or dreamer. The Lord your God is testing you to find out whether you love him with all your heart and with all your soul. It is the Lord your God you must follow, and him you must revere. Keep his commands and obey him; serve him and hold fast to him.' In 2 Chron 18:21, we are told, 'I will go and be a deceiving spirit in the mouths of all his prophets,' he said. ''You will succeed in enticing him,' said the Lord. 'Go and do it..'

Jesus said, 'Beware of false prophets, who come to you in sheep's clothing, but inwardly they are ravenous wolves. You will know them by their fruits' (Mt 7:15-16). In Mt 24:11 Jesus warned that, 'many false prophets will appear and deceive many people.' Speaking about the approach of the end times he stated, 'false prophets will appear and perform great signs and miracles to deceive even the elect - if that were possible. See, I have told you ahead of time' (Mt 24:24-25). A false prophet is someone who presumes to speak on God's behalf. Not only has he or she failed to receive a divine revelation, what is said contradicts the teaching of the scriptures and the Church. The law of love is pre-eminent in Christianity. So, anyone who utters a prophetic word which is animated by conscious or unconscious inner states such as human jealousy, envy, judgment, condemnation, resentment or a desire to please or to impress is not from the Holy Spirit. Arguably, the prophet has unwittingly become the mouthpiece of the evil one. As Paul said, 'if I have the gift of prophecy... but have not love, I am nothing' (1 Cor 13:2-3).

E. Don't practice what they proclaim

Jesus suggested that false prophecies came from hypocritical people who did not practice what they proclaimed. 'Beware of false prophets,' he said, 'who come to you in sheep's clothing but inwardly are ravenous wolves. You will know them by their fruits. Are grapes gathered from thorns, or figs from thistles? So, every sound tree bears good fruit, but the bad tree bears evil fruit. A sound tree cannot bear evil fruit, nor can a bad tree bear good fruit' (Mt 7:15). This is an interesting observation because the charism of prophecy is given, not as a sign that the speaker is holy, but as a means of sanctifying the listeners. In the Old Testament a sinful pagan like Balaam, was used by God to speak a genuine prophecy (cf. Num 24:17).

That said, Jesus warned, 'Not everyone who says to me, 'Lord, Lord,' will enter the kingdom of heaven, but only he who does the will of my Father who is in heaven. Many will say to me on that day, 'Lord, Lord, did we not prophesy in your name,... Then I will tell them plainly, 'I never knew you. Away from me, you evildoers!' In par. 1107 of her *Diary*, St Faustina wrote, 'Neither graces, nor revelations, nor raptures, nor gifts granted to a soul make it perfect, but rather the intimate union of the soul with God. These gifts are merely ornaments of the soul, but constitute neither its essence nor its perfection. My sanctity and perfection consist in the close union of my will with the will of God.' It would seem therefore, that normally, only people who are trying to live holy lives in conformity with the will of God will utter genuine prophecies. If an evil person utters a true prophecy, he or she will receive no reward from God.

F. Misinterpreting and Misapplying Genuine Prophecy

Scripture scholar Jack Deere makes a perceptive observation when he says in his book *The Beginner's Guide to the Gift of Prophecy*, that gift consists of three things, a prophetic revelation, its interpretation and its application.[11] He says that although a person may receive a genuine prophecy he or she may misunderstand its implications. Deere himself gives a good example. On one occasion when he was ministering to others he got a revelatory word about a blood pressure problem. He felt it was to be addressed to a particular woman in the congregation. He asked her if she was suffering from high blood pressure and she said no. Then he asked if her husband suffered from high blood pressure. Again the answer was no. Finally, he asked if anyone beside the woman suffered from high blood pressure. Once again the answer was no. Deere was embarrassed and puzzled, because he thought the word of revelation was genuine. When the service was over the woman to whom he had first addressed his question approached him and said, 'you know my husband suffers from low blood pressure.' This taught Deere that although the prophetic message he had received was genuine, he had misinterpreted it. He felt in retrospect that he should have asked the Lord, 'What do you mean by a blood pressure problem, and what do you want me to do about it?'

G. Genuine Prophecy and Deeds of Power

St Thomas Aquinas said that evangelisation consisted in three things, firstly, prophetic revelation; secondly, the verbal proclamation of what had been revealed; and thirdly, demonstration of the supernatural origin of the word proclaimed by means of supernatural deeds of power such as exorcism, healing and miracle working. With regard to the latter, it is interesting to note that when John the Baptist sent messengers to Jesus to ask, ''Are you the one who was to come, or should we expect someone else?'' (Lk 7:20), Jesus replied, 'Go back and report to John what you have seen and heard: The blind receive sight, the lame walk, those who have leprosy are cured, the deaf hear, the dead are raised, and the good news is preached to the poor' (Lk 7:22-23). In other words, Jesus was saying, if you want to know whether I'm the Messiah, the one inspired by God, look at the supernatural things I'm doing. On another occasion he said in similar vein, 'I am God's Son' Do not believe me unless I do what my Father does. But if I do it, even though you do not believe me, believe the miracles, that you may know and understand that the Father is in me, and I in the Father' (Jn 10: 36-39). The implication of this point was made clear by St Paul when he said, 'For the kingdom of God is not a matter of talk [prophecy] but of power' (1 Cor 4:19-20), and again, 'My [prophetic] message and my preaching were not with wise and persuasive words, but with a demonstration of the Spirit's power [i.e. healings and miracles], so that your faith might not rest on men's wisdom, but on God's power' (1 Cor 2:4-5). Prophets will sometimes demonstrate that their words came from God by performing deeds of power. As Jesus said, 'these signs will accompany those who believe: In my name they will drive out demons... they will place their hands on sick people, and they will get well' (Mk 16:17-18). This topic is explored in another chapter.

THE CHARISM OF DISCERNMENT OF SPIRITS

In 1 Cor 12:10 St Paul said that to some was given the ability to distinguish between spirits. The Greek words used probably refer to the gift of recognising whether words of revelation are genuine or not. Understood in that way, discernment is a gift which is given to some members of the community which enables them to recognise whether a prophecy has originated in God, the speaker's human nature, or is due to the illusions and false inspirations of the evil one, who, as Paul warns us, can appear as an angel of light (cf. 2 Cor 11:14). The discernment of Spirits that Paul speaks about is akin to what is referred to as connatural knowledge in Catholic theology, i.e., an instinctive ability to distinguish, good from bad, godly from ungodly, natural from supernatural which is the result of union with God.[12] Anyone who is interested in the subject of the discernment of private revelations, especially of a prophetic kind, would be well advised to read chapters twenty to twenty three in Augustin Poulain's wonderful book, *The Graces of Interior Prayer*. I know of no more detailed, perceptive, balanced and helpful treatment of this important topic.[13]

MOHAMMED AND JOSEPH SMITH

Followers of Islam, a non-Christian religion, refer to their founder Mohammed (570-629 AD), as The Prophet, or The Messenger. They regard him as the last and greatest of the prophets sent by God to mankind. He claimed that the Archangel Gabriel began to reveal many religious and ethical truths to him when he was forty years of age. Christians do not accept that Mohammed was a genuine prophet because his teachings are not in accord with Biblical truth and some of the predictions he made were not fulfilled. Followers of The Church of Jesus Christ of Latter-day Saints, a religion which has many Christian characteristics, believe that their founder, Joseph Smith (1805-44 AD), received the *Book of Mormon* as a result of a revelation by the angel Moroni.

They regard it as an inspired companion to the Bible. Smith claimed to have received a further revelation in 1843 which sanctioned polygamy. His teachings were not orthodox, and a number of his prophetic predictions failed to be fulfilled.

Although both men may have had a prophetic spirit, Christians regard the teachings of both prophets to be false. As such they were either the product of their natural minds or the evil spirit. In 2 Jn 1:9 we read, 'Anyone who runs on ahead [of God] and does not abide in the doctrine of Christ [who is not content with what He taught] does not have God' *(Amplified Bible)*. St. Paul added in Gal 1:6-9, 'I am astonished that you are so quickly deserting him who called you in the grace of Christ and are turning to a different gospel - not that there is another one, but there are some who trouble you and want to distort the gospel of Christ. But even if we or *an angel from heaven* [my italics] should preach to you a gospel contrary to the one we preached to you, let him be accursed. As we have said before, so now I say again: If anyone is preaching to you a gospel contrary to the one you received, let him be accursed.' The teachings of Mohammed and Smith are contrary to what is taught in the new Testament.

CONCLUSION

In the New Testament it is clear that not only was the gift of prophecy esteemed, it was also widely exercised. The believers knew they were living in the age of the Spirit when the promise of Joel was being fulfilled, when sons and daughters would prophesy (cf. Acts 2:17). Is it any wonder that St Paul said in 1 Cor 14:5, 'I would like every one of you to speak in tongues, but I would rather have you prophesy.' As St Paul said, 'The one who prophesies speaks to people for their up-building and encouragement and consolation' (1 Cor 14:3).

For a century or more after the New Testament was written, the gift of prophecy continued to be exercised in the Church. For example, Justin Martyr (100-165 AD) boasted to the Jew Trypho 'the prophetic gifts remain with us.' St. Irenaeus (120-200 AD) also bore witness to the presence of the gifts of the Spirit. He wrote, 'We have heard of many of the brethren who have foreknowledge of the future, visions, and prophetic utterances; others, by laying-on of hands, heal the sick and restore them to health.' On another occasion he wrote, 'We hear of many members of the church who have prophetic gifts, and, by the Spirit speak with all kinds of tongues, and bring men's secret thoughts to light for their own good, and expound the mysteries of God.' Finally he wrote, 'It is impossible to enumerate the charisms which throughout the world the church has received from God.'

Literature such as the *Letters of Ignatius* and the *Didache* and the writings of Tertullian indicate that while prophecy was still of a feature of Church life, it was in decline. The *Didache* which was written around the mid or late first century said, 'Appoint therefore for yourselves bishops and deacons worthy of the Lord, meek men, and not lovers of money, and truthful and approved, for they also minister to you the ministry of the prophets and teachers.'[14] So it would seem that already the charism of prophecy was being subsumed into more institutional forms of ministry. This is what sociologist Max Weber referred to as the ritualisation of prophecy.

The advent of Montanism in the late 2nd century, known as the 'New Prophecy,' also had a very negative effect when the Church adjudicated that it was heretical. It gave all charisms a bad name, especially prophecy. In any case, at the same time the Church was becoming more structured and institutionalised with the result that the faithful increasingly relied on the clergy and official church teaching for guidance. In fact the gift of prophecy became virtually synonymous with the *magisterium* of the Church. However, as Niels Christian Hvidt points out in his book, *Christian Prophecy: The Post Biblical Tradition,* although the exercise of the charism of prophecy went into steep decline, it never disappeared completely. Down the centuries, there were outstanding men and women such as Saints Anthony of the desert, Francis of Assisi, Bridget of Sweden, Vincent Ferrer, Catherine of Sienna, Don Bosco etc. who exercised this gift. As Raniero Cantalamessa, has observed, the charism of prophecy was moved out 'of the ambit of *ecclesiology* into the area of *hagiography*.'[15] The Church anticipated the revival of the charisms in general and the gift of prophecy in particular, in par. 12 of the Vatican II, *Dogmatic Constitution on the Church.* When the Charismatic Renewal began in the Catholic Church in 1967 a revival began in the exercise of the gifts of the Spirit, including that of prophecy, among the faithful of the Church.

NOTES

1. Arnold Bittlinger, *Gifts and Ministries* (London: Hodder and Stoughton, 1974), 65.
2. (Colorado Springs: The Sienna Institute Press, 1998).
3. Ibid., 45-46.
4. *On Joel, 2:28.*
5. *On Zecharaiah* (preface).
6. *Romans, The Anchor Bible,* vol. 33 (New Haven: Yale University Press, 2008), 647.
7. Cf. Wayne Grudem, *'Prophecy and Teaching'* in *The Gift of Prophecy in the New Testament and Today* (Wheaton: Crossway, 2000).
8. (London: T & T Clark, 2003), 583.
9. Bruce Yocum, *Prophecy* (Ann Arbor: Servant, 1976), 79.
10. *Come, Creator Spirit: Meditations on the Veni Creator* (Collegeville: Liturgical Press, 2003), 233.
11. (Ventura: Regal, 2008), 81-82.
12. Cf. Pat Collins *Guided by God,* (Luton: New Life, 2015), 129-131.
13. Augustin Poulain, S.J., *The Graces of Interior Prayer: A Treatise on Mystical Theology* (London: Kegan Paul, Trench, Trubner, 1910), 299-399.
14. *'The Didache,'* sec. 15, in *The Apostolic Fathers in English,* ed. Michael W. Holmes (Grand Rapids: Baker Academic, 2006), 170-1.
15. *Come Creator Spirit: Meditations on the Veni Creator* (Collegeville: Liturgical Press, 2003), 184.

FIVE

TWO STREAMS OF MESSIANIC PROPHECY

Mark Neugebauer grew up in a conservative Jewish home in suburban Toronto, He regularly attended synagogue on Sabbaths and high holy days, and lived a committed Jewish life. His father was a Polish Holocaust survivor from Auschwitz, and his mother's family escaped the organised massacres of Jews in Russia. He recounts how, 'One day I picked up a volume by the Yiddish writer Sholem Asche called *The Nazarene*. I was awestruck by the Jewish Yeshua who in no way resembled those who apparently hated us for two thousand years. Watching the film *Jesus of Nazareth* confirmed this discovery, and listening yearly to Handel's Messiah began to deepen my awareness of who He was. As I examined the scriptural libretto of that magnificent oratorio, these words caused me to ponder, 'He was wounded for our transgressions, bruised for our iniquities. The chastisement for our peace was on him, and by his stripes we are healed.' Subsequently, Mark met two messianic Jews. He recounts how, 'they began to expound on the ancient prophecies in the Hebrew Scripture concerning the Messiah, but I didn't hear a word they said. What I did hear was what the Lord spoke to my heart when He revealed Himself to me personally, saying, 'Jesus is the Messiah; He is Lord.' My two friends brought me to the fledgling Messianic fellowship that met in our neighbourhood, and I confessed to being a believer in

Yeshua as Messiah.' In recent years Mark has been led to join the Catholic Church.

This contemporary testimony is reminiscent of the story in Lk 24:13-33 which describes how two disillusioned disciples met Jesus on the road to Emmaus. At one point in the narrative we are told that, 'beginning with Moses and all the Prophets, he explained to them what was said in all the Scriptures concerning himself' (Lk 24:27). What a marvellous exposition that must have been. Later the disciples observed, 'Were not our hearts burning within us while he talked with us on the road and opened the Scriptures to us?' (Lk 24:32). What is sometimes overlooked is the fact that shortly after this incident had taken place the risen Jesus appeared to the apostles. On that occasion we are told that, 'He said to them, 'This is what I told you while I was still with you: Everything must be fulfilled that is written about me in the Law of Moses, the Prophets and the Psalms. Then he opened their minds so they could understand the Scriptures' (Lk 24:44-45). Jesus said something similar in Jn 5:39-40, 'You diligently study the Scriptures because you think that by them you possess eternal life. These are the Scriptures *that testify about me.*' We are told that on one particular occasion Jesus spoke about himself as the fulfilment of the messianic prophecies when he, 'turned to his disciples and said privately, 'Blessed are the eyes that see what you see. For I tell you that many prophets and kings wanted to see what you see but did not see it, and to hear what you hear but did not hear it' (Lk 10:23-24).

Over the years I have often wondered what messianic texts Jesus referred to and what he had to say about them. Some time ago I came across an approximate answer when I read *The First Apology* of St. Justin Martyr (100-165 AD). This post-apostolic father of the Church was keen to prove to his readers that Jesus was the promised Messiah. One of his main proofs was the fact that Jesus fulfilled the messianic prophecies in the Old Testament. As he said, 'There were certain persons among the Jews, who were prophets of God, through whom the prophetic Spirit announced beforehand things that were to come to pass before they happened.'[1] Then he went on to refer to many of the prophets and to comment on the meaning and implications of what they had foretold. I felt that in doing so, Justin had provided his readers with a survey reminiscent of the one Jesus had shared, firstly, with the two disciples, and later with the apostles.

When Jesus referred to Messianic texts in the Old Testament, he quoted from three kinds of inspired literature, the law; the prophets; and what are referred to as the writings, e.g., the psalms. In this chapter I intend to refer to two streams of messianic prophecy which have impressed me and many others over the years. This subjective treatment is intended to be indicative rather than scholarly and comprehensive. That said, I hope that you will be as impressed and edified, as I have been, by these amazing anticipations of God's saving activity in and through the person of Jesus.[2] As Origen Adamantius (184-254 AD) wrote in his *First Principles*, 'If anyone ponders over the prophetic sayings with all attention and reverence they deserve, it is certain that in the very act of reading and diligently studying them his mind and feelings will be touched by a divine breath and he will recognise that the words he is reading are not the utterances of man but the language of God; and so he will perceive from his own experience that these books have been composed not by mortal eloquence but, if I may so speak, in a style that is divine.'[3]

The Messiah as Son of David

The story of David's rise to the throne of Israel is recounted in 1 Samuel 16 – 2 Samuel 4. He is shown to be God's chosen one and is anointed king by Samuel and, 'from that day on, the Spirit of the Lord rushed upon David' (1 Sam 6:13). That act signalled the founding of the Davidic dynasty. The anointing of David was important for an understanding of the Old Testament idea of the Messiah. The rule of David as God's anointed one was used by the prophets to picture the coming of an eschatological king.

After a lot of fighting David captured Jerusalem about 3,000 years ago and brought the ark of the covenant into the city, and God gave him rest from all his enemies. At that time, David met with Nathan the prophet and expressed his desire to build a temple to house the ark. As he said in 2 Sam 7:2-3, 'Here I am, living in a palace of cedar, while the ark of God remains in a tent.' At first Nathan agreed. 'Whatever you have in mind,' he said, 'go ahead and do it, for the Lord is with you.' It would seem that in saying this, Nathan was relying on his natural judgment. But as a result of a subsequent dream of a revelatory kind he changed his mind. He told David that he should not build the temple, but added, 'The Lord declares to you that the Lord himself will establish a house for you: When your days are over and you rest with your fathers, I will raise up your offspring to succeed you, who will come from your own body, and I will establish his kingdom. He is the one who will build a house for my Name, and I will establish the throne of his kingdom forever... Your house and your kingdom will endure forever before me; your throne *will be established forever* [my italics]' (2 Sam 7:11-16). David responded by saying to God, 'Now be pleased to bless the house of your servant, that it may continue forever in your sight; for you,

O Sovereign Lord, have spoken, and with your blessing the house of your servant will be blessed forever' (2 Sam 7:29). God's assurance that David's dynasty would last forever was one of the remarkable promises in the Old Testament and it was repeated on a number of occasions. For example:

- 'You will have a son who will be a man of peace and rest, and I will give him rest from all his enemies on every side. His name will be Solomon, and I will grant Israel peace and quiet during his reign. He is the one who will build a house for my Name. He will be my son, and I will be his father. And I will establish the throne of his kingdom over Israel forever' (1 Chron 22:9-10).
- 'Don't you know that the Lord, the God of Israel, has given the kingship of Israel to David and his descendants forever' (2 Chron 13:5).
- 'This is what the Lord says: 'David will never fail to have a man to sit on the throne of the house of Israel' (Jer 33:17).
- 'I have made a covenant with my chosen one, I have sworn to David my servant, 'I will establish your line forever and make your throne firm through all generations' (Ps 89:3-4).

Following David's death he was succeeded by as many as eighteen kings, among them Solomon, who built the temple. But then, around 605 BC, the land of Israel was conquered by the Babylonians and most of the population was sent into exile. We are told in 2 Kings 24:13-14 that, 'Nebuchadnezzar removed all the treasures from the temple of the Lord and from the royal palace, and took away all the gold articles that Solomon king of Israel had made for the temple of the Lord. He carried into exile all Jerusalem: all the officers and fighting men, and all the craftsmen and artisans - a total of ten thousand. Only the poorest people of the land were left.' During that time of exile one prophet wrote, 'In the first year of Darius son of Xerxes, who was made ruler over the Babylonian kingdom - in the first year of his reign, I, Daniel, understood from the Scriptures, according to the word of the Lord given to Jeremiah the prophet, that the desolation of Jerusalem would last seventy years' (Dan 9:1-2). That prophecy was fulfilled when in 538 BC, king Cyrus the Great issued an edict that allowed the Israelites to return home. Surprisingly, the pagan king ordered the rebuilding of the Temple in Jerusalem. When the Jews returned, the house of David was not restored. In this connection it is interesting to note that Hos 3:4-5 had foretold that, 'The Israelites will live many days without king or prince, without sacrifice or sacred stones... Afterward the Israelites will return and seek the Lord their God and David their king.'

It looked as if the promise that David's dynasty would last forever had not been fulfilled. Nevertheless, because of a number of prophecies the Jewish people came to believe that a messiah was coming, a man who would be a descendant of king David.

- 'The days are coming,' declares the Lord, 'when I will raise up to David a righteous Branch, a King who will reign wisely and do what is just and right in the land. In his days Judah will be saved and Israel will live in safety. This is the name by which he will be called: The Lord Our Righteousness' (Jer 23:5-6).
- 'Of the increase of his government and of peace there will be no end, on the throne of David and over his kingdom, to establish it and to uphold it with justice and with righteousness from this time forth and forever more.

The zeal of the Lord of hosts will do this' (Is 9:7).

- 'In my vision at night I looked, and there before me was one like a son of man, coming with the clouds of heaven. He approached the Ancient of Days and was led into his presence. He was given authority, glory and sovereign power; all peoples, nations and men of every language worshipped him. His dominion is an everlasting dominion that will not pass away, and his kingdom is one that will never be destroyed' (Dan 7:13-14).

Joseph and Mary were descended from David

In Rom 1:3, Paul said that Jesus was, 'descended from David according to the flesh.' If we turn the pages of the Bible until we get to the gospels we see how the messianic prophecies were finally fulfilled. Luke 1:26-27 tells us that, 'In the sixth month, God sent the angel Gabriel to Nazareth, a town in Galilee, to a virgin pledged to be married to a man named Joseph, a descendant of David.' Speaking about Jesus, the angel Gabriel said to Mary, 'He will be great and will be called the Son of the Most High. The Lord God will give him *the throne of his father David,* and he will reign over the house of Jacob forever; *his kingdom will never end*' (Lk 1:32-33). The place where Jesus was born was significant. Luke tells us that, 'Joseph also went up from the town of Nazareth in Galilee to Judea, to Bethlehem the town of David, because *he belonged to the house and line of David*' (Lk 2:4). It is clear that Luke's nativity account is saying clearly that Jesus was a descendant of David through his legal, if not his biological father. It is thought that Mary, the mother of Jesus, may have been a descendant of David because St. Paul said that he was referring to, 'The Good News which is about his Son. In his earthly life he was born into

King David's family line' (Rm 1:3). As a result, commentators tell us that in the text 'in the sixth month the angel Gabriel was sent from God…to a virgin espoused to a man whose name was Joseph, of the house of David' (Lk 1:26-27); the last clause 'of the house of David' refers not to Joseph, but to the virgin who is the principal person in the narrative; thus we would have an inspired testimony to Mary's Davidic descent.[4]

The gospels testify on many occasions to the kingship of Jesus. Here are a number of relevant texts:

- 'After Jesus was born in Bethlehem in Judea, during the time of King Herod, Magi from the east came to Jerusalem and asked, 'Where is the one who has been born king of the Jews?' (Mt 2:1-2).
- 'Nathanael declared, 'Rabbi, you are the Son of God; you are the King of Israel' (Jn 1:49).
- 'The whole crowd of disciples began joyfully to praise God in loud voices for all the miracles they had seen: 'Blessed is the king who comes in the name of the Lord!' (Lk 19:37-38).
- 'You are a king, then!' said Pilate. Jesus answered, 'You are right in saying I am a king' (Jn 18:37).
- 'Do you want me to release to you the king of the Jews?' asked Pilate' (Mk 15:9).
- 'They put a staff in his right hand and knelt in front of him and mocked him. 'Hail, king of the Jews!' they said' (Mt 27:29).
- 'Above his head they placed the written charge against him: This is Jesus the king of the Jews' (Mt 27:37-38).
- 'The chief priests of the Jews protested to Pilate, 'Do not

write 'The King of the Jews,' but that this man claimed to be king of the Jews.' Pilate answered, 'What I have written, I have written' (Jn 19:21-22).

- 'He saved others,' they said, 'but he can't save himself! He's the King of Israel! Let him come down now from the cross, and we will believe in him' (Mt 27:42).

What the New Testament was saying was that the messianic promise made to David had been fulfilled. Jesus, a descendant of king David, was the messiah king whose throne lasts forever because he had ascended to his Father in heaven.

THE SUFFERING SERVANT

There is another major stream of messianic prophecy in the Old Testament. Around 700 BC Isaiah wrote these amazing words, 'He grew up before him like a tender shoot, and like a root out of dry ground. He had no beauty or majesty to attract us to him, nothing in his appearance that we should desire him. He was despised and rejected by men, a man of sorrows, and familiar with suffering. Like one from whom men hide their faces he was despised, and we esteemed him not. Surely he took up our infirmities and carried our sorrows, yet we considered him stricken by God, smitten by him, and afflicted. But he was pierced for our transgressions, he was crushed for our iniquities; the punishment that brought us peace was upon him, and by his wounds we are healed. We all, like sheep, have gone astray, each of us has turned to his own way; and the Lord has laid on him the iniquity of us all. He was oppressed and afflicted, yet he did not open his mouth; he was led like a lamb to the slaughter, and as a sheep before her shearers is silent, so he did not of his descendants? For he was cut off from the land of the living; for the transgression of my people he was stricken. He was assigned a grave with the wicked, and with the rich in his death, though he had done no violence, nor was any deceit in his mouth' (Is 53:2-9).

There is another messianic prophecy which seems to refer to Christ as the Suffering Servant. It is in Wis 2:12-20. In his commentary on this passage Addison G. Wright, says that it is probably based on Isaiah's prophecy. It reads as follows. 'Let us lie in wait for the righteous one, because he is annoying to us; he opposes our actions, Reproaches us for transgressions of the law and charges us with violations of our training. He professes to have knowledge of God and styles himself a child of the Lord. To us he is the censure of our thoughts; merely to see him is a hardship for us, because his life is not like that of others, and different are his ways. He judges us debased; he holds aloof from our paths as from things impure. He calls blest the destiny of the righteous and boasts that God is his Father. Let us see whether his words be true; let us find out what will happen to him in the end. For if the righteous one is the son of God, God will help him and deliver him from the hand of his foes. With violence and torture let us put him to the test that we may have proof of his gentleness and try his patience. Let us condemn him to a shameful death; for according to his own words, God will take care of him.' Those words find an echo in Ps 42:10, where the psalmist says in a messianic way, 'As with a deadly wound in my bones, my adversaries taunt me, while they say to me continually, 'Where is your God?'

Plato on the suffering servant

It is worth mentioning that there is a passage in the writings of Plato's *Republic*, book 2, (360 BC) which is surprisingly reminiscent of the one in Wisdom 2:12-20. Aeschylus, a man of simplicity and moral integrity, wants to be actually good and not merely to appear to give the impression of being good. His envious opponents say to themselves, 'We must, indeed, not allow him to seem good, for if he does he will have all the rewards and honours paid to the man who has a reputation for justice, and we shall not be able to tell whether his motive is love of justice or love of the rewards and honours. No, we must strip him of everything except his justice, and our picture of him must be drawn in the opposite way to our picture of the unjust man; for our just man must have the worst of reputations even though he has done no wrong. So we shall be able to test his justice and see if it can stand up to unpopularity and all that goes with it; we shall give him an undeserved and lifelong reputation for wickedness, and make him stick to his chosen course until death ... The just man, then, as we have pictured him, will be scourged, tortured, and imprisoned, his eyes will be put out, and after enduring every humiliation he will be crucified, and learn at last that in the world as it is we should want not to be, but to seem, just.'

This passage is intriguing. It is so similar to the one in Wisdom that two questions arise. Firstly, was Plato aware of the prophecy about the suffering servant in Is 53:2-9 or was the author of Wisdom aware of Plato's *Republic*? Apparently it is highly unlikely that Plato had read Isaiah because the Old Testament hadn't been translated into Greek before the time of his death. The second question is this, did the author of Wisdom, supposedly an Alexandrian Jew, read Plato's *Republic*, or was he told about it? We don't know the answer. It would appear that Plato was a bit like Balaam, a pagan who received a prophetic revelation about the coming messiah, or like king Nebuchadnezzar who had a number of prophetic dreams which were interpreted by the prophet Daniel. St. Justin Martyr seemed to think that a pagan could receive such a grace. Having mentioned Plato, the Stoics, and Greek poets Justin said, 'For each person spoke well, according to the part present in him of the divine logos, the Sower.' The Sower mentioned by Justin is the Lord who can sow the seed of truth, not only in the hearts of Jews and Christians, but also in the hearts of sincere pagans who conscientiously seek truth and love in their lives. In another place Justin said, 'They who lived with the *logos* are Christians, even though they have been thought to have been atheists.'[5] In this connection it is worth noting that Pope Benedict XIV said, 'The recipients of prophecy may be angels, devils, men, women, children, heathens, or gentiles; nor is it necessary that a man should be gifted with any particular disposition in order to receive the light of prophecy provided his intellect and senses be adapted for making manifest the things which God reveals to him. Though moral goodness is most profitable to a prophet, yet it is not necessary in order to obtain the gift of prophecy.'[6] This authoritative teaching seems to imply that a pagan could be graced with a genuine revelation of a prophetic kind by God.

Conclusion

I don't know about you, but speaking for myself, I'm amazed that, for over a thousand years before the coming of Jesus, Jewish prophets from Moses onwards had predicted his advent in such an amazingly accurate way. There is an informative and moving video available in English on Youtube entitled, 'The Messiah - Prophecy Fulfilled.'[7] It shows how so many of the details of Jesus' life were fulfillments of what the prophets had foretold. Blaise Pascal (1623-1662) was aware of this. In a chapter entitled, 'The Prophecies,' in his famous *Pensees,* he referred to the way in which Messianic prophecies have been fulfilled, 'If one man alone had made a book of predictions about Jesus Christ, as to the time and the manner, and Jesus Christ had come in conformity to these prophecies, this fact would have infinite weight. But there is much more. Here is a succession of men during four thousand years who, consequently and without variation, come, one after another, to foretell this same event. Here is a whole people who announce it, and who have existed for four thousand years, in order to give corporate testimony of the assurances which they have, and from which they cannot be diverted by whatever threats and persecutions people may make against them. This is far more important.'[8]

NOTES

1. Justin Martyr, *The First and Second Apologies,* vol. 56, eds., Burghardt, Dillon & McManus (New York: Paulist, 1997), 43.
2. Cf., Raymond Brown, 'A Brief History of the Development of the Royal Messianic Hope in Israel,' in *An Introduction to New Testament Christology* (London: Geoffrey Chapman, 1994), 155-161.
3. Origen on *First Principles* (Glouster, Mass: Peter Smith, 1973), 265.
4. Cf. Marcus Bockmuehl, 'The Son of David and the Gospel' in *Introduction to Messianic Judaism,* eds. David Rudolph & Joel Willitts (Grand Rapids: Zondervan, 2013), 264-271.
5. *The Second Apology,* par. 13; *The First Apology* par. 46 in St. Justin Martyr, *The First and Second Apologies* (New York: Paulist Press, 1997), 83; 55.
6. *Heroic Virtue,* vol. 3, op. cit.
7. *https://www.youtube.com/watch?v=Q1tRF4HfsHc (Accessed 22/12/2015).*
8. *Pensees,* book eleven, par. 710.

SIX

Jesus as Fulfillment of Messianic Prophecy

When Jesus began his public ministry we are told that, 'Philip found Nathanael and told him, 'We have found the one Moses wrote about in the Law, and about whom the prophets also wrote - Jesus of Nazareth, the son of Joseph' (Jn 1:45). Clearly, these two disciples came to the conviction that Jesus was the promised messiah. But what kind of messiah, a political and military king like David, or a suffering servant who endures much on behalf of the people? In his book, *Jesus was a Jew,* messianic Jew, Arnold G. Fruchtenbaum, says that many rabbis came to the conclusion that the prophets had spoken about two different messiahs. The messiah who was to suffer and die was Messiah son of Joseph, and the second, who would follow the first, was Messiah son of David. This latter one would raise the first messiah to life and establish the Messianic Kingdom of peace on earth. Fructenbaum says that since the Talmudic period the Jewish people focused almost exclusively on the Son of David stream of prophecy while overlooking the suffering servant stream of Isaiah.[1]

Although, Jesus knew that he was the descendant of David, his call to be the suffering servant was confirmed at his baptism when he heard the Father say, 'This is my Son, whom I love; with him I am well pleased' (Mt 3:17). In speaking these words, the

Father was drawing attention to two messianic scripture references to the Suffering Servant, 'Here is my servant, whom I delight, I will put my Spirit on him' (Is 42:1) and 'He said to me, 'You are my Son; today I have become your Father' (Ps 2:7). It could be argued that when Jesus was tempted by the devil in the wilderness, the evil one tried on three separate occasions to seduce him into abandoning his vocation to be the suffering servant. He tried to do this in order to get Jesus to revert to being the Davidic messiah of popular Jewish expectation, the one who would wield political and military power in order to conquer the enemies of Israel and set up a Messianic Kingdom of peace and prosperity.

It is noticeable in the gospels that Jesus was not keen on being addressed as son of David, not because it was untrue, but rather because it was a misleading title. As David Aune explains, 'The Davidic Messiah of popular expectation was conceived as a military figure whose primary tasks were the defeat of Israel's enemies, the purification of Jerusalem and the temple, and the in-gathering of dispersed Israelites as a prelude for a golden age. This messianic figure did not function as a prophet, a preacher of repentance, or a miracle worker.'[2] In any case, people didn't normally recognise that Jesus was the messiah. An exception was the occasion when Jesus asked the apostles who they thought he was, and St. Peter exclaimed, 'You are the Christ [i.e. anointed messiah], the Son of the living God.' Jesus replied, 'Blessed are you, Simon son of Jonah, for this was not revealed to you by man, but by my Father in heaven' (Mt 16:16-18). In other words, as a result of receiving a prophetic revelation Peter recognised who Jesus really was.

In Luke's Gospel Jesus added, 'The Son of Man must suffer many things and be rejected by the elders, chief priests and teachers of the law, and he must be killed and on the third day be raised to life' (Lk 9:22). As soon as Jesus talked about being the suffering servant going to meet his destiny in Jerusalem, 'Peter took him aside and began to rebuke him. But when Jesus turned and looked at his disciples, he rebuked Peter. 'Get behind me, Satan!' he said. 'You do not have in mind the things of God, but the things of men' (Mk 8:32-33). In saying what he did, Jesus felt that Peter was echoing the temptations which he had already been subjected to shortly after his baptism in the Jordan. It was as if Peter was saying, 'forget about being the suffering servant, it is too difficult, it would be better if you acted like the son of David.' Arguably, Jesus himself was tempted on similar lines in Gethsemane when the thought of what he would have to endure as the Suffering Servant was emotionally overwhelming. 'Abba, Father,' he prayed, 'everything is possible for you. Take this cup from me. Yet not what I will, but what you will' (Mk 14:36). It was if Jesus was asking God to allow him to switch from being the Suffering Servant to being a Davidic type messiah.

It is surprising to find that although he was the promised Messiah, Jesus didn't tell people who he was. There is one moving exception, however, in the Gospel of John. We are told that having dialogued with the Samaritan woman at the well of Jacob she said, 'I know that Messiah' (called Christ) is coming. When he comes, he will explain everything to us.' Then Jesus declared, 'I who speak to you am he' (Jn 4:25-26). I find this disclosure intensely moving. The Samaritan woman had opened her heart to Jesus, and he reciprocated by revealing to her who he really was. Perhaps one reason he did so, was the fact that she would have been unlikely to misunderstand what Jesus meant by his words.

SOME MORE MESSIANIC PROPHECIES

Having heard the messianic prophecies of the Old Testament being recalled and explained by Jesus, no wonder the two disciples on the road to Emmaus could say, 'Were not our hearts burning within us while he talked with us on the road and opened the Scriptures to us?' (Lk 24:32). They can have much the same effect on contemporary readers. Although, the two complementary streams of revelation about the coming messiah were of major importance in the Old Testament, there were other striking prophecies about the coming of the messiah. At this point I will mention some of them.

A. PLACE OF JESUS' BIRTH

In Mic 5:2 we read this messianic prophecy, 'But you, Bethlehem Ephrathah, though you are small among the clans of Judah, out of you will come for me one who will be ruler over Israel.' It was fulfilled in the New Testament. Matt 2:1-5 says, 'After Jesus was born in Bethlehem in Judea, during the time of King Herod, Magi from the east came to Jerusalem and asked, 'Where is the one who has been born king of the Jews? We saw his star in the east and have come to worship him.' It is worth saying in passing that it is quite possible that the wise men of the East were influenced by the memory of Daniel's messianic prophecies in Babylon. When King Herod heard what the Magi had to say he was disturbed, and all Jerusalem with him. When he had called together all the people's chief priests and teachers of the law, he asked them where the Christ was to be born. 'In Bethlehem in Judea,' they replied, 'for this is what the prophet has written.' In Lk 2:4 we read, 'So Joseph also went up from the town of Nazareth in Galilee to Judea, to Bethlehem the town of David, because he belonged to the house and line of David.'

B. MASSACRE OF THE INNOCENTS

In Ex 1:22 we are told how Pharaoh gave this order to all his people: 'Every boy that is born you must throw into the Nile, but let every girl live.' Moses survived because his family put him in a basket and floated him down the Nile. He was discovered by Pharaoh's daughter who adopted him. Jesus was the new Moses. Following his birth, we are told that, 'When Herod realised that he had been outwitted by the Magi, he was furious, and he gave orders to kill all the boys in Bethlehem and its vicinity who were two years old and under, in accordance with the time he had learned from the Magi' (Mt 2:16). Jesus survived because, obedient to a prophetic dream, Joseph his adoptive father, brought him and his mother Mary to Egypt until Herod died. However between ten and twenty boys were killed in Bethlehem. 'Then what was said through the prophet Jeremiah was fulfilled: 'A voice is heard in Ramah, weeping and great mourning, Rachel weeping for her children and refusing to be comforted, because they are no more' (Mt 2:17-18).

C. JESUS BETRAYED FOR THIRTY PIECES OF SILVER

In Zech 11:12-13 we read, 'I told them, 'If you think it best, give me my pay; but if not, keep it.' So they paid me thirty pieces of silver. And the Lord said to me, 'Throw it to the potter'-the handsome price at which they priced me! So I took the thirty pieces of silver and threw them into the house of the Lord to the potter.' There is an echo of that text in Jer 19:1-2, 'Go and buy a clay jar from a potter. Take along some of the elders of the people and of the priests.' St. Matthew tells us how this messianic prophecy was fulfilled, 'The chief priests picked up the coins and said to Judas who received thirty pieces of silver, 'It is against the law to put this into the treasury, since it is blood money.' So they decided to use the money to buy the potter's field as a burial place for foreigners. That is why it has been called the Field of Blood to this day. Then what was spoken by Jeremiah the prophet was fulfilled: 'They took the thirty silver coins, the price set on him by the people of Israel, and they used them to buy the potter's field, as the Lord commanded me' (Mt 27:6-10).

D. Jesus the new Moses

Deut 18:18 says, 'I will raise up for them a prophet like you from among their brothers; I will put my words in his mouth, and he will tell them everything I command him.' St. Peter recounted what Moses had said and then went on to state that his words had been fulfilled in the coming of Jesus The Messiah, 'The Lord your God will raise up for you a prophet like me from among your own people; you must listen to everything he tells you. Anyone who does not listen to him will be completely cut off from among his people.' 'Indeed, all the prophets from Samuel on, as many as have spoken, have foretold these days. And you are heirs of the prophets and of the covenant God made with your fathers.' He said to Abraham, 'Through your offspring all peoples on earth will be blessed.' 'When God raised up his servant, he sent him first to you to bless you by turning each of you from your wicked ways' (Acts 3: 22-26).

E. Death of the Suffering Servant

Speaking about the crucifixion of Christ, Ps 22:18 prophesied, 'They divide my garments among them and cast lots for my clothing.' Mt 27:35 tells us how those words were fulfilled. 'When they had crucified him, they divided up his clothes by casting lots.' In Ps 22:1-2 these words of dereliction are spoken, 'My God, my God, why have you forsaken me? Why are you so far from saving me, so far from the words of my groaning? O my God, I cry out by day, but you do not answer, by night, and am not silent.' When Jesus was nearing the end of his life he cried out on the cross, *'Eloi, Eloi, lama sabachthani?'* - which means, 'My God, my God, why have you forsaken me?' (Mt 27:46). Speaking of the bones of the messiah Jn 19:33 informs us that, 'But when they came to Jesus and found that he was already dead, they did not break his legs.' This fulfils what was said in Ps 34:20, 'He keeps all his bones; not one of them is broken.'

F. The Heart of Jesus Pierced by a Lance

In Zech 12:10-11 there is a passage which seems to be messianic. It says, 'And I will pour out on the house of David and the inhabitants of Jerusalem a spirit of grace and supplication. They will look on me, the one they have pierced, and they will mourn for him as one mourns for an only child, and grieve bitterly for him as one grieves for a firstborn son. On that day the weeping in Jerusalem will be great.' As the *NIV Zondervan Study Bible* says in a footnote, this prophecy gains even greater meaning for Christians who see its fulfillment in the piercing of Jesus on the cross by a Roman soldier's spear (cf. Jn 19:34-37). After Jesus' death, God's Spirit was poured out on God-fearing Jews in Jerusalem, who were 'cut to the heart' and repented (cf Acts 2:32-37).

G. The Resurrection of Jesus

The Amplified Bible which brings out nuances implicit in the original Hebrew text, tells us that David prophesied, 'I will bless the Lord, Who has given me counsel; yes, my heart instructs me in the night seasons. I have set the Lord continually before me; because He is at my right hand, I shall not be moved. Therefore my heart is glad and my glory [my inner self] rejoices; my body too shall rest and confidently dwell in safety, for You will not abandon me to *Sheol* [the place of the dead], neither will You suffer Your holy one to see corruption. You will show me the path of life; in Your presence is fullness of joy, at Your right hand there are pleasures for evermore' (Ps 16:7-11). St Peter quoted these words from Ps 16: 8-11 on Pentecost Sunday to show that the Old Testament had foretold the resurrection of Jesus (cf. Acts 2:25-32).

Why many Jews did not accept that Jesus fulfilled messianic prophecies

These are only a selection from the many messianic prophecies in the Old Testament which have been fulfilled in the New Testament. As Heb 1:1-3 attests, 'In the past God spoke to our forefathers through the prophets at many times and in various ways, but in these last days he has spoken to us by his Son, whom he appointed heir of all things.' In Acts 3:24-25, Peter said something very similar, 'Indeed, all the prophets from Samuel on, as many as have spoken, have foretold these days. And you are heirs of the prophets and of the covenant God made with your fathers.' In the *Living Bible* version of Rm 1:2-3 we read, 'This Good News was promised long ago by God's prophets in the Old Testament. It is the Good News about his Son, Jesus Christ our Lord, who came as a human baby, born into King David's royal family line.' At this juncture two points can be made about the fulfilled prophecies of the Old Testament.

As we know the first believers in Jesus were Jewish. Unlike Gentile converts, the Messianic Jews continued to practice their traditional faith while augmenting it with new elements which reflected their belief in Jesus and his teachings. Scholars have long held that the Jerusalem community, headed firstly by Peter and then by James, lived strictly according to the Torah. It is believed that they intended to spark a Jewish renewal movement for Jesus, the Son of David, within the Jewish religion. However, they did not realise their dream because the Gentile Christians wanted them to drop their distinctively Jewish practices. By the fourth century the Messianic Jewish community had more or less faded away. However, it is heartening and significant to see that in recent years there has been a rebirth of Messianic Judaism. In other words, an increasing number of Orthodox Jews are accepting Jesus as their Messiah and reading the New Testament as inspired scripture while continuing to practice as Jews.[3]

It is really surprising, not to say disappointing, however, that from the beginning so many Orthodox Jews failed, and still fail, to acknowledge the fact that Jesus fulfilled the messianic prophecies. Speaking about some reasons for this, par. 576 of the *Catechism of the Catholic Church* explains that, firstly, in the eyes of many in Israel, Jesus seemed to be acting against essential institutions of the Chosen People such as submission to the whole of the Law in its written commandments and, for the Pharisees, in the interpretation of the oral tradition. Secondly, mindful of the centrality of the Temple at Jerusalem as the holy place where God's presence dwelt in a special way they could not accept that it would be replaced by the living temple of Christ's body on earth. Thirdly, because the Jews had faith in the one God whose glory no man could share, they could not accept the doctrine that there were three persons in the one God. It was as if the spiritual ears and eyes of many Jews had been deafened and blinded to what otherwise seemed rather obvious. As Jesus said, quoting the prophet Isaiah, 'seeing they do not see, and hearing they do not hear, nor do they understand' (Mt 13:13-14). St Paul said much the same in Rom 11:7-8, 'What Israel sought so earnestly it did not obtain, but the elect did. The others were hardened, as it is written: 'God gave them a spirit of stupor, eyes so that they could not see and ears so that they could not hear, to this very day.'

One could also argue that, by and large, the Jews at the time of Jesus expected a political and military messiah like David, and so when Jesus came as the suffering servant, they couldn't accept that he was the one promised by God. It could also be said that the Jews did not expect the Messiah to be divine, and so they rejected any implicit or explicit claim of that kind by Jesus because they believed it was blasphemous. However, Blaise Paschal commented in his *Pensees*, 'The Jews, in slaying Him in order not to receive Him as the Messiah, have given Him the final proof of being the Messiah. And in continuing not to recognise Him, they made themselves irreproachable witnesses. Both in slaying Him and in continuing to deny Him, they have fulfilled the prophecies (Is. 60; Ps. 71).'[4] Luke said much the same in Acts 13:27-28, 'The people of Jerusalem and their rulers did not recognise Jesus, yet in condemning him they fulfilled the words of the prophets that are read every Sabbath.'

Paul prophesied, that the spiritual blindness and deafness of many orthodox Jews would be embraced by divine providence. Firstly, it would prove to be a 'happy fault' which would lead to the evangelisation of the Gentiles. Secondly, much later their rejection would give way to the acceptance of Christ by many Jews. As Paul prophesied in Rom 11:25-27, 'Israel has experienced a hardening in part until the full number of the Gentiles has come in. And so all Israel will be saved, as it is written: 'The deliverer will come from Zion; he will turn godlessness away from Jacob. And this is my covenant with them when I take away their sins.'

I believe that in God's providence, the immense sufferings of the Jewish people, especially in the Holocaust, are becoming a springboard for a great outpouring of God's grace, not only on Jewish people, but through them on the world. As Paul said in Rm 5:20, 'Where sin increased grace overflowed all the more.' The blessing has begun to be poured out in two interrelated steps.

Firstly, in Is 66:8 we read, 'Who has ever heard of such a thing? Who has ever seen such things? Can a country be born in a day or a nation be brought forth in a moment? Yet no sooner is Zion in labour than she gives birth to her children.' Some biblical scholars believe that this prophecy was fulfilled on the 14th of May 1948 when the modern state of Israel was re-established and Hebrew was resurrected as the official language of the state. Arguably, this was also a fulfillment of Ezek 37:21-23 which says, 'This is what the Sovereign Lord says: I will take the Israelites out of the nations where they have gone. I will gather them from all around and bring them back into their own land. I will make them one nation in the land, on the mountains of Israel. There will be one king over all of them and they will never again be two nations or be divided into two kingdoms.' The re-establishment of Israel was a key prophecy which had to be fulfilled before the other end time prophecies could be fulfilled.

Secondly, since the 1970s, there have been a growing number of Jews who have accepted Jesus as their messiah. It is thought that there may be as many as 15,000 of them in Israel in 150 or so congregations.[5] Arguably, this unexpected development is a prophetic indication that we are on the run-in to the end times. That however, does not necessarily imply that the end is near. I also believe that Messianic Jews have a great deal to teach Christians about the deeper meaning of the scriptures. I find that every time a Messianic Jew interprets the New Testament in the light of the Old, either in print or in speech, I understand it in a more insightful way. Finally, I believe that from now on Messianic Jews will have to be included in Christian ecumenical discussions. Furthermore, I wouldn't be surprised if they play an increasingly important role as mediators, precisely because they were not involved in the internal disputes that divided Christianity down the centuries. Our divisions are foolish. We are not enemies of one another. The real enemy is militant secularism which leads many people to be 'without hope and without God in the world' (Eph 2:12).

Conclusion

When reading the messianic prophecies, it is important to avoid the hermeneutics of suspicion, i.e. a sceptical form of interpretation which presupposes that the New Testament writers, conformed their accounts of the events of Christ's life to the Old Testament prophecies rather than seeing the actual events of his life as a fulfilment of those prophecies. Unless one can prove that the inspired writers were either involved in deliberate deception, or badly deluded, their way of understanding how the messianic prophecies were fulfilled is trustworthy. Speaking about his own interpretation of messianic texts St. John testified, 'He who saw it has borne witness - his testimony is true, and he knows that he is telling the truth - that you also may believe. For these things took place that the Scripture might be fulfilled' (Jn 19:35-36).

Peter Stoner was chairman of the mathematics and astronomy departments at Pasadena City College until 1953 when he moved to Westmont College in Santa Barbara, California. There he served as chairman of the science division. During that time he wrote a book entitled, *Science Speaks: Scientific Proof of the Accuracy of Prophecy and the Bible.* Among other things his book examined eight messianic prophecies and how they were fulfilled. He calculated that the odds against their accidental fulfillment in one person was 1 in 10 to the power of 28. Stoner said that written out 'it is 1 in ten trillion.'[6]

It would be quite a mistake to believe that private revelation, of a prophetic kind, in the modern world is equal in authority to the prophetic revelations in the scriptures. As St. Paul observed, 'our prophecy is imperfect' (1 Cor 13:9). So it would have to be said that those who have a charism of prophetic utterance do not speak with absolute divine authority, in the way that Old or New Testament prophets did. They simply report any message the Lord has revealed to their hearts. As was noted in a previous chapter, such revelations are subject to a number of possible shortcomings. Although some of a prophecy may have been revealed by God, other parts of it may be what is called 'non-prophecy' or even 'false prophecy' because it originated, either in the person's own human nature, or it may even have been prompted by the devil by means of illusions and false inspirations. An otherwise authentic prophecy can be misinterpreted by the one who received it or those who hear it.

The prophet can also misapply the prophecy he or she has received.

NOTES

1. (San Antonio: Ariel, Ministries, 2014), 15-16.
2. *Prophecy in Early Christianity and the Ancient Mediterranean World* (Grand Rapids: Eerdmans, 1983), 123.
3. Cf. David Rudolph, 'Messianic Judaism in Antiquity and in the Modern Era,' in *Introduction to Messianic Judaism, Its Ecclesial Context and Biblical Foundations,* eds, David Rudolph & Joel Willitts (Grand Rapids: Zondervan, 2013), 21-36.
4. Book fourteen, par. 761.
5. *Charisma Magazine* October 29, 2013.
6. (Chicago: Moody Press, 1969). 105.

SEVEN

PROPHECY IN THE TEACHING OF THE CHURCH

I'm not so sure where I was born. I know it was Dublin City, but I don't know the exact location. I do know, however, when and where I was baptised. It was the day after my birth, March first 1945, in the Church of the Sacred Heart, Donnybrook. To the best of my knowledge a Jesuit uncle of mine, who was home from the missions in Zambia, administered the sacrament. Although my father was present, my mother was still in the nursing home. But on that blessed day, I became a Christian and began, for the first time, to share in the kingly, priestly and prophetic roles of Jesus Christ.

Catholic theology maintains that Jesus was a king (cf. Ps 2), priest (cf. Ps 110:1-4) and prophet (cf. Deut 18:14-22). Speaking of the kingship of Christ Mt 27:11 says, 'Now Jesus stood before the governor, and the governor questioned Him, saying, 'Are You the King of the Jews?' And Jesus said to him, 'It is as you say.' As king, Jesus leads us on the right path, by giving guidance. Speaking of the priesthood of Jesus Heb. 9:11 says, 'But when Christ appeared as a high priest of the good things to come, He entered through the greater and more perfect tabernacle, not made with hands, that is to say, not of this creation.' As priest, Jesus sanctifies by re-establishing the lost link between God and humanity. Speaking of his prophetic role, Mt 13:57 tells us that, 'they took offence at

Him. But Jesus said to them, 'A prophet is not without honour except in his home town, and in his own household.' As a prophet, Jesus speaks and embodies divine truth.

Christians are baptised into Christ's saving death and resurrection. The words of the Baptismal Rite say, 'As Christ was anointed Priest, Prophet and King, so may you live always as a member of his body, sharing everlasting life.' Par. 2 of the Decree on *Apostolate of the Laity* spells out some of the implications of that prayer, 'In the Church there is a diversity of ministry but a oneness of mission. Christ conferred on the Apostles and their successors the duty of teaching, sanctifying, and ruling in His name and power. But the laity likewise share in the priestly, prophetic, and royal office of Christ and therefore have their own share in the mission of the whole people of God in the Church and in the world.' The mission of the Church, therefore, is to participate in Christ's priestly, sanctifying function; prophetic, teaching function; and royal, ruling function.

Writing about the prophetic office, in which all baptised Christians share, par. 35 of the *Dogmatic Constitution of the Church* says, 'Christ, the great Prophet, who proclaimed the Kingdom of His Father both by the testimony of His life and the power of His words, continually fulfils His prophetic office until the complete manifestation of glory. He does this not only through the hierarchy who teach in His name and with His authority, but also through the laity whom He made His witnesses and to whom He gave understanding of the faith and an attractiveness in speech so that the power of the Gospel might shine forth in their daily social and family life.' The organisation of the 1983 *Code of Canon Law* was very much influenced by the three functions, already mentioned. Of particular interest, where this chapter is concerned, is the fact that in the Code, canons 747-833 on the teaching office of the Church, the gift of prophecy is virtually synonymous with such things as preaching, teaching and catechesis. It could be said that this approach is very institutional and needs to be augmented by an appreciation of the charism and ministry of prophecy.

However, it is worth noting that when he promulgated the *Code of Canon Law*, Pope John Paul II explained that it, 'is in no way intended as a substitute for faith, grace, *charisms* [my italics], and especially charity in the life of the Church and of the faithful. On the contrary, its purpose is rather to create such an order in the ecclesial society that, while assigning the primacy to love, grace, and *charisms,* it at the same time renders their organic development easier in the life of both the ecclesial society and the individual persons who belong to it.' Talking about the charisms, including that of prophecy, pars. 799-800 of the *Catechism of the Catholic Church,* say, 'Whether extraordinary or simple and humble, charisms [especially prophecy] are graces of the Holy Spirit which directly or indirectly benefit the Church, ordered as they are to her building up, to the good of men, and to the needs of the world. Charisms are to be accepted with gratitude by the person who receives them and by all members of the Church as well. They are a wonderfully rich grace for the apostolic vitality and for the holiness of the entire Body of Christ, provided they really are genuine gifts of the Holy Spirit and are used in full conformity with authentic promptings of this same Spirit, that is, in keeping with charity, the true measure of all charisms.' In a letter proclaiming the Year of Priests in 2009, Pope Benedict XVI wrote, 'In his gifts the Spirit is multifaceted. He breathes where he wills. He does so unexpectedly, in unexpected places, and in ways previously *unheard of* [my italics].' Surely, the Pope was balancing the institutional with the charismatic dimension of the Church. Needless to say, pre-eminent among the charisms he referred to is that of prophecy.

That said, the subject of the charism and ministry of prophecy is largely neglected. Archbishop Rino Fisichella has said that theological reflection on prophecy has been like, 'wreckage after shipwreck.'[1] That largely non charismatic approach is reflected in Niels Christian Hvidt's, otherwise excellent book, *Prophecy: The Post-Biblical Tradition*.[2] As a result it is not surprising that many well intentioned Christian groups, communities and leaders have little or no appreciation of how to exercise the prophetic gift in such a way that it would enable them to tune in to the mind and heart of God. In this chapter we will look at some of the things that the Church has said down the centuries about the charism of prophecy.

The Post Apostolic Fathers on Prophecy

In the years after the death of the apostles, a number of Christian authors wrote spiritual documents which are important and interesting because they afford us an insight into the development and beliefs of the early Church. Three documents in particular are of interest as far as the charism of prophecy is concerned, *The Didache* (c. 80-120 AD)[3] *The Shepherd of Hermas* (c. 140-150 AD),[4] and Origen's *On the First Principles* (225 AD).[5] It is fairly apparent from these documents that the Church was in a transitional period between the time of the wandering apostles and Christian prophets and the establishment of a hierarchical organisation of ecclesiastical government. While these documents do not have much to say about the nature and exercise of the gift of prophecy, which was still evident in Christian communities, they have interesting things to say on the subject of how to recognise a true from a false prophet.

The Didache is recognised as an early church manual which was used to instruct new candidates for a specific Christian community. In sec. 13:1-7 the anonymous author deals with the subject of apostles and prophets. Speaking specifically about prophets he said, 'Do not test or examine any prophet who is speaking in a spirit. Every genuine prophet who wants to live among you is worthy of support. So also, every true teacher is, like a workman, entitled to his support. Every first fruit, therefore, of the products of vintage and harvest, of cattle and of sheep, should be given as first fruits to the prophets, for they are your high priests. But if you have no prophet, give it all to the poor. If you bake bread, take the first loaf and give it according to the commandment. If you open a new jar of wine or of oil, take the first fruit and give it to the prophets. If you acquire money or cloth or any other possession, set aside a portion first, as it may seem good to you, and give according to the commandment.'[6]

Scholars usually consider the text of *The Shepherd of Hermas* to be an early example of Christian apocalyptic literature which sought to reveal hidden truths about the end times to its readers. In sec. 43:1-21 of the document there is a relatively long passage on prophecy where we are told how to distinguish true from false prophets. Among other things it asks, 'How then, will a man know which of them is the prophet, and which the false prophet?' 'I will tell you,' says he, 'about both the prophets, and then you can try the true and the false prophet according to my directions.

Try the man who has the Divine Spirit by his life. First, he who has the Divine Spirit proceeding from above is meek, and peaceable, and humble, and refrains from, all iniquity and the vain desire of this world, and contents himself with fewer wants than those of other men, and when asked he makes no reply; nor does he speak privately, nor when man wishes the spirit to speak does the Holy Spirit speak, but it speaks only when God wishes it to speak. When, then, a man having the Divine Spirit comes into an assembly of righteous men who have faith in the Divine Spirit, and this assembly of men offers up prayer to God, then the angel of the prophetic Spirit, who is destined for him, fills the man; and the man being filled with the Holy Spirit, speaks to the multitude as the Lord wishes. Thus, then, will the Spirit of Divinity become manifest. Whatever power therefore comes from the Spirit of Divinity belongs to the Lord.

Hear, then,' says he, 'in regard to the spirit which is earthly, and empty, and powerless, and foolish. First, the man who seems to have the Spirit exalts himself, and wishes to have the first seat, and is bold, and impudent, and talkative, and lives in the midst of many luxuries and many other delusions, and takes rewards for his prophecy; and if he does not receive rewards, he does not prophesy. Can, then, the Divine Spirit take rewards and prophesy? It is not possible that the prophet of God should do this, but prophets of this character are possessed by an earthly spirit. Then it never approaches an assembly of righteous men, but shuns them. And it associates with doubters and the vain, and prophesies to them in a corner, and deceives them, speaking to them, according to their desires, mere empty words: for they are empty to whom it gives its answers.'[7]

Origen was one of the great scholars in the early Christian Church who wrote an enormous number of books, scripture commentaries and homilies. St Jerome referred to him as 'The greatest teacher of the Church after the Apostles.'[8] One of his seminal works is entitled *On First Principles.* In a chapter on the spirits, good and bad, which can influence people, he spoke about prophecy and how to discern genuine from false messages. 'A man admits the energy and control of a good spirit when he is moved and incited to what is good and inspired to strive towards things heavenly and divine; just as the holy angels and God himself worked in the prophets, inciting and exhorting them by holy suggestions to strive towards better things, though certainly in such a way that it rested with man's own will and judgment whether or not he was willing to follow God's call to the heavenly and divine. From this we learn to discern clearly when the soul is moved by the presence of a spirit of the better kind, namely, when it suffers no mental disturbance or aberration whatsoever as a result of the immediate inspiration and does not lose the free judgement of the will. Such for example were the prophets and apostles, who attended upon the divine oracles without any mental disturbance.'[9]

ST THOMAS AQUINAS ON PROPHECY

St. Thomas Aquinas (1225-1274) lived in an age when the charismatic gifts were not much in evidence, except in the lives of saints. It is thought that heretical Albigenses known as Cathari, who flourished in parts of France during Thomas's lifetime, were interested in the gifts of the Spirit. Furthermore, St. Domnic Guzman, the founder of the Order of Preachers, was endowed with many charisms. That said, the Church of the time mainly focused on those gifts of the Spirit which are mentioned in

Is 11:2. Nevertheless, in a 'Treatise on the Gratuitous Graces,' in the *Summa Theologiae* II-II, questions. 171-179, St. Thomas devoted more than 32,000 words to an examination of the charisms mentioned by St. Paul, especially, in 1 Cor 12:8-10. He also wrote about them in his *Commentary on the First Epistle to the Corinthians,* and in book 3, art. 155, of the *Summa Contra Gentiles.* Nevertheless, it is surprising to find that the teaching of the Church's premier theologian on the gifts is, largely, neglected.

The first thing to say about Thomas's treatment of the gift of prophecy is that he saw it within a more general theological context. I think it would be true to say that in Thomas's view the gifts have an evangelistic purpose. He said, 'Some charisms freely given relate to knowledge, some to words, some to deeds.'[10] Another way of putting it would be to say that there are gifts of revelation, proclamation and demonstration. Gifts of revelation enable evangelisers to know what to say, gifts of proclamation enable them to preach and teach effectively, and gifts of demonstration enable them to authenticate what they proclaim by means of such things as works of mercy, action for justice and deeds of power like healing and miracle working. St. Thomas talked about the gift of prophecy in two interrelated ways as a gift of revelation on the one hand and of verbal proclamation on the other. He said, 'Prophecy consists first and foremost in knowing certain far-off things outside the normal knowledge of men and women. But secondarily it involves speech, since a prophet proclaims to others what God has taught him or her in order to build them up.' Then he added, 'Prophets sometimes work miracles to confirm their prophecies.'[11] Thomas believed, in an evangelistic way, that the function of prophecy was to instruct people in whatever was necessary for salvation. It would probably be true to say that for him, the gift of prophecy was the most important of the charisms, a keystone in the charismatic bridge. That is evident in the *Summa Theologica* II-II, questions 175-178 which deal with the relationship of prophecy to the other charisms.

A. The Nature of Prophecy.

Thomas talks about the nature of the prophetic gift in a number of places. He sees it as knowledge, which is supernaturally given, of truths exceeding the ability of the mind, its intelligence, learning or experience which are revealed by God for the benefit of the community. In his commentary on 1 Cor 12:10, which refers to the charism of prophecy, Thomas says, 'In verse 10b Paul says, to another is given prophecy, which is divine revelation, announcing future events with unshakable truth.' This would be the conventional point of view. However, Thomas provided a more nuanced definition in his *Summa Theologica* where he wrote, 'Prophecy consists first and foremost in knowing certain far-off things outside the normal knowledge of men.'[12] In another place he said, 'it is in the revelation of future events that prophecy above all consists and to which it owes its name. But in a broad sense the subject of prophecy is whatever a person knows by God's revelation... Prophecy is knowledge imprinted on the prophet's mind by the teaching of God's revelation... anything whatever can be the subject of prophetic revelation... which involves the removal of the veils of darkness and ignorance so that the prophet can see what God is revealing.'[13]

B. How Prophetic Knowledge is Received

Having described what prophetic knowledge is, St. Thomas, had interesting things to say about the ways it can be received.

He outlined them in his *Summa Contra Gentiles*. For the sake of clarity what he said will be itemised and commented on. He wrote, 'As the natural light of the understanding renders a man certain of what he observes by that light, so does this supernatural light convey certainty of the objects which it reveals: for we cannot securely publish to others what we are not certain of ourselves. This light, which inwardly enlightens the mind, is sometimes borne out by other aids to knowledge as well, exterior or interior.

There may be formed by divine power some utterance, or locution, heard by the external senses.' In other words, the person may hear an external, audible voice saying something revelatory. For example, in Mt 17:5 Peter, James and John heard the Father say in an audible way, 'This is my Son, whom I love; with him I am well pleased. Listen to him!' Or it may be inner speech. The person may hear an inner voice telling him or her something revelatory. Sometimes the words will be accompanied by an image like a photograph, or with a vision like a short video.

Another possibility is that there may be bodily appearances, external and visible. The prophecy may come as a result of an apparition like those experienced by Catherine Laboure in the Rue de Bac in Paris in 1830, or such bodily appearance may be inwardly depicted in fantasy by means of an inner image, e.g., Acts 10:9-16 recounts the vision Peter had when he prayed on a roof. Thomas said that no one could be accounted a prophet because God had represented something to him or her in an image, but only when God enlightens the mind as to its meaning and significance.

By these means, aided by the light inwardly impressed on his mind, 'man receives a knowledge of divine things. Hence, without the inner light, these aids are insufficient for the knowledge of divine things; whereas the inner light is sufficient of itself without them.'[14]

C. Prophetic knowledge is not necessarily a sign of sanctifying grace

St Thomas said more than once that all the charisms, including that of prophecy, are given to help others to grow in sanctifying grace, but that doesn't necessarily mean that the person exercising the gift is him or herself in a state of grace. In his commentary on 1 Cor 12, Thomas quotes Heb 2:4 which says, 'God also testified to his word by signs, wonders and various miracles, and gifts of the Holy Spirit distributed according to his will.' Then he observed that a prophet, in whom the Holy Spirit does not dwell, could be enabled not only to prophesy but also to perform miracles in order to show that the faith of the Church which he or she proclaims is true. However, in his *Summa Theologica* he added this observation, 'Morally wicked feelings and behaviour can hinder prophecy; for a prophet's mind must be lifted up wholly to the contemplation of spiritual things, and strong passions and inordinate concern for external things are obstacles to that.'[15]

St John of the Cross

St. John of the Cross (1542-1591) a Carmelite, and one of thirty seven Doctors of the Church, was the author of many influential books. In one of them *The Ascent of Mount Carmel*, he had a good deal to say about the gift of prophecy. Writing about revelation in Bk. 2, ch. 25, he said that it is the manifestation of some secret or mystery, as when God imparts understanding of some truth to the intellect, or discloses one of his past, present or future deeds.' Speaking about this form of revelation he said, that it 'bears great resemblance to the spirit of prophecy.' Later in ch. 26 he seems to describe prophetic words of knowledge when he says, 'Although spiritual persons cannot know naturally the thoughts of others, or their interior state, they can know this clearly through supernatural enlightenment.' In ch. 27, he said, 'In our time God grants revelations to whom he wills. He will reveal to some the number of days they have to live, or the trials they will have to endure, or something that will befall a particular person or kingdom, etc.'

It would have to be said that St. John has many misgivings about the exercise of the prophetic gift, e.g., because it could be so easily influenced by the malign activity of the evil one. In bk. 3, ch 31, he says, 'He, then, that has supernatural gifts and graces ought to refrain from desiring to practice them, and from rejoicing in so doing, nor ought he to care to exercise them; for God, who gives himself to such persons, by supernatural means, for the profit of his Church and of its members, will move them likewise supernaturally in such a manner and at such time as he desires. As he commanded his faithful ones to take no thought as to what they were to say, or as to how they were to say it, since this is the supernatural business of faith, it will likewise be his will (as these operations are no less a supernatural matter) that a man should wait and allow God to work by moving his heart, since it is in the virtue of this working that there will be wrought all virtue.'

It seems to me that although at times St. John does not seem enthusiastic about the exercise of the gift of prophecy, his caution may have been due, in part, to the influence of the Alumbrados, i.e. The Illuminated, a term used to describe practitioners of a mystical form of Christianity in Spain during the 15th and 16th centuries. They declared, that worship was superfluous, reception of the sacraments, useless, and sin impossible when a person was in a state of complete union with God. Persons in this state, they asserted like the Manicheans of old, could indulge their sexual desires without sinning. Not surprisingly, the Church condemned this group, but in doing so any claim of receiving prophetic revelations became suspect. However, it is worth remembering a Latin saying in this context, *abusus non tollit usum*, 'abuse of anything does not invalidate its proper use.'

PROSPERO LAMBERTINI ON PROPHECY

Prospero Lambertini was born in Bologna in 1675.[16] By the age of 19 he had received doctorates in theology, canon law and civil law. He was so widely read that he was reputed to be one of the most erudite men of his time. He lived in the Age of Enlightenment when the Church was being attacked by rationalist philosophers and challenged by absolutist rulers. In 1712 he was appointed canon theologian at the Vatican and assessor of the Congregation of Rites. In 1731 he became Archbishop of his native city. Later in 1740 he was elected Pope following a consistory which lasted six months! He took the name of Benedict XIV and is considered by many scholars as the most learned Pope the Church has ever had. He died in 1758 at the age of 83.

While he was at the Congregation of Rites, Cardinal Lambertini had the responsibility of assessing the causes of people who had been put forward for possible beatification and canonisation. It raised the question in the bishop's mind, what criteria should be used? Eventually, he wrote a massive work entitled *On the Beatification and Canonisation of the Servants of God*. In 1850, a British scholar translated some of the Latin version in three volumes, with the collective title *Heroic Virtue*. The last of these, dealt mainly with the charisms in 1 Cor 12:8-10. Chapters six to eight deal specifically with various aspects of the charism of prophecy.[17] Although he was heavily influenced by St. Thomas, Cardinal Lambertini did not classify the gifts as his theological mentor had done. Whereas Thomas looked at the gifts in relationship to the universal call to evangelise, Cardinal Lambertini looked at them in relationship to the universal call to holiness.

It strikes me that Lambertini's treatise is a very important reflection on the nature of prophecy because it is an authoritative expression of the ordinary magisterium of the Church. Speaking about the latter, par. 25 of the *Dogmatic Constitution on The Church* says, 'Although the bishops, taken individually, do not enjoy the privilege of infallibility, they do, however, proclaim infallibly the doctrine of Christ on the following conditions: namely, when, even though dispersed throughout the world but preserving for all that amongst themselves and with Peter's successor the bond of communion, in their authoritative teaching concerning matters of faith or morals.' Surely the fact that Cardinal Lambertini was subsequently elected Pope added an even greater gravitas to what he had already written as a bishop.

A. The Nature of Prophecy

Writing about the nature of prophecy Cardinal Lambertini said, 'Prophecy is the foreknowledge of future events, but it sometimes extends to past events, of which there is no recollection nor any certain indications; and to present events distant in place and hidden, and to the inward thoughts of the heart; so that he is a prophet who divinely knows those things which are removed from sense and the natural knowledge of men, and is able to make them known.'[18]

Like Thomas before him, Cardinal Lambertini said that prophecy is pre-eminently a knowledge of future events. Notice that the Archbishop says that besides being about the future, prophecy can also be about events past or present. Speaking about prophetic knowledge of past events he cited as an example the fact that Jesus knew that the woman at Jacob's well had been married to five husbands (cf. Jn 4:18). Referring to prophecy as knowledge of some reality in the present Cardinal Lambertini cited the example of the way in which Jesus knew what Simon the Pharisee was thinking.

Although the Church teaches that public revelation ended with the writing of the last inspired book of the New Testament, it also teaches that private revelation of a prophetic kind, is not only possible but useful for spelling out the implications of public revelation for the times in which we live.[19] Speaking about this subject, Cardinal Lambertini wrote, 'He to whom that private revelation is proposed and announced, ought to believe and obey the command or message of God, if it be proposed to him on sufficient evidence.'[20]

B. How prophetic knowledge is received

Cardinal Lambertini described how prophetic revelation is received in much the same way as St. Thomas had done. He said that it could occur in three ways. Firstly, by means of the sense of sight and hearing such as external apparitions and locutions, e.g., Daniel not only seeing the writing on the wall but also being able to interpret its prophetic meaning for Belshazzar (cf. Dan 5:24-28). Secondly, by the inward senses of sight and hearing, such as inner locutions, visions, images and dreams, e.g., in Acts 16: 9-10 where St. Luke said that, 'During the night Paul had a vision of a man of Macedonia standing and begging him, 'Come over to Macedonia and help us.' After Paul had seen the vision, we got ready at once to leave for Macedonia, concluding that God had called us to preach the gospel to them.' Thirdly, by intellectual representation, i.e. unmediated reception of a prophetic revelation in the mind, e.g. knowing that someone has just died.

C. Prophetic knowledge is not necessarily a sign of sanctifying grace

It is of the essence of true prophecy, that the prophet should not only know what has been revealed to him or her, but also that it is God who does the revealing and that no natural disposition is required for such prophetic knowledge; that union with God by grace is not required in order to have the gift of prophecy, and thus it was at times bestowed even upon sinners. However, Archbishop Lambertini said that, 'We readily admit that a good and modest life is not necessary as an evidence of true prophecy; for there are well known instances of some most wicked men, whom God made use of as instruments to publish his oracles, as we have seen in the case of Balaam and Caiaphas; but these instances are rare.' But Cardinal Lambertini added, 'For the most part the gift of prophecy is bestowed on holy people.'[21] In saying this he was echoing what Origen (185-254 AD) had written in his

On First Principles, 'As holy and stainless souls, when they have devoted themselves to God with entire affection and entire purity and have kept themselves apart from all contact with daemons (spirits) and purified themselves by much abstinence and have been steeped in pious and religious exercises, acquire thereby a communion with the divine nature and win the grace of prophecy and other divine gifts.'[22]

D. The role of angels in prophecy

It may come as a surprise to know that, like St Thomas Aquinas, Prospero Lambertini thought that angels were instrumental in prophetic revelation. After all, scripture maintains that the Holy Spirit leads us into the truth. What Cardinal Lambertini seemed to be suggesting is the fact that the revelations of the Holy Spirit can be conveyed to people by the angels who are the messengers of God. Cardinal Lambertini wrote, 'prophetic revelation is made by means of the angels.'[23] A little later he stated that the angels are mediators between God and people. He wrote, 'prophetic illuminations are ministered by God through the angelic spirits, who not only enlighten and move the imagination interiorly toward divine appearances, but also from within speak to the prophets, to whom also they show themselves frequently in human form, foretelling future events, and instructing them in many things to be done.'[24]

E. Discernment of spirits

Having quoted: 'Do not put out the Spirit's fire, do not treat prophecies with contempt. Test everything. Hold on to the good' (1 Thess 5:19), Prospero Lambertini went on to suggest three main criteria that could be used in the assessment of a prophecy. Firstly, was it in accord with the teachings of Jesus, the Apostles, and

Church law? Secondly, what was the interior state of the prophet when he or she spoke? False prophets, he observed, speak when their minds are disturbed, because they cannot cope with the assaults of the devil, who can influence them sometimes as an angel of light. But he added: 'they whom God moves, speak with gentleness, humility and modesty.' Thirdly, how can we know when a message has been spoken by the Lord? Archbishop Lambertini responded, 'If what a prophet proclaims in the name of the Lord does not take place or come true, then a genuine message has not been spoken.' He added, that it needs to be established, 'Whether the predictions were beyond human knowledge... or whether he who foretold them could have conjectural knowledge of them from signs, guesses, or experience. Again whether he revealed the future hesitatingly, by using such words as 'perchance,' 'perhaps,' or 'it may be.' Whether also in revealing and foretelling, he made use of human reasons in proof of what he said, or in doing this, whether he was subject to any human affection, as for instance, the hope, or the possible hope of temporal advantage; or to mental agitation; and lastly, whether he truly knew, if not all, at least some of those things of which he prophesied. All these questions must be very minutely investigated before it can be pronounced to have been real prophecy.'[25]

In answer to the question, what credence should be given to private revelation of a prophetic kind, Benedict XIV referred to the teaching of Cardinal Cajetan (1469-1524) when he wrote, 'Human actions are of two kinds, one of which relates to public duties, and especially to ecclesiastical affairs, such as preaching, celebrating Mass, pronouncing judicial decisions, and the like; with respect to these the question is settled in the canon law, where it is said that no credence is to be publicly given to him who says he has privately received a mission from God, unless he confirms it by a miracle or a special testimony of Holy Scripture. The other class of human actions consists of those of private persons, and speaking of these, he distinguishes between a prophet who enjoins or advises them, according to the universal laws of the Church, and a prophet who does the same without reference to those laws. In the first case every man may rely on his own conscience as to whether or not to direct his actions according to the will of the prophet; in the second case a prophet is not to be listened to'.[26]

CONCLUSION

Although it would be true to say that, by and large, the gift of prophecy has been overlooked, in the Church's theology and pastoral practice, there are outstanding exceptions as we have seen. Thomas Aquinas, John of the Cross and Benedict XIV, in particular, have devoted a surprising amount of attention to the subject. That said, even most Catholic Charismatics are not familiar with the important things they have to say about the charism of prophecy. It also strikes me that the approach of both Thomas and Prospero Lambertini was largely academic rather than experiential because they lived at a time when the charisms were not really being exercised in the Church. As a result their writings need to be read in the light of what contemporary scripture scholars and theologians, especially those who have personal experience of the charism of prophecy, have written about the subject.

NOTES

1. 'Prophecy' in *Dictionary of Fundamental Theology* (New York: The Crossroad Publishing Company, 2000), 788.
2. (Oxford: Oxford University Press, 2007)
3. See 'The Teaching of the Twelve Apostles: The *Didache*' in Clayton N. Jefford, *Reading the Apostolic Fathers: An Introduction* (Peabody: Hendrickson, 2007), 32-51.
4. Ibid., 134-158.
5. (Gloucester, Mass: Peter Smith, 1973).
6. *The Apostolic Fathers in English,* ed. Michael W. Holmes (Grand Rapids: Baker Academic, 2006), 169-70.
7. *On the First Principles,* op. cit., 227.
8. Jerome, Praef. in Hom. Orig. in Ezech (Lommatzsch XIV 4). Rufinus, Apol. II. 13 (Migne P.L., XXI), 596.
9. *On the First Principles,* op. cit., 227.
10. *Summa Theologiae: A Concise Translation,* ed. Timothy McDermott (London: Methuen, 1989), 444.
11. Ibid., 444
12. Ibid., 445.
13. Ibid., 445-6.
14. *Summa Contra Gentiles,* book 3, chapt., 155.
15. *Summa Theologiae: A Concise Translation,* op.cit.,447.
16. Renee Haynes, *Philosopher King: The Humanist Pope Benedict XIV* (London: Weidenfeld & Nicholson, 1970).*17*. Prospero Lambertini,
17. (Benedict XIV), *Heroic Virtue,* vol.3., (London: Thomas Richardson and Son, 1852), 135-211.
18. Prospero Lambertini, *Heroic Virtue* op. cit. 135.
19. On this see, Pat Collins, C.M., 'Private Revelation', in *Guided by God: Ordinary and Charismatic Ways of Discovering God's Will* (Luton: New Life, 2015), 189-210.
20. *Heroic Virtue,* op.cit., 394.
21. Ibid., 1291.
22. Origen, *On First Principles* (Gloucester, Pass: Peter Smith, 1973), 226.

23. Prospero Lambertini, *Heroic Virtue* op.cit., 142.
24. Ibid., 144.
25. Ibid., 194.
26. *Heroic Virtue*, III, op. cit., 192.

EIGHT

THE CONTEMPORARY CHURCH ON PROPHECY

Ever since the advent of Pentecostalism and the Charismatic Movement there has been a notable increase of interest in the charism of prophecy. Both scripture scholars such as Wayne Grudem, and David Aune, and theologians such as Cardinal Newman, Karl Rahner and Niels, Christian Hvidt, have been writing in an illuminating and helpful way about the gift. This chapter will be devoted to some of the things that the contemporary Church has had to say about the gift of prophecy.

Private revelation

The Church distinguishes between public and private revelation. Public revelation came to an end with the ascension of Jesus into heaven and the writing of the last book in the New Testament. The phrase, private revelation refers to all the visions and revelations which have taken place since the completion of the New Testament. Rather than adding to public revelation which is already complete, it merely draws out its implications for modern day living. Par 66 of the *Catechism of the Catholic Church* says, 'Even if revelation is complete it has not been made fully explicit; it remains for Christian faith gradually to grasp its full significance over the course of the centuries.' Par. 67 went on to add, 'Throughout the ages, there have been so-called 'private' revelations, some of which have been recognised by the authority of the Church... It is not their role to complete Christ's definitive revelation, but to help live more fully by it in a certain period of history.' When he was still cardinal prefect of the Congregation for the Doctrine of the Faith, Joseph Ratzinger wrote a very interesting article on the subject of private revelation.[1] He also spoke about the subject in an interview with Niels Christian Hvidt during which he said, 'the 'revelations' of Christian mystics and prophets can never aspire to the same level as biblical Revelation; they can only lead to it and they must measure themselves by it. But that does not mean that these types of revelation are not important for the Church in its entirety. Lourdes and Fatima are the proof that they are important. In the final analysis, they are but an appeal to the biblical Revelation and, for this very reason, they are important.'[2]

Subsequently, Pope Benedict XVI included a very helpful section on the subject of private revelation of a prophetic kind in par. 14 of his Apostolic Exhortation, *'On the Word of God in the Life and Mission of the Church.'* There, the Pope said that the charism of prophecy is a form of private revelation. He wrote, 'In every age the Church has received the charism of prophecy, which must be scrutinised but not scorned. On this point, it should be kept in mind that prophecy in the biblical sense does not mean to predict the future but to explain the will of God for the present, and therefore show the right path to take for the future... The prophet... declares the will of God as an indication and demand for the present time. In this case, prediction of the future is of secondary importance.' In another place he wrote, 'What is a prophet? A prophet is not a soothsayer; the essential element of the prophet is not the prediction of future events. The prophet is someone who tells the truth on the strength of his contact with

God - the truth for today, which also, naturally, sheds light on the future. It is not a question of foretelling the future in detail, but of rendering the truth of God present at this moment in time and of pointing us in the right direction.'[3] The Pope added that prophets can receive private revelation by means of three forms of perception 'with the senses, and hence exterior bodily perception, interior perception, and spiritual vision.' This threefold distinction is reminiscent of similar ones in the writings of St Thomas Aquinas and Prospero Lambertini.

Not surprisingly, the Pope broached the subject of how to discern whether prophecies are true or false. He wrote, 'The criterion for the truth and value of a private revelation is therefore its orientation to Christ himself. When it leads us away from him, when it becomes independent of him or even presents itself as another and better plan of salvation, more important than the Gospel, then it certainly does not come from the Holy Spirit, who guides us more deeply into the Gospel and not away from it.'[4]

Is prophecy fore-telling or forth-telling?

In modern theology there is a tendency to say that, rather than being a matter of fore-telling future events, prophecy is a matter of forth-telling, i.e., seeing implications for the future which are implicit in something that is revealed about the present. For example, Joseph Ratzinger wrote, 'it should be kept in mind that prophecy in the biblical sense does not mean to predict the future but to explain the will of God for the present, and therefore show the right path to take for the future.'[5] He reiterated that point in the 'Introduction' of his *Jesus of Nazareth* where he says of the prophet, 'His task is not to report on the events of tomorrow or the next day in order to satisfy human curiosity or the human need for security. He shows the face of God, and in so doing he shows us the path we have to take... Prophecy in this sense is a strict corollary to Israel's monotheism. It is the translation of this faith into the everyday life of a community before God and on the way to him.'[6]

I just wonder why Pope Benedict downplays the notion of prophecy as prediction of future events. In the Old Testament there are a number of prophesies about the future. For example, in Jer 25:9-12 we read, 'This whole country will become a desolate wasteland, and these nations will serve the king of Babylon seventy years. But when the seventy years are fulfilled, I will punish the king of Babylon and his nation, the land of the Babylonians, for their guilt,' declares the Lord, 'and will make it desolate forever.' In Jer 29:10 there is a similar prediction, 'This is what the Lord says: 'When seventy years are completed for Babylon, I will come to you and fulfil my gracious promise to bring you back to this place.' The seventy-year prophecy of Jeremiah is referred to in Dan 9:1-3 where we read, 'In the first year of Darius son of Xerxes, who was made ruler over the Babylonian kingdom -- in the first year of his reign, I, Daniel, understood from the Scriptures, according to the word of the Lord given to Jeremiah the prophet, that the desolation of Jerusalem would last seventy years. So I turned to the Lord God and pleaded with him in prayer and petition, in fasting, and in sackcloth and ashes.' Scholars point out that what Jeremiah had in mind was the fact that in 609 BC the Assyrian empire was defeated and the Babylonian empire dominated until 539 BC when it too was defeated. That was a period of 70 years. It was also clear from the prophecies mentioned in the chapter on messianic prophecy that they actually were fulfilled in the future.

Furthermore, we noted earlier in this chapter how both St. Thomas Aquinas, and Prospero Lambertini both said that prophecy was often about the future. For instance, Saint Thomas wrote, 'It is in the revelation of future events that prophecy above all consists.'[7] In the *Summa Contra Gentiles* he said, 'a gift of prophecy was necessary, whereby they might know and reveal to others, through God's revelation, future events and things generally concealed from men.'[8]

There have been other prophecies in recent times which were also about the future. Here is a notable example. Smith Wigglesworth (1859-1947) was a 20th century British Pentecostal who was well known for his great faith, healing, and prophetic gifts. In 1936 he visited South Africa and met a young Pentecostal minister called David du Plessis. Early one morning David was in his office. He described what happened next, 'All of a sudden the door flew open and there stood Brother Wigglesworth. He walked forward, stood upright and looked straight into my eyes. I had no choice but to stare back at him. He began to speak, and I knew that he was prophesying. 'I have been sent by the Lord to tell you what he has shown me this morning. Through the old-line denominations will come a revival that will eclipse anything we have known throughout history. No such things have happened in times past as will happen when this begins.' Wigglesworth's prophecy continued. Without breaking stride, he plunged ahead in his rapid-fire manner. 'It will eclipse the present-day, twentieth-century Pentecostal revival that already is a marvel to the world, with its strong opposition from the established church. But the same blessing will become acceptable to the churches and they will go on with this message and this experience beyond what the Pentecostals have achieved. You will live to see this work grow to such dimensions that the Pentecostal movement itself will be a light thing in comparison with what God will do through the old churches. There will be tremendous gatherings of people, unlike anything we've seen, and great leaders will change their attitudes and accept not only the message but also the blessing.' 'He paused' ever so slightly, and his eyes burned into mine. 'The Lord said to me that I am to give you warning that He is going to use you in this movement. You will have a very prominent part'.'[9] Having uttered this amazing prophecy which was about future events, Wigglesworth told du Plessis that it would not begin to be fulfilled until after his death. That event took place in 1947 when Wigglesworth was 87 years of age. What he had foretold began to be fulfilled immediately after his death.

In the 1950's and early 1960's, God began opening doors for Du Plessis, firstly in mainline Protestant churches and then in the Catholic Church. In his book *Simple and Profound,* du Plessis explained how he first came in contact with the Catholic Church. In 1952 he was invited to speak to the Commission of Faith and Order of the World Council of Churches in Scotland. During his address he spoke about the need for baptism in the Spirit. Fr. Bernard Leeming, S.J., attended the meeting as an observer. He introduced himself to du Plessis and explained that he had been sent as a delegate by the Church. He said to the South African, 'I've been a priest for 40 years, and in Rome for 11 of them, and I've never heard anyone call Jesus the Baptiser in the Holy Spirit.' As far as I know, Leeming asked to be prayed with that he might receive the outpouring of the Spirit.

Some years later preparations were being made for Vatican II. Fr

Leeming spoke to a fellow Jesuit, Cardinal Bea, about du Plessis who invited him to visit the Vatican. When he answered the invitation Bea asked him, 'What do Pentecostals want to say to Rome?' Du Plessis replied, 'Cardinal, I have come, humbly, to beg of you and the Council, if possible, to change the order of things and liberate the Bible and make it available to all Catholics, everywhere in the world, in their own language. If Catholics will read the Bible, then Pope John's prayer for the renewal of the Church will be answered. That will change the Church... Only the Word of God is the basis for Renewal.' When he heard this Bea exclaimed, 'write that down. We'll tell the Holy Father what this holy man says.'[10] Later, du Plessis was invited to attend the final session of the Council during which Catholics were not only encouraged to read and pray the scriptures but also to be open to receive the gifts of the Spirit which are mentioned in 1 Cor 12: 8-10.

In 1967 the Catholic Charismatic Movement came into existence. It is estimated that by the year 2000 over 100 million Catholics had been baptised in the Holy Spirit. It is worth noting that when the Council ended du Plessis was involved in a theological dialogue between Pentecostals and Catholics. In 1983, he was honoured with the *Benemerenti Medal* by Pope John Paul II for his outstanding service to all of Christianity. It was the first time this award had been given to a non-Catholic. Wigglesworth's prophecy had been fulfilled to the letter. As the *Catechism of the Catholic Church* says in par. 2115, 'God can reveal the future to his prophets or to other saints. Still, a sound Christian attitude consists in putting oneself confidently into the hands of Providence for whatever concerns the future, and giving up all unhealthy curiosity about it.'

That said, many prophecies in the Bible were about the Lord's perspective on current events. The same could be said about private revelation of a prophetic kind in the contemporary church. More often than not, it conveys God's attitude to what is happening in the here and now. For example, in 1977 this memorable prophecy was spoken by Ralph Martin in Kansas, 'Mourn and weep, for the body of my Son is broken. Come before me with sackcloth and ashes, come before me with tears and I would have made you one new man, but the body of my Son is broken. I would have made you a light on a mountaintop, a city glorious and splendorous that all the world would have seen, but the body of my Son is broken. The light is dim. My people are scattered. The body of my Son is broken. Turn from the sins of your fathers. Walk in the ways of my Son. Return to the plan of your Father, return to the purpose of your God. The body of my Son is broken.'[11] That prophecy was about the present day scandal of division in the body of Christ and the Lord's desire to see it overcome in the future.

Prophecy and Mysticism

A detailed study of the interconnection of prophecy and mysticism is will not be possible here.[12] Evelyn Underhill wrote,

> 'Mysticism, according to its historical and psychological definitions, is the direct intuition or experience of God; and a mystic is a person who has, to a greater or less degree, such a direct experience – one whose religion and life are centered, not merely on an accepted belief or practice. But on that which he regards as first hand personal knowledge.'[13]

Professor Bernard McGinn is probably the most authoritative contemporary scholar writing about mysticism in English. He is the author of five volumes in his *Presence of God: A History of Western Christian Mysticism* series. Speaking about mysticism he explained,

> 'I set forth my understanding of mysticism as that part or element of Christian belief and practice that concerns the preparation for, the consciousness of, and the effect of what the mystics themselves have described as a direct and transformative presence of [the Christian] God.'[14]

That being so, surely we can say that the prophets not only had direct, transformative experience of God, but that God revealed hidden truths to their hearts, which they conveyed to the people. Ezekial was a case in point. In Ezek 1:1-2:2 the prophet writes, 'In the thirtieth year, in the fourth month, on the fifth day of the month, as I was among the exiles by the Chebar canal, the heavens were opened, and I saw visions of God'. He saw four living creatures. Then he added, 'over their heads there was the likeness of a throne, in appearance like sapphire; and seated above the likeness of a throne was a likeness with a human appearance... Such was the appearance of the likeness of the glory of the Lord. And when I saw it, I fell on my face, and I heard the voice of one speaking. And he said to me, 'Son of man, stand on your feet, and I will speak with you.' Surely, this was a powerful mystical experience. Evelyn Underhill believed that the other Old Testament prophets were also mystics. For example, writing about Jeremiah, she said, 'The profound sense of the intercourse of spirit with Spirit is strongly marked in Jeremiah, who is perhaps the most mystical of the prophets.'[15]

When one reads the Christian mystics, it is obvious that many of them received revelation from God. Speaking about them Bernard McGinn has observed, 'The mystic wants to penetrate to the living source of the biblical message, that is, to the Divine Word who speaks in and through human words and texts. This means that the Bible has been both the origin and the norm for Christian mystics down the ages.'[16] For example Dame Julian of Norwich (1343-1416) became dangerously ill when she was thirty years of age. During her health crisis she fell into a trance, lasting five hours, during which she received a number of visions to do with the scriptural description of the passion of Jesus Christ. Following years of reflection upon the visions and their implications she finally wrote her *Revelations of Divine Love*. Arguably, her visions or showings were prophetic in the sense that they were gratuitous revelations, whereas her meditations upon them were a form of theological reflection. Because of the role of such things as intelligence, learning and meditation, her book, though rooted in prophetic revelation, was not strictly speaking prophetic in expression. Meanwhile in Italy, Catherine of Sienna (1347-1380), a contemporary of Julian, also experienced many visions which she recorded in *The Dialogue of Divine Providence*. Unlike Julian, Catherine was politically active. For instance, in 1376, she wanted to convince Pope Gregory XI, to come back from Avignon to Rome. She did so by walking with some of her followers from Italy to France. There she reminded the Pope of a vow he had made, but which he had never revealed to anyone. Catherine's prophetic gifts both surprised and persuaded Gregory to return to Italy. So I think that Spanish Carmelite Ciro Garcia was correct when he said, 'Mysticism and prophecy are two essentials, closely connected dimensions of every religious identity. The first is more directly projected towards union with God, the second is more immediately oriented to the fulfilment of God's will here and now.'[17]

In his book *Christian Mysticism: The Future of a Tradition,* Harvey Egan, S.J., says succinctly in a section entitled, 'Christian Mysticism and Unusual Phenomena' that, 'Private revelations often presuppose the gift of prophecy. Prophetic revelations commission the mystic to address the entire Church, or a significant portion. He must deliver a message, plead for a particular devotion, call for conversion and penance, warn against certain aberrations in Church life and teaching, suggest new styles of life or spiritual doctrine, or foretell the future. These post apostolic, prophetic revelations, therefore, apply the faith in a practical way to daily Christian living.'[18]

PROPHECY AND THEOLOGY

The foregoing section leads to a related question. What is the relationship, if any, between theology and prophecy? In the course of a fairly long interview with Niels Christian Hvidt Joseph Ratzinger offered an insightful perspective on the issue. He pointed out that many well known theologians in bye gone years were influenced by a prophetic perspective. When one thinks of some of the great theologians of the past such as Sts Augustine, Thomas Aquinas, and Bonaventure, it is evident that they were men who enjoyed a mystic sense of contact with the living God. As St Thomas explained, 'The object of faith is not the statement but the reality.'[19] Not surprisingly people like Thomas were open to divine inspiration and revelation.

Then there are theologians who are influenced by mystics and prophets. For example, in 1940 influential Catholic theologian

Hans Urs von Balthasar (1905-1988) was introduced to a twice-married, Protestant medical doctor called Adrianne von Speyr. He received her into the Catholic Church in 1945. Together they founded a religious society for men and women, called the Community of Saint John. Von Speyr was a mystic and shared many of her prophetic revelations with her friend and collaborator. By doing so, said Ratzinger, she exercised a big influence on von Balthasar's theological writings. Then he observed, 'I believe that it can be proven that for all the great theologians any new theological elaboration is only possible if the prophetic element has first paved the way. While one proceeds with the mind only, nothing new will ever happen. Increasingly more definite systems may well be constructed, increasingly subtle questions raised but the true and proper way from which great theology may again flow is not generated by the rational side of theological work but by a charismatic and prophetic thrust. And it is in this sense, I believe, that prophecy and theology go hand in glove together. Theology, as theological science in the strict sense, is not prophetic but may only truly become living theology under the thrust and illumination of a prophetic impulse.'[20] Arguably, Pope Benedict's muse was his personal assistant for many years, Dr. Ingrid Stampa, a former professor at the conservatory of Hamburg who speaks at least three languages and has an advanced degree in ancient music. Unmarried, she is a lay affiliate of the German Schoenstatt Sisters of Mary and has been the Pope's trusted friend, confidant and collaborator ever since the death of his sister Maria in 1991. Having read many theological books, I'd have to say that, while some of them are scholarly and insightful, many of them seem to lack a prophetic dimension, unlike those of Benedict XVI.

CONCLUSION

Although some theologians and scripture scholars have written in an illuminating way about the charism and ministry of prophecy, by and large, they are still neglected gifts in the Church. In this connection one is reminded of what is said in 1 Sam 3:1, 'In those days the word of the Lord was rare; there were not many visions,' and in Ps 74:9, 'no prophets are left,' and in Lam 2:4, 'her prophets no longer find visions from the Lord.' Happily, since the advent of the Charismatic Renewal Movement, there has been a revival in the exercise of the gift of prophecy. Not only has it helped to complement the institutional aspects of the Church it has also enlivened the writing of Christian theology, and given believers a sense of what on earth God is doing for heaven's sake. As we have seen in this chapter prophecy provides truth for the present and light for the future.

NOTES

1. 'Theological Commentary,' in *The Message of Fatima,* published by the Congregation for the Doctrine of the Faith.
2. *http://tlig.org/en/spirituality/prophecy/intratz1/ (Accessed 5/11/2015).*
3. Joseph Ratzinger, 'Foreword' to Niels Christian Hvidt's *Christian Prophecy* (Oxford: Oxford University Press, 2007), vii.
4. Benedict XVI Apostolic Exhortation *Verbum Domini (The Word of God),* par. 14.
5. Joseph Ratzinger, *Theological Commentary on the Third Secret of Fatima,* Congregation for the Doctrine of the Faith, https: / /www. ewtn.com / fatima / apparitions / Third_Secret / Fatima.htm (Accessed 4 / 10 / 2015).
6. *Jesus of Nazareth: From the Baptism in the Jordan to the Transfiguration* (London: Bloomsbury, 2007), 4.
7. *Summa Theologiae: A Concise Translation,* op. cit., 445
8. 5 Chapt. 154, par. 10.
9. *http://smithwigglesworth.com/pensketches/prophecy.html (Accessed 25/10/2015).*
10. David du Plessis, *Simple and Profound* (Orleans, Mass: Paraclete Press, 1986), 181.
11. https: / / www.renewalministries.net / files / freeliterature / Prophecy _KansasCity_1977.pdf (accessed 16th March, 2018).
12. Pat Collins, C.M., 'Introduction to Mysticism,' in *Spirituality for the 21st Century* (Dublin: Columba, 1999), 65-85; Robert J. Egan, 'The mystical and the prophetic Dimensions of Christian existence,' in *The Way* (Supplement, 2002): 92-106.
13. *Mystics of the Church* (Cambridge: Clarke & Co, 1975), 9-10.
14. Bernard McGinn, 'Introduction' *The Essential Writings of Christian Mysticism* (New York: Modern Classics, 2006), xiv.
15. *Mystics of the Church,* op., cit. 31.
16. *The Essential Writings of Christian Mysticism,* op. cit., 3.
17. *National Catholic Reporter* (May 7th 2010).
18. (New York: Pueblo Publishing, 1984), 311.
19. *Summa Theologica I-II,* qq. 1, a. 2, ad 2.
20. *http://tlig.org/en/spirituality/prophecy/intratz1/ (Accessed 5/11/2015).*

NINE

FIVE RECENT POPES ON THE SIGNS OF THE TIMES

The late Anthony de Mello told a memorable story to highlight the notion of divine providence. There was a Chinese farmer who used an old horse to plough his fields. One day, the horse escaped into the hills and when the farmer's neighbours sympathised with the old man over his bad luck, the farmer replied, 'Bad luck? Good luck? Who knows?' A week later, the horse returned with a herd of horses from the hills and this time the neighbours congratulated the farmer on his good luck. His reply was, 'Good luck? Bad luck? Who knows?' Then, when the farmer's son was attempting to tame one of the wild horses, he fell off its back and broke his leg. Everyone thought this was very bad luck. Not the farmer, whose only reaction was, 'Bad luck? Good luck? Who knows?' Some weeks later, the army marched into the village and conscripted every able-bodied youth they found there. When they saw the farmer's son with his broken leg, they left him behind. Now was that good luck or bad luck? Who knows?[1]

The notion of divine providence was of central importance in the teaching of Jesus. It contained two interrelated convictions. Firstly God has a benevolent plan for our lives. In Jer 29:11-12 we read, 'For I know the plans I have for you,' declares the Lord, 'plans to prosper you and not to harm you, plans to give you hope and a future.' Secondly, God provides for those who trust in him by giving them the natural and supernatural means of carrying out the divine plan. As Jesus promised, 'seek first God's kingdom and his righteousness, and all these things will be given to you as well' (Mt 6:33). All of us have to try, with God's help, to tune in to what God is doing. As Jesus said in Mt 16:2-3, 'When it is evening, you say, 'When evening comes it will be fair weather, for the sky is red,' and in the morning, 'Today it will be stormy, for the sky is red and overcast.' You know how to interpret the appearance of the sky, but you cannot interpret the signs of the times.'

The signs of the times are those events, phenomena, or movements in a given era that are characteristic of that period and bring about a new awareness of God's purposes. The signs of the times are like so many dots, so to speak, which prophetic people can join together in such a way that they discern the outline of what God is doing. The ability to do this is the result of divinely given revelation. This notion was often referred to during and after the Second Vatican Council. For example, in par. 4 of the *Pastoral Constitution on the Church in the Modern World* we read, 'the Church has always had the duty of scrutinising the signs of the times and of interpreting them in the light of the Gospel. Thus, in language intelligible to each generation, she can respond to the perennial questions which men ask about this present life and the life to come, and about the relationship of the one to the other.'

While serving as prefect of the Congregation for the Doctrine of the Faith, Pope Benedict XVI commented on the connection between prophecy and the signs of the times, 'The prophetic word is a warning or a consolation, or both together. In this sense there is a link between the charism of prophecy and the category of 'the signs of the times,' which Vatican II brought to new light... To interpret the signs of the times in the light of faith means to recognise the presence of Christ in every age. The private revelations approved by the Church help us to understand the signs of the times and to respond to them rightly in faith.'[2] At this point we will look at some of the ways in which five recent Popes seemed to have had the ability, not only to read the signs of the times in a prophetic way, but also to join the dots and interpret their providential significance.

1. Pope Leo XIII's vision

On October 13th, 1884, Pope Leo XIII had finished celebrating Mass in his private Vatican Chapel. He suddenly stopped at the foot of the altar. He stood there for about ten minutes, as if in a trance, his face ashen white. When asked what had happened, he explained that, as he was about to leave the foot of the altar, he suddenly heard voices - two voices, one kind and gentle, the other guttural and harsh. They seemed to come from near the tabernacle. As he listened, he heard the following conversation: The guttural voice, the voice of Satan in his pride, boasted to Our Lord: 'I can destroy your Church.' The gentle voice of Our Lord said, 'You can? Then go ahead and do so.' Satan replied, 'To do so, I need more time and more power.' Our Lord asked, 'How much time? How much power? Satan responded, '75 to 100 years, and a greater power over those who will give themselves over to my service.' Our Lord said, 'You have the time, you will have the power. Do with them what you will.'[3]

The implications of this vision remind one of some words spoken by Jesus to St. Peter, 'Satan has asked to sift you as wheat. But I have prayed for you,... that your faith may not fail' (Lk 22:31-32).

As a result of his prophetic revelation, Pope Leo decreed that the prayer to St. Michael the archangel be said at the end of Mass. His instruction was carried out until 1970 when the new rite of the Mass was introduced. It is worth mentioning that the prayer to Michael the Archangel, with which so many Catholics are familiar, is an edited version of a much longer prayer which was composed by Pope Leo. One section contains these striking words about the Vatican, ' In the Holy Place itself, where has been set up the See of the most holy Peter and the Chair of Truth for the light of the world, they [the evil spirits] have raised the throne of their abominable impiety, *with the iniquitous design that when the Pastor* [the Pope] *has been struck, the sheep may be scattered* (my italics). Arise then, O invincible prince, bring help against the attacks of the lost spirits to the people of God, and bring them the victory.'[4] The meaning and implications of those prophetic words, especially those in italics, are well worth pondering. Leo XIII also personally wrote a prayer of exorcism that is included in the Roman Ritual. He recommended that only bishops and priests say it on a regular basis in their dioceses and parishes. Apparently, he often recited it himself.

Blessed Elena Guerra (1835-1914), was from a wealthy, aristocratic family in Lucca, Italy, and founder of the Oblate Sisters of the Holy Spirit. Like Pope Leo she was blessed with a prophetic gift. Over a period of eight years, around the turn of the twentieth century, she wrote no less than 13 letters to Pope Leo XIII. They were prompted by private revelation of a prophetic kind, which she had received. She urged him to encourage devotion to the Holy Spirit. Leo was thus prompted in 1895 to call the faithful to participate in an annual novena to the Holy Spirit in preparation for Pentecost. Two years later, he wrote a short encyclical on the Holy Spirit, *Divinum Illud Munus*. When the bishops failed to take the Pontiff's instructions to heart, Sr. Guerra observed in her sixth letter to Pope Leo, 'It is true that right after the publication of that encyclical, which I believe was dictated by the Holy Spirit, many bishops thanked Your Holiness... And this was good. But wouldn't it have been better to obey?' As a result, Sr. Elena sent more letters to the Pope. In one of them, dated October 15, 1900, she wrote: 'May the new century begin with a *Veni Creator Spiritus*... sung either at the beginning of the Midnight Mass, or before the first Mass to be celebrated in every Church on the first day of the year.' As a result Pope Leo took two more steps. On January 1, 1901, in St. Peter's Basilica, he chanted the *Veni Creator Spiritus*, invoking the Holy Spirit over all Christians. Lastly, in 1902, the Roman Pontiff, now 92, had a copy of his 1897 encyclical sent to the bishops, with a cover letter which urged them to recite the Pentecost Novena for the unity of all Christians. Surely, these collaborative actions were prophetic and later bore fruit in the form of the ecumenical and charismatic movements in the twentieth and twenty first centuries. For example, on the very day that Pope Leo sang the *Veni Creator Spiritus* in St. Peter's, halfway around the world in Topeka, Kansas, at the Bethel College and Bible School, an outpouring of the Holy Spirit occurred which is generally accepted as the beginning of Pentecostalism. Then the Azusa Street revival of 1906 began to spread Pentecostalism across the continents. It is estimated that nowadays there are over 500 million Pentecostals and Charismatics worldwide.

2. Pope St Pius X

In 1909, during an audience for the general chapter of the Franciscan Order, St. Pope Pius X suddenly fell into a trance.

The audience waited in reverent silence. When the trance ended, the Pope cried out, 'What I see is terrifying! Will it be myself? Will it be my successor? What is certain is that the Pope will quit Rome, and in leaving the Vatican he will have to walk over the dead bodies of his priests. 'Do not tell anyone this while I am alive.'

Just before his death on August 20, 1914, Pope Pius X had another vision, 'I have seen one of my successors,' he said, 'of the same name, who was fleeing over the bodies of his brethren. He will take refuge in some hiding place; but after a brief respite he will die a cruel death. Respect for God has disappeared from human hearts. They wish to efface even God's memory. This perversity is nothing less than the beginning of the last days of the world.'

3. Joseph Ratzinger (Benedict XVI)

We continue with Joseph Ratzinger. In the 1960s he was a priest theologian with a growing reputation as a result of having participated in the recent council as theological consultant to Cardinal Frings of Cologne. In 1969 Ratzinger, who would later become Pope Benedict XVI, gave a prophetic talk on German Radio entitled, 'What Will the Church Look Like in 2000?'[5] He began by saying, 'The theologian is no soothsayer, nor is he a futurologist who makes a calculation of the future based on the measurable facts of the present.' Among other things Ratzinger said that in the future the Church would go through a painful time of purification. Perhaps it is presumptuous on my part but for the sake of clarity I'm going to break what he said into three parts.

a) DARKNESS FOR THE CHURCH

'From the crisis of today the Church of tomorrow will emerge - a Church that has lost much. She will become small and will have to start afresh more or less from the beginning. She will no longer be able to inhabit many of the edifices she built in prosperity. As the number of her adherents diminishes, so will she lose many of her social privileges. In contrast to an earlier age, she will be seen much more as a voluntary society, entered only by free decision. As a small society, she will make much bigger demands on the initiative of her individual members. Undoubtedly she will discover new forms of ministry and will ordain to the priesthood approved Christians who pursue some profession.' Ratzinger went on to predict that, 'The Church will be a more spiritual Church, not presuming upon a political mandate, flirting as little with the Left as with the Right. It will be hard going for the Church . . . It will make her poor and cause her to become the Church of the meek.' A little later he added in hopeful terms, 'When this sifting is past, a great power will flow from a more spiritualised and simplified Church.'

b) DARKNESS FOR THE SECULAR WORLD

People in a totally planned world will find themselves unspeakably lonely, said Ratzinger. If they have completely lost sight of God, they will feel the whole horror of their poverty, at a spiritual and psychological level. It is interesting to note that in 1985 Cardinal Ratzinger talked about the connection between ethics and economics in a lecture entitled 'Market Economy and Ethics.' Toward the end of his presentation he predicted rather than prophesied that failure to respect the intimate connection between morality and economics could lead to abuses that would cause the system to 'implode.' As we know the banking system did collapse in 2008 and it may do so again.

c) *THE CHURCH A LIGHT IN THE WORLD*

Ratzinger went on to say that they [i.e. lonely and disillusioned people in the secular world] will discover the little flock of believers as something wholly new. They will discover it as a hope that is meant for them, an answer for which they have always been searching in secret. 'And so it seems certain to me that the Church is facing very hard times... she may well no longer be the dominant social power to the extent that she was until recently; but she will enjoy a fresh blossoming and be seen as man's home, where he will find life and hope beyond death.' He said on another occasion, 'An age in which Christianity is quantitatively reduced can bring a more conscious Christianity to a new vitality. In this sense it is true that we are standing before a new kind of Christian era. I won't venture to makes prophecies about when this will happen, whether it can happen slowly or quickly.'[6] When one remembers that most of these words were spoken about half a century ago they seem remarkably prescient and still surprisingly relevant today.

4. KAROL WOJTYLA (JOHN PAUL II)

In 1994 author and broadcaster Karen Armstrong interviewed me for a Channel 4 T.V. programme entitled, 'The Pope's Divisions,' which was about John Paul II. When she asked me whether I thought the Pope was a fundamentalist, her disappointment was evident when I said, 'You must be joking. John Paul has two doctorates. He is a profound and subtle theological thinker. Rather than being a fundamentalist, John Paul is a prophet. And it is precisely because he is a prophet that many people both within and outside the Church reject what he has to say.' Interestingly, although her producer and camera men commended me afterwards on how well I had done in the interview, nothing of what I had to say appeared in the broadcast programme. On the 12th November of that same year *The Independent* newspaper in England reported that the ITV Authority had upheld many complaints about the broadcast. It said, 'Our principal concern is one of fairness. In this regard we find that, whilst the case advanced by Karen Armstrong was supported by the evidence of a number of interviewees, at no stage was it challenged or tested against other views.' Although I had offered an alternative point of view, in an apparently competent way, it had not been included! I have believed for a long time that John Paul II had such an inspired insight into the signs of the times that he was capable of revealing in a prophetic way what God's perspective is on current and future events. But there were, and still are, those who do not want to hear what he had to say. It is not easy to summarise the prophetic utterances of Pope John Paul II. I will look at them in a chronological way while providing a number of headings which are intended to highlight aspects of his understanding of the signs of the times.

a) *THE FINAL CONFRONTATION*

On November 11th 2013, Archbishop Vigano, the Papal Nuncio to the United States, addressed the following remarks to the American bishops. 'At this point, I would like to call your attention to the words of the then-Cardinal Wojtyla which he is reported to have given in an address in 1976 for the Bicentennial celebration of the signing of the Declaration of independence. It seems to be *so profoundly prophetic* (my italics). What Cardinal Wojtyla said was this, 'We are now standing in the face of the greatest historical confrontation humanity has ever experienced. The wide circle of the Christian Community realise this fully. We are now facing the final confrontation between the Church and the anti-church, between the gospel and the anti-gospel, between Christ and the antichrist. The confrontation lies within the plans of Divine Providence. It is, therefore, in God's Plan, and it must be a trial which the Church must take up, and face courageously. It is a trial of the Church but in a sense a test of 2,000 years of culture and Christian civilisation with all its consequences for human dignity, individual rights, human rights and the rights of nations.' Ralph Martin has written an insightful booklet on this subject entitled, *The Final Confrontation.*[7] In it, he says that it is already obvious that we are involved in a significant confrontation of the kind described by St. John Paul. Whether it is the definitive one or not still remains to be seen.

Two years after his dramatic statement at the Eucharistic Congress, Carl Wojtyla was elected Pope and came to Ireland the following year. While in the country he gave many memorable addresses. The one that made the biggest impact on me was one he delivered in the course of a sermon in Limerick. Although I said earlier in this book that prophecy is not inspired preaching, there can be times when teaching becomes prophecy. I feel that this happened at one point during John Paul's homily when he began to talk about the signs of the times. What he said in effect, was that the Irish, like the people in other Catholic countries such as Spain, France and Italy, are caught up in the drama of the final confrontation. He said prophetically, 'Your country must choose, you the present generation must decide; your choice must be clear and your decision firm. Let the voice of your forefathers, who suffered so much to maintain their faith in Christ and thus to preserve your country's soul, resound today in your ears through the voice of the Pope when he repeats the words of Christ: 'What will it profit a man, if he gains the whole world, and forfeits his life?' (Mt 16 :26). What would it profit your country to go the easy way of the world and suffer the loss of her own soul? Your country seems in a sense to be living again the temptations of Christ: Ireland is being asked to prefer the 'kingdoms of the world and their splendour' to the Kingdom of God (cf. Mt 4:8). Satan, the Tempter, the Adversary of Christ, will use all his might and all his deceptions to win your country for the way of the world. What a victory he would gain, what a blow he would inflict on the Body of Christ in the world, if he could seduce men and women away from Christ. Now is the time of testing for your country. This generation is once more a generation of decision. Dear sons and daughters of your country, pray, pray not to be led into temptation.'[8] We can see in retrospect that the Pope's words were prescient. As prosperity has increased in the intervening years, so has apostasy from the Irish church. For instance, the practice rate in Ireland in 1979 was over 80%. By 2016 it had fallen back to around 20-25%, while abortion and gay marriage had been introduced as a result of referendums.

B) *A DANGEROUS CRISIS OF TRUTH*

In 1994 Pope John Paul II wrote in par. 13 of his *Letter to Families* 'Who can deny that our age is one marked by a great crisis, which appears above all as a profound 'crisis of truth'? A crisis of truth means, in the first place, a crisis of concepts. Do the words 'love', 'freedom', 'sincere gift', and even 'person' and 'rights of the person,' really convey their essential meaning? This is why the Encyclical *'Splendour of the Truth'* has proved so meaningful and important for the Church and for the world - especially in the West.' Nearly a quarter of a century later there have been many references to the fact that we live in a post truth society. The term 'post-truth' was The *Oxford Dictionary*'s word of the year for

2016. It was defined as 'relating to or denoting circumstances in which objective facts are less influential in shaping public opinion than appeals to emotion and personal belief.' It is a way of thinking that denies that we can know absolute truth about anything, in science, philosophy or religion. Pope John Paul II referred to it in par. 91 of his encyclical, *Faith & Reason* when he commented, 'The currents of thought which claim to be postmodern merit appropriate attention. According to some, the time of certainties is irrevocably past, and the human being must now learn to live in a horizon of total absence of meaning, where everything is provisional and ephemeral.' It would appear, therefore, that modern culture is adrift on a sea of subjectivity where the umbilical cord connecting the human mind with objective truth has been severed. John Paul feared that this hiatus would have disastrous consequences. Speaking to the American bishops on the 24th of October 1998 he said, 'The violent history of this century is due in no small part to the closure of reason to the existence of ultimate and objective truth. The result has been a pervasive scepticism and relativism, which have not led to a more 'mature' humanity but to much despair and irrationality.' A little later he added, 'If reason cannot attain ultimate truths, faith loses its reasonable and intelligible character and is reduced to the realm of the non-definable, the sentimental and the irrational. The outcome is fideism. Detached from its relationship to human reason, faith loses its public and universal validity and is limited to the subjective and private sphere. In the end, theological faith is destroyed.'

C) Alienation from God and one's true self

John Paul's best known biographer, American George Weigel, has pointed out in *Witness to Hope*, that the future pontiff believed that the Christian anthropology implicit in pars 22 and 24 of *The Church in the Modern World,* was the theological linchpin of Vatican II.[9] Those paragraphs maintain that we can only know our deepest selves in and through total self-giving to Christ and one another. For example, in par. 25 of *Rosary of the Virgin Mary* he said: 'Anyone who contemplates Christ through the various stages of his life cannot fail to perceive in him the truth about man. This is the great affirmation of the Second Vatican Council which I have so often discussed in my own teaching.'

Because he believed that we discover our deepest spiritual self through union with Christ, John Paul felt that separation from Christ led to separation from one's deepest human identity and potential. As a result he was very worried by the decline of religious faith in Europe and other parts of the world. In par. 38 of *Faith and Reason* he wrote 'When God is forgotten the creature itself grows unintelligible.' Later in par. 90 he spoke about some of the likely consequences of unbelief, 'It makes it possible to erase from the countenance of men and women the marks of their likeness to God and thus leads them little by little either to a destructive will to power or to a solitude without hope.'

The Pope warned in *The Gospel of Life* that the destructive will to power can find expression in evils such as suicide, abortion, euthanasia and modern warfare. Speaking in a homily about life without hope, which he gave on Dec 11th 2003, St. John Paul said, 'Isn't existential solitude perhaps the profound source of all the dissatisfaction we also perceive in our day? So much insecurity, so many thoughtless reactions originate in our having abandoned God, the rock of our salvation.' In par. 9 of his apostolic exhortation *The Church in Europe* he wrote, 'We are witnessing the emergence of a new culture, largely influenced by the mass media, whose content and character are often in conflict with the Gospel and the dignity of the human person. This culture is also marked by a widespread and growing religious agnosticism, connected to a more profound moral and legal relativism rooted in confusion regarding the truth about man as the basis of the inalienable rights of all human beings.' As a result of these worrying trends, Pope John Paul felt that there was an urgent need for a new evangelisation, one that would not judge or condemn people who have drifted away from the Church and in many cases from the Gospel too, but rather to proclaim to them the divine mercy which was spoken about so eloquently by his fellow Pole, Sr. Faustina Kalowska (1905-38).

D) *An Immense danger*

With this in mind, it is well worth noting that in 1980 Pope John Paul said in par. 15 of, *Rich in Mercy*, 'If any of our contemporaries do not share the faith and hope which lead me, as a servant of Christ and steward of the mysteries of God, to implore God's mercy for humanity in this hour of history, let them at least try to understand the reason for my concern. It is dictated by love for man, for all that is human and which, according to the intuitions of many of our contemporaries, *is threatened by an immense danger* (my italics).' Unfortunately, John Paul did not mention what contemporaries he had in mind or what precise danger was impending. However, in 1980, shortly before the attempt on his life in St. Peter's Square, he chatted with a group of Catholics in Fulda, Germany. In response to a question about the secrets of Fatima he seemed to amplify what he had already said in his recent encyclical. 'We must prepare ourselves,' he warned, 'to suffer great trials before long, such as will demand of us a disposition to give up even life, and a total dedication to Christ and for Christ. With your and my prayer it is possible to mitigate this tribulation, but it is no longer possible to avert it, because only thus can the Church be effectively renewed.'[10]

It seems to me that the immense danger he talked about was a chastisement that was going to come upon the world, not as a punishment by a just God, but as the inevitable consequence of a materialistic form of humanism that is built on the sand of false beliefs and values which will crumble and collapse, sooner or later, with catastrophic consequences. This notion would tie in with Joseph Ratzinger's mention of the unbearable loneliness and spiritual poverty of those who, in the words of St Paul, live, 'separate from Christ, excluded from citizenship in Israel and foreigners to the covenants of the promise, without hope and without God in the world' (Eph 2:12).

d) *A NEW SPRINGTIME TO COME*

Although Pope John Paul had forbidding things to say about the present and future, he did so in a spirit of Christian hope. When he spoke about the final confrontation, he added, 'The confrontation lies within the plans of Divine Providence. It is, therefore, in God's Plan, and it must be a trial which the Church must take up, and face courageously.' St John Paul had a prophetic sense that the tribulations of the Church and the world would lead to blessing. 'As the third millennium of the redemption draws near,' he wrote in par. 86 of *Mission of the Redeemer*, 'God is preparing a great springtime for Christianity, and we can already see its first signs. In fact, both in the non-Christian world and in the traditionally Christian world, people are gradually drawing closer to gospel ideals and values, a development which the Church seeks to encourage. Today in fact there is a new consensus among peoples about these values: the rejection of violence and war; respect for the human person and for human rights; the desire for freedom, justice and brotherhood; the surmounting of different forms of racism and nationalism; the affirmation of the dignity and role of women.' In his 1995 address to the United Nations, he added, 'the tears of this century have prepared the ground for a new springtime of the human spirit.' And in 1998 he said to pilgrims gathered in Rome for Pentecost, that the Holy Spirit was bringing about 'a new springtime in the Church.' John Paul believed that docility to the Spirit and engagement in the new evangelisation he had repeatedly called for, would be instrumental in bringing about the new springtime. He wrote, 'The new evangelisation that can make the twenty-first century a springtime of the gospel is a task for the entire People of God, but will depend in a decisive way on the lay faithful being fully aware of their baptismal vocation and their responsibility for bringing the good news of Jesus Christ to their culture and society.'

5. Jorje Bergolio (Francis)

At times it seems as if the Holy Spirit is speaking through Pope Francis to the Church and the world. Indeed, he has spoken about the gift of prophecy. On Dec 15th 2013, he said in the course of a homily that, 'A prophet is someone who listens to the words of God, who reads the spirit of the times, and who knows how to move forward towards the future. True prophets hold within themselves three different moments: past, present, and future. They keep the past promise of God alive, they see the present suffering of their people, and they bring us the strength to look ahead.'

His Papal Bull, *The Face of Mercy* declared that there would be a special Year of Jubilee devoted to the mercy of God, beginning on Dec 8th 2015 and ending on the feast of Christ the King, 2016. In par. 11, Francis referred to John Paul's encyclical *Rich in Mercy*. I found it remarkable that although the encyclical is long and contains so many different points, Francis singled out this one point when he stated, 'Saint John Paul II pushed for a more urgent proclamation and witness to mercy in the contemporary world: 'It is dictated by love for man, for all that is human and which, according to the intuitions of many of our contemporaries, is threatened by an immense danger.' Clearly, Francis was buying into and endorsing John Paul's reading of the signs of the times, namely, that the world is threatened by an immense danger and needs to hear the Gospel of mercy in order to come to its senses, and return to God in order to avoid the danger that threatens it at present.

I think that Francis's urgency about having a jubilee of mercy is prompted, at least in part, by the fact that he believes that Word War III has already begun. During his visit to Korea in August 2014 he said rather ominously, 'Today we are in a world at war everywhere. A man said to me, 'Father, we are in World War III, but spread out in small pockets everywhere.' He was right,' In November 2013, Francis visited a cemetery near Venice to commemorate soldiers who died in World War I. In the course of his homily he said, ' War is irrational; its only plan is to bring destruction: it seeks to grow by destroying,' he added 'Greed, intolerance, the lust for power. These motives underlie the decision to go to war and they are too often justified by an ideology.' Then he added, 'Even today, after the failure of a second world war, perhaps one can speak of a third war, one fought piecemeal, with crimes, massacres, destruction... the plotters of terrorism, the schemers of conflicts, just like arms dealers, have engraved in their hearts, 'What does it matter to me?" Then again, in June 2015, Pope Francis spoke in Sarajevo and said that many conflicts across the planet amount to 'a kind of Third World War being fought piecemeal and, in the context of global communications, we sense an atmosphere of war... Some wish to incite and foment this atmosphere deliberately... War means children, women and the elderly in refugee camps; it means forced displacement, destroyed houses, streets and factories. Above all countless shattered lives.' Pope Francis has also drawn attention to the fact that one result of this world wide conflict is the unprecedented persecution of Christians mainly at the hands of Islamic extremists. Surely, there is a distinct danger that the war which is currently being waged piecemeal will develop into a more general conflict, one which could have devastating consequences for millions of people.

In a sermon in November, 2013, Pope Francis, like Benedict XVI before him,[11] praised the novel, *Lord of the World*, which was published by Englishman Monsignor Robert Hugh Benson in 1907.[12] Apparently, Mgr Benson was influenced by four lectures of Cardinal Newman entitled, 'The Patristical Idea of Antichrist.'[13] Writing about the novel Joseph Pearse has said, 'The world depicted in *Lord of the World* is one where creeping secularism and godless humanism have triumphed over traditional morality. It is a world where philosophical relativism has triumphed over objectivity; a world where, in the name of tolerance, religious doctrine is not tolerated. It is a world where euthanasia is practised widely and religion hardly practiced at all. The lord of this nightmare world is a benign-looking politician intent on power in the name of 'peace', and intent on the destruction of religion in the name of 'truth.' In such a world, only a small and shrinking Church stands resolutely against the demonic '*Lord of the World*.'[14] In the course of a homily he gave on Nov 18th 2013, Francis said, 'Robert Hugh Benson, son of the Archbishop of Canterbury Edward White Benson, speaks of the spirit of the world that leads to apostasy 'almost as though it were a prophecy, as though he was envisioning what would happen.' In early 2015, Pope Francis further revealed Benson's influence upon his thinking. Among other things, he said that the book contains a scary vision of the future. It culminates in the final battle between secular humanism and Catholicism, which eventually leads to Armageddon. He advised all of those on a flight back from the Philippines in January 2015 to read it. Journalist John Allen has suggested that Francis's 'fondness for the novel seems to chime with his belief that humanity is making some definitive choices today.' In other words, Francis seems to be endorsing John Paul's notion of the final confrontation.

CONCLUSION

My late mother was a devout Catholic, well read and reflective. When I was a teenager, or a little older, I noticed one of my mother's books on a shelf at home. It was about prophecy, and contained many predictions about the future. I cannot remember the title, but it was similar to Yves Dupont's, *Catholic Prophecy: The Coming Chastisement*.[15] While my mother, like many other Catholics, was interested in what seers like Michel de Nostradamus (1503-1566) had to say, I don't think she took them too seriously. As far as I can remember, she didn't discuss the prophecies with me or my siblings. However, I suspect that if she were alive today, not only would she be interested in what the five recent popes had to say, like many others, she would take their words seriously as being credible and important.

NOTES

1. *Sadhana: A Way to God* (Gujarat: Anand Press, 1983), 134.
2. *Thomas Petrisko, Fatima's Third Secret Explained* (NcKees Rocks: St Andrew's Productions, 2001), 69.
3. Fr. Domenico Pechenino, quoted in the 1955 Roman journal *Ephemerides Liturgicae V. LXIX, pp 54–60). 2.*
4. *'Prayer to St Michael'* Wikipedia, https://en.wikipedia.org/wiki/Prayer_to_Saint_Michael (Accessed 14/12/2015).
5. 'What Will the Church Look Like in 2000?' in *Faith and the Future* (San Francisco: Ignatius Press, 2009). *It is available online at, https://matiane.wordpress.com/2015/08/29/joseph-ratzinger-what-will-the-church-look-like-in-2000/ (accessed 3/9/2015).*
6. Joseph Cardinal Ratzinger, *Salt of the Earth: The Church at the End of the Millennium* (San Francisco: Ignatius Press, 1977), 268-269.
7. (Ann Arbor: Renewal Ministries, 2015).
8. Homily of Pope John Paul II Greenpark Racecourse, Limerick, 1979.
9. (London: Harper/Collins, 2001), 224.
10. October 1981 issue of the German magazine *Stimme des Glaubens* reported on a discussion that Pope John Paul II had with a select group of German Catholics, in November of 1980.
11. During a lecture he gave at the Catholic University in Milan on February 6th, 1992.
12. (London: Dodd Meade & Company, 1908).
13. *Discussions and Arguments on Various Subjects* (London: Pickering, 1872), 44-108.
14. *Literary Giants, Literary Catholics* (San Francisco: Ignatius Press, 2005), 141.
15. (Rockford; Tan, 2009).

TEN

Some modern prophecies about the present and future

A medieval Jewish astrologer, prophesied that the king's favourite horse would die soon. Sure enough, the horse expired a short time later. The king was angry with the astrologer, certain that his prophecy had brought about the horse's death. He summoned the astrologer and commanded him, 'Prophecy and tell me when you will die! Realising that the king was planning to kill him no matter what answer he gave, he responded, 'I do not know when I will die I only know that whenever I die, the king will die three days later.'

On a more serious note, we saw in the foregoing chapter how both John Paul II and Francis have referred to the intuitions of contemporaries who warned about immense dangers that may have to be faced in the future. They didn't make it clear who those contemporaries were or what they had said. At this point it is worth mentioning a few possible candidates in chronological order. It is important to remember a point made in the introduction, namely, that Catholics are not bound to believe anything these prophets have written. That said, it is well worth our while to attend to what they have to say.

The Message of la Salette

This is part of a message that was reported by two children, Maxim Giraud and Melanie Calvat at La Salette-Fallavaux,

France in 1846. Speaking about the messages, Pope John Paul II stated, 'As I wrote on the occasion of the 150th anniversary, 'La Salette is a message of hope, for our hope is nourished by the intercession of her who is the Mother of mankind.' Part of the revelation which has Church approval, reads, 'I address a pressing appeal to the earth: I call upon the true disciples of the God living and reigning in the heavens; I call upon the true imitators of Christ made man, the one true Saviour of men; I call upon my children, my true devotees, those who have given themselves to me so that I may lead them to my Divine Son, those whom I bear as it were in my arms, those who have lived in my spirit; finally, I call upon the Apostles of the latter times, the faithful disciples of Jesus Christ who have lived in contempt of the world and of themselves, in poverty and humility, in contempt and silence, in prayer and mortification, in chastity and in union with God, in suffering, and unknown to the world. It is time for them to emerge and come enlighten the earth. Go, show yourselves to be my dear children; I am with you and in you, provided your faith is the light enlightening you in these evil times. May your zeal make you zealous for the glory and honour of Jesus Christ. Do battle, children of light, you, the few who see thereby; for the time of times, the end of ends, is at hand.

'The Church will be eclipsed, the world will be in consternation. But there are Enoch and Elias, they will preach with the power of God, and men of good will believe in God, and many souls will be comforted; they will make great progress by virtue of the Holy Spirit and will condemn the diabolical errors of the Antichrist. 'Woe to the inhabitants of the earth. There will be bloody wars, and famines; plagues and contagious diseases; thunders which will demolish cities; earthquakes which will engulf countries; voices will be heard in the air; men will beat their heads against the walls; they will call on death, yet death will constitute their torment; blood will flow on all sides. Who could overcome, if God doesn't shorten the time of trial? At the blood, tears and prayers of the righteous, God will relent; Enoch and Elias will be put to death; pagan Rome will disappear; the fire of Heaven will fall and consume three cities; the whole universe will be struck with terror, and many will allow themselves to be seduced because they didn't adore the true Christ living in their midst. It is time; the sun is darkening; Faith alone will survive.'

THE SECRETS OF FATIMA

The apparitions in Fatima in 1917 were undoubtedly among the most prophetic of modern times. Pope John Paul II said, 'Our Lady's call to conversion and penance, issued at the start of the twentieth century, remains timely and urgent today. The Lady of the message seems to read the signs of the times - the signs of our time - with special insight.'[1] The first and second parts of the 'secret referred especially to the frightening vision of hell, devotion to the Immaculate Heart of Mary, the Second World War, and finally the prediction of the immense damage that Russia would do to humanity by abandoning the Christian faith and embracing Communist totalitarianism. The third part of the secret was revealed at the Cova da Iria-Fátima, on 13 July 1917. Lucy who was one of the three children present on that occasion recounted it as follows:

'After the first two parts which I have already explained, we saw an Angel with a flaming sword in his left hand at the left of Our Lady and a little above; flashing, it gave out flames that looked as though they would set the world on fire; but they died out in contact with the splendour that Our Lady radiated towards her from the angel's right hand: pointing to the earth with his right hand, the Angel cried out in a loud voice: 'Penance, Penance, Penance!'. And we saw in an immense light that is God: 'something similar to how people appear in a mirror when they pass in front of it was a Bishop dressed in White. We had the impression that it was the Holy Father.' Other Bishops, Priests, men and women religious going up a steep mountain, at the top of which there was a big Cross of rough-hewn trunks as of a cork-tree with the bark; before reaching there the Holy Father passed through a big city half in ruins and half trembling with halting step, afflicted with pain and sorrow, he prayed for the souls of the corpses he met on his way; having reached the top of the mountain, on his knees at the foot of the big Cross he was killed by a group of soldiers who fired bullets and arrows at him, and in the same way there died one after another the other Bishops, Priests, men and women Religious, and various lay people of different ranks and positions. Beneath the two arms of the Cross there were two Angels each with a crystal vessel for holy water in his hand, in which they gathered up the blood of the Martyrs and with it sprinkled the souls that were making their way to God.'[2]

Joseph Ratzinger wrote a detailed commentary on this third secret, in the course of which he said, 'The purpose of the vision is not to show a film of an irrevocably fixed future. Its meaning is exactly the opposite: it is meant to mobilise the forces of change in the right direction... the vision speaks of dangers and how we might be saved from them.'[3] In a letter Sr. Lucia wrote to Pope John Paul II, in 1982, she seemed to endorse Cardinal Ratzinger's point when she said, 'let us not say that it is God who is punishing us in this way; on the contrary it is people themselves who are preparing their own punishment. In his kindness God warns us and calls us to the right path, while respecting the freedom he has given us; hence people are responsible.'

Around 4pm on January 3rd, 1944 St, Lucia asked Jesus to let her know His will. She says that while she was in the chapel, 'I felt my spirit flooded by a light-filled mystery which is God and in Him I saw and heard: the point of the flame-like lance which detaches, touches the axis of the earth and it [the earth] shakes: mountains, cities, towns and villages with their inhabitants are buried. The sea, rivers and clouds leave their bounds, they overflow, flood and drag with them into a whirlpool, houses and people in a number unable to be counted; it is the purification of the world from the sin it is immersed in. Hatred, ambition, cause destructive wars. Afterward I felt in the increased beating of my heart and in my spirit a quiet voice which said: 'in time, one faith, one baptism, one Church, Holy, Catholic, Apostolic. Heaven in eternity!' This word, 'Heaven,' filled my heart with peace and happiness, so much so that, almost without realising it, I continued to repeat for some time: Heaven, Heaven!'

On February 16, 2008, an interview with Cardinal Carlo Caffara of Bologna, was reported in '*Voce di Padre Pio*' (March, 2008). It began, 'there is a prophecy by Sister Lucia dos Santos, of Fatima, which concerns the final battle between the Lord and the kingdom of Satan. Apparently the battlefield is the family. We know that you were given charge by John Paul II to plan and establish the Pontifical Institute for the Study on Marriage and the Family.' The Archbishop responded, 'Yes, I was. At the start of this work entrusted to me by the Servant of God John Paul II, I wrote to Sister Lucia of Fatima through her Bishop as I couldn't do so directly. Inexplicably however, since I didn't expect an answer, seeing that I had only asked for prayers, I received a very long letter with her signature – now in the Institute's archives. In it we find written: 'the final battle between the Lord and the reign of Satan will be about marriage and the family. Don't be afraid, she added, because anyone who works for the sanctity of marriage and the family will always be fought and opposed in every way, because this is the decisive issue.' And then she concluded, however, 'Our Lady has already crushed its head.' Clearly this revelation complements what Pope John Paul II said about the final confrontation.

St Faustina Kowalska

Many prophetic messages sound rather harsh and forbidding. In that context it is worth looking at what Our Lord said to St. Faustina Kowalska, 'In the Old Covenant I sent prophets wielding thunderbolts to My people. Today I am sending you with My mercy to the people of the whole world. I do not want to punish suffering mankind, but I desire to heal it, pressing it to My Merciful Heart. I use punishment when they themselves force Me to do so; My hand is reluctant' *(Diary, 1588)*.

It is instructive to recall some more thematically related messages of an apocalyptic kind which were given to St. Faustina. 'Speak to the world about My mercy; let all mankind recognise My unfathomable mercy. It is a sign for the end times; after it will come the day of justice. While there is still time, let them have recourse to the fountain of My mercy' *(Diary, 848)*. 'You will prepare the world for My final coming' *(Diary, 429)*. 'Tell souls about this great mercy of Mine, because the awful day, the day of My justice, is near' *(Diary, 965)*. 'Before the Day of Justice, I am sending the Day of Mercy' *(Diary, 1588)*. 'Let people profit from the Blood and Water which gushed forth for them' *(Diary, 848)*. 'Before I come as a just Judge, I first open wide the doors of My mercy. He who refuses to pass through the doors of My mercy must pass through the doors of My justice' *(Diary, 1146)*. Lastly, she wrote, 'I am prolonging the time of mercy for the sake of sinners. But woe to them if they do not recognise this time of My visitation' *(Diary, 1160)*.

On two other occasions St Faustina was told, 'You have to speak to the world about His great mercy and prepare the world for the Second Coming of Him who will come, not as a merciful Saviour, but as a just Judge. Oh how terrible is that day! Determined is the day of justice, the day of divine wrath. The angels tremble before it. Speak to souls about this great mercy while it is still the time for granting mercy' *(Diary, 635)*. At another time she was told, 'Before I come as a just judge, I am coming first as the King of Mercy. Before the day of justice arrives, there will be given to people a sign in the heavens of this sort: All light in the heavens will be extinguished, and there will be great darkness over the whole earth. Then the sign of the cross will be seen in the sky, and from the openings where the hands of feet of the Saviour were nailed will come forth great lights which will light up the earth for a period of time. This will take place shortly before the last day' *(Diary, 83)*.

Pope John Paul II was of the opinion that St. Faustina was one of the great prophets of the 20th century. In the homily he gave at the time of her canonisation, he stressed that Jesus Christ's message to Sister Faustina was placed in time between two World Wars and is was very much linked to the history of the 20th century. What will be the future of man on earth, he asked, 'It is not given to us to know it. It is true, however, that along with the new progresses we will not lack painful experiences. However, the light of Divine Mercy, which the Lord wished virtually to give again to the world through the charism of Sister Faustina, will illumine the path of the men of the third millennium.'

THE PROPHECY OF BL. ELENA AIELLO

Elena Aiello (1895-1961) of Montalto Uffugo, Italy, assisted her father in his tailoring shop following the death of her mother. She entered the Sisters of the Most Precious Blood at the age of twenty-five, but health problems compelled her to return to her family nine months later. On Friday, 2nd March 1923, Elena was meditating upon the Passion of Christ when she received the stigmata of the crown of thorns and the bloody sweat of Gethsemane, a mystical experience that lasted three hours. From then on, to the end of her life, she received the stigmata annually on each Friday of Lent, and most intensely on Good Friday. Elena later became the founder of a new congregation, the Sisters Minims of the Passion of Our Lord Jesus Christ. Mother Elena died on 19th June 1961. Pope Benedict XVI beatified her on September 14, 2011.

During her lifetime Elena received many prophecies. In 1940, she was given a message by Jesus and was asked to deliver it to Premier Benito Mussolini. It urged him not to join forces with Hitler in World War II. Here are two of her more apocalyptic messages. 'Russia will march upon all the nations of Europe, particularly Italy, and will raise her flag over the Dome of

St. Peter's. Italy will be severely tried by a great revolution, and Rome will be purified in blood for its many sins, especially those of impurity! The flock is about to be dispersed and the Pope must suffer greatly!... If the people do not recognise in these scourges the warnings of Divine Mercy, and do not return to God with truly Christian living, another terrible war will come from the East to the West. Russia with her secret armies will battle America; will overrun Europe... Oh, what a horrible vision I see! A great revolution is going on in Rome! They are entering the Vatican. The Pope is all alone; he is praying. They are holding the Pope. They take him by force.'

On another occasion Our Lady said to her, 'My Heart is sad for so many sufferings in an impending world in ruin... The wrath of God is near. Soon the world will be afflicted with great calamities, bloody revolutions, frightful hurricanes and the overflowing of rivers and the seas... the world will be overturned in a new and more terrible war. Arms most deadly will destroy peoples and nations. The dictators of the earth, specimens infernal, will demolish the churches and desecrate the Holy Eucharist, and will destroy things most dear. In this impious war, much will be destroyed of that which has been built by the hands of man.'

Sr. Agnes Sasagawa's Prophetic Message

Sr. Agnes Sasagawa, a nun in Akita Japan, who had already experienced a number of private revelations, received a message from Our Lady on October 13, 1973. Sister Agnes related how she entered the convent chapel and had barely finished making the sign of the cross with her rosary when she heard a voice of indescribable beauty come from the statue of Our Lady. From the first word, Sister Agnes prostrated herself on the ground and concentrated on the message being given to her. 'My dear daughter, listen well to what I have to say to you. You will inform your superior.' After a short silence our Lady said, 'As I told you, if men do not repent and better themselves, the Father will inflict a terrible punishment on all humanity. It will be a punishment greater than the deluge, such as one will never have seen before. Fire will fall from the sky and will wipe out a great part of humanity, the good as well as the bad, sparing neither priests nor faithful. [This could be a reference to atomic war or an asteroid crashing into the planet] The survivors will find themselves so desolate that they will envy the dead. The only arms which will remain for you will be the Rosary and the Sign left by My Son. Each day recite the prayers of the Rosary. With the Rosary, pray for the Pope, the bishops and priests. The work of the devil will infiltrate even into the Church in such a way that one will see cardinals opposing cardinals, bishops against bishops. The priests who venerate me will be scorned and opposed by their confreres... churches and altars will be sacked; the Church will be full of those who accept compromises and the demon will press many priests and consecrated souls to leave the service of the Lord. The demon will be especially implacable against souls consecrated to God. The thought of the loss of so many souls is the cause of my sadness. If sins increase in number and gravity, there will be no longer pardon for them. With courage, speak to your superior. He will know how to encourage each one of you to pray and to accomplish works of reparation. It is Bishop Ito, who directs your community.' And she smiled and then said 'You have still something to ask? Today is the last time I will speak to you in a living voice. From now on you will obey the one sent to you by Father Yasuda [her spiritual director] and your superior.

Pray very much the prayers of the rosary. I alone am able to save you from the calamities that approach. Those who place their confidence in me will be saved.'[4] There are obvious similarities between the prophecy of St Lucia of Fatima, and Sr. Sasagawa of Akita.

A number of miraculous signs were associated with Sr. Sasagawa. The statue of our Lady wept and bled. Samples of the blood and tears were sent to the laboratory of Akita University for analysis on January 29th 1979. According to signed testimony the blood was type B and the body fluids type AB. Teresa Chun, a Korean woman who was reduced to a vegetative state because of a brain tumour was cured miraculously as was Sr Agnes herself, when her deafness was cured instantly. Having investigated these events the local bishop of Niigata diocese, John Shojiro Ito, issued a pastoral letter declaring the events of Akita to be supernatural.

Prophecies of Ralph Martin and Bruce Yocum

On the Monday following Pentecost in 1975, the words of the five popes examined in the previous chapter seemed to be echoed by a two part prophecy which was spoken by Americans Dr. Ralph Martin and Bruce Yocum in St. Peter's Basilica in Rome in the presence of Pope Paul VI and Cardinal Suenens.

'Because I love you I want to show you what I am doing in the world today. I want to prepare you for what is to come. Days of darkness are coming on the world, days of tribulation... Buildings that are now standing will not be standing. Supports that are there for my people will not be there. I want you to be prepared, My people, to know only me and to cleave to me and to have me in a way deeper than ever before. I will lead you into the desert... I will strip you of everything that you are depending on now, so you depend just on me. A time of darkness is coming on the world, but a time of glory is coming for my church, a time of glory is coming for my people. I will pour out on you all the gifts of My Spirit. I will prepare you for spiritual combat; I will prepare you for a time of evangelism that the world has never seen. And when you have nothing but Me, you will have everything: land, fields, homes and brothers and sisters and love and joy and peace more than ever before. Be ready, my people, I want to prepare you.

I speak to you of the dawn of a 'new age' for My church. I speak to you of a day that has not been seen before... Prepare yourselves for the action that I begin now, because things that you see around you will change; the combat that you must enter now is different; it is new. You need wisdom from Me that you do not yet have.

You need the power of my Holy Spirit in a way that you have not possessed it; you need an understanding of My will and of the ways that I work that you do not yet have. Open your eyes, open your hearts to prepare yourselves for Me and for the day that I have now begun. My church will be different; My people will be different; difficulties and trials will come upon you. The comfort that you know now will be far from you, but the comfort that you will have is the comfort of My Holy Spirit. They will send for you, to take your life, but I will support you. Come to Me. Band yourselves together, around Me. Prepare, for I proclaim a new day, a day of victory and of triumph for your God. Behold, It is begun.

I will renew my Church. I will renew my people. I will make My people one. I am calling you to turn away from the pleasure of the world. I am calling you to turn away from seeking the approval of the world in your lives. I want to transform your lives... I have a word for My church. I am sounding My call. I am forming a mighty army... My power is upon them. They will follow My chosen shepherd(s).

Be the shepherds I have called you to be... I am renewing My church. I will free the world. Know that I, your God, brought Peter and Paul to Rome to witness to My glory. I have chosen you also and have brought you to Rome to bear witness to My glory, confirmed now by your shepherd. Go forth to the healing of the nations. Know that I am with you; and though you may pass through tribulation and trial, I will be with you even to the end. I am preparing a place for you in glory. Look to Me and I will deliver you from the power of the evil one. Behold I am with you now, all days, even till the end of time.

You have known the truth these days. You have experienced the truth these days. It is clear to you at this moment what the truth is. It is the truth of My kingdom, My kingdom that will prevail... I want you to take that truth, to rest in that truth, to believe in that truth, not to compromise it, not to lose it in confusion, not to be timid about it, but to stand simply, in love, firmly rooted in the truth as foundation stones upon which My church can have new life and new power.'[5]

It would be true to say that these combined prophecies have influenced a large number of Catholics, including myself. Not only do they mirror what Joseph Ratzinger had said on German radio in 1969, they have evoked an answering amen in many a heart. I'm probably over simplifying when I say that they fall into three parts.

- Firstly great difficulties are going to afflict and purify the Church.
- Secondly, there is going to be a great and disillusioning upheaval in the world which could involve war, economic difficulties or worldwide disease.
- Thirdly, as a result of the darkness in the secular world, where many people live without hope and without God, large numbers will be open to the saving meaning and hope that comes from believing in Jesus and his Gospel. That period will lead to widespread evangelisation which will help to bring about the new springtime in Christianity which was spoken about in a prophetic way by John Paul II.

Prophetic utterances of Jonathan Cahn

Jonathan Cahn is a Messianic Jewish rabbi in the United states. He is the author of two very successful, but questionable books, *The Harbinger* and *The Mystery of the Shemitah*. Many people regard him as a modern prophet. Time will tell. Cahn predicted that on Sept 15th 2015, it was likely that there would be an economic collapse in America. That date has since passed, and the economic collapse has not taken place as foretold. In the course of a keynote address at the January Presidential Inaugural Breakfast, February 4th, 2013, he said like a latter day John the Baptist, 'As the people of ancient Israel, in the midst of their blessings, committed a fatal error, so have we. We too, as a nation, have turned from God. We too, as a nation, have removed Him from our lives. Step by step we too have ruled Him out of our culture, out of our government, out of our economy. We too have ruled Him out of the instruction and lives of our children. We too have made God a stranger. And as we have driven God from our national life, we have brought in other gods and idols to replace Him - gods of sensuality, violence, wealth, carnality, sexual promiscuity. And as did Israel, so too we have abandoned the ways of God and the laws of God for the ways of immorality.' What he said about America, could also be said about many other Western countries. But Cahn went on to warn that this kind of forgetfulness of God and God's will, is likely to bring misfortune.

When the justices of The American Supreme Court issued a judgment in 2015 which said that gay marriage should be a right in every state in the U.S., Cahn said that they were like the Israelites who, 'drove God out of their government, out of their public squares, out of their culture, and out of the lives of their children. They worshipped idols and served other gods. They celebrated immorality and persecuted the righteous. They lifted up their children on the altars of foreign gods. And the blessings of God were removed from the land and replaced with judgment.' Then he went on to add, 'It is two and half thousand years later, and America has made the same mistake. We, too, have turned away from God. We, too, have driven Him out of our government, out of our public squares, out of our culture, and out of the lives of our children. We too have profaned the sacred and sanctified the profane. And we, too, have killed our most innocent, over fifty five million of our unborn children, and our collective hands are covered with blood. What we were warned never to do, we now have done.' Later, Cahn warned, 'Can you, with man-made verdicts, overrule the eternal laws of God? There is another court, and there is another judge. And before

Him, all men and all judges will give account. If a nation's high court should pass judgment on the Almighty, should you then be surprised if the Almighty should pass judgment on that court and that nation.' Cahn has suggested that contemporary Americans are like those in Isa 9:10. They say, 'The bricks have fallen down, but we will rebuild with dressed stone; the fig trees have been felled, but we will replace them with cedars.' He feels that the collapse of the twin towers and the economic crisis of 2008 were a divine warning. But instead of repenting people built the One World Trading Centre, the tallest skyscraper in the Western hemisphere, and continued to ignore the revealed will of God in order to do their own worldly thing. As a result he feels that people will bring a purifying chastisement upon themselves.

Prophecies of Vassula Ryden

Vassula Rydén, a member of the Greek Orthodox Church, was born in 1942. She claims to receive messages from Jesus Christ and the Blessed Virgin. Her writings frequently call for people 'to repent, love God, and unify the churches.' Writing about her, Niels Christian Hvidt says, 'Few other contemporary mystics exhibit the prophetic charism as does Mrs. Ryden.' It should be said, that although she is not a member of the Catholic Church, her writings were investigated by the Congregation of the Doctrine of the Faith in the Vatican. In a 1996 it issued a notification which said that Vassula's messages were 'merely the result of private meditation.' Subsequently, Cardinal Ratzinger said, 'The notification is a warning, not a condemnation... There are some debatable apocalyptic elements and unclear ecclesiological aspects. Her writings contain many good things but the grain and chaff appear to be mixed. That is why we invite Catholics to view it with all with a prudent eye and measure it with the yardstick of the constant faith of the Church.' Ryden is of the opinion that currently we are witnessing a mass apostasy, a veritable rebellion against God. She believes that human sinfulness is not only destructive of people it makes even nature to turn against them. On Christmas Eve 1991, Ryden was given these words, 'I come today and offer all mankind My Peace, but very few listen. Today I come with peace-terms and a message of Love, but the peace I am offering is blasphemed by the earth, and the Love I am giving them is mocked and jeered in this Eve of My Birth. Mankind is celebrating these days without My Holy Name. My Holy Name has been abolished and they take the day of My Birth as a great holiday of leisure, worshipping idols. Satan has entered into the hearts of My children, finding them weak and asleep. I have warned the world.'

On February 18th 1993 she received this austere message, 'See the days are coming when I am going to come by thunder and fire but I will find, to My distress, many of you unaware and in deep sleep! I am sending you through creation, messenger after messenger to break through your deafness, but I am weary now of your resistance and your apathy. I am ever so weary of your coldness; I am weary of your arrogance and your inflexibility when it comes to assembling for unity - you filled and overflowed now the Cup of Stupor. Intoxicated by your own voice you have opposed My Voice but it shall not be forever - soon you shall fall for you have opposed My Voice by your voice, misleading nonsense; naturally My Church is in ruin because of your division and the earth will shake and like a shooting star, will reel from its place, tearing mountains and islands out of their places. Entire nations will be annihilated; the sky will disappear like a scroll rolling up as you saw it in your vision, daughter. A great agony will fall on all the citizens, and woe to the unbeliever! Hear Me: and should men say to you today: 'Ah, but the Living One will have Mercy upon us, your prophecy is not from God but from your own spirit', tell them: although you are reputed to be alive, you are dead; your incredulity condemns you, because you refused to believe in My time of Mercy and prohibited My Voice to spread through My mouthpieces to warn and save My creatures.'

Commenting on messages of this kind Ryden says that 'Our Lord is warning us that, because of our apostasy, we are endangering the cosmos - not only the earth, but the entire cosmos, provoking nature to rebel against us.' Although some of her prophecies are apocalyptic, Ryden says that they, 'are not prophecies of doom and gloom. God gives them to us in these times of mercy to shake us up; they are a call out of the sublime Love of God. God will not allow us forever to offend His Holy Name. This is the reason why He comes, in His mercy, to give us many warnings.' She also adds that, 'Jesus tells us: 'Many of you have seen many signs, these signs are to be observed, they are the signs of the end of Times, they are not the signs of the end of the world, they are the signs of the end of an era.'[6] This being so, Vassula says that she is not a prophet of doom and gloom, but rather a messenger of hope.

Conclusion

I am well aware that my choice of messengers and messages has been subjective and perhaps a little arbitrary. There are many others I could have adverted to such as Fr Gobbi, Pedro Regis etc. One way or the other, when one reads prophecies of this kind it is important to notice whether any overall message emerges. In the light of these interpretations of the signs of the times what is needed? Firstly, the members of the Church require spiritual renewal and a willingness to make personal and structural changes which will better facilitate the church's evangelising mission. As Faustina, John Paul II, and Francis have indicated, we have to proclaim the message of divine mercy. Secondly, we need to listen to the Lord. As Paul prayed in Col 1:9-10, 'we have not stopped praying for you and asking God to fill you with the knowledge of his will through all spiritual wisdom and understanding. And we pray this in order that you may live a life worthy of the Lord and may please him in every way.' The Lord can answer that prayer in many ways, e.g., by means of inspirations, promptings and prophetic revelations. Thirdly, while a time of disillusioning chastisement is probably coming upon the world, providentially, it could lead many of those who have completely lost sight of God, to feel in the words of Joseph Ratzinger, 'the whole horror of their poverty.' Then they may turn to the purified community of believers as something wholly new and attractive. The evangelisation that will occur as a result, may well inaugurate the new springtime for Christianity which was spoken about repeatedly by Popes John Paul and Benedict. Understood in this way, although many of the prophecies cited may be forbidding, they are also redolent with hope.

NOTES

1. Pope John Paul II, Message for the 1997 World Day of the Sick.
2. Congregation for the Doctrine of the Faith: *The Message of Fatima.*
3. http://www.vatican.va/roman_curia/congregations/cfaith/documents/re_con_cfaith_doc_20000626_message-fatima_en.html.
4. http://www.catholicrevelations.org/PR/akita.htm (Accessed 23/12/2015).
5. http://www.freerepublic.com/focus/f-religion/3089486/posts (Accessed 24/12/2015).
6. Message given on Jan 31st 1990. in Vassula Ryden's, *True Life in God* (New York/Bath: Alexian, 2013). The book has the nihil obstat and the imprimatur which indicate that it is free from doctrinal or moral error.

ELEVEN

PROPHECY AND WORDS OF KNOWLEDGE IN THE BIBLE

In November 2015 I visited Palermo in Sicily. While I was there I was asked to lead a healing service for about seven hundred people. I spent some time, beforehand, praying for guidance. Two of the thoughts that came spontaneously to mind were that one woman would attend who would be suffering from an irrational fear of fire and that another would be afflicted by an arthritic disc in her neck. During the healing service I mentioned both of these complaints. The following day, I discovered that not only were those two women present, it appeared that they had both been healed. A couple of days later I went to Cefalu to speak at a weekend conference on the New Evangelisation. Right in the middle of one of my talks, the image of an elderly woman came into my mind. Then it occurred to me that she had a painful nerve in her back. When I thought about it for a moment it occurred to me that she was suffering from shingles. I stopped and said, 'I know it is a strange question to ask, but is there a woman here who is recovering from a painful dose of shingles?' As soon as my interpreter had translated what I had said, a woman raised her hand. I urged everyone to join me in saying a brief prayer for her. Then I continued to give the talk. The next day the woman informed us that the pain in her infected nerves had ceased.

This chapter is about a mysterious but wonderful phenomenon, what is referred to by Pentecostal and Charismatic Christians as 'a word of knowledge.' As many readers may be unfamiliar with the term, we begin with a definition. Writing in *The New International Dictionary of Pentecostal and Charismatic Movements*, scripture scholar Francis Martin says,

> 'We may define the gift of 'word of knowledge' as being the charismatically endowed capacity to express some aspect of God's plan as it is at work in creation here and now, revealing something of God.' A little later Martin adds, 'In our own day' it is, 'a very special gift, that of knowing what God is doing at this moment in another's soul or body, or of knowing the secrets of another's heart is often described as a 'word of knowledge.'[1]

Anglican bishop, David Pytches, states that the word of knowledge is a

> 'supernatural revelation of facts about a person or situation, which is not learned through the efforts of the natural mind, but is a fragment of knowledge freely given by God, disclosing the truth which the Spirit wishes to be made known concerning a particular person or situation.'[2]

Scripture on the Prophetic Word of Knowledge

There is one verse in St. Paul's writings that I find particularly helpful when it comes to understanding the prophetic word of knowledge. In 1 Cor 2:10-11 he writes: 'The Spirit searches all things, even the deep things of God.' Paul seems to be suggesting that the Spirit has an intimate knowledge, both of all created things and the mystery of God. The word 'intimate' in English is derived from Latin and could loosely be translated as 'to publish to make known that which is innermost.' Implicit in that etymology is the belief that the Spirit of God is familiar with the hidden essence of everything that exists. Like an X-ray it penetrates in a loving, affirming way to the core of all things. In this context one is reminded of a verse in Wis 1:7 which says: 'For the spirit of the Lord fills the world, and that which holds everything together, knows every word said.' If that is true of creation in general, it is particularly true of human beings. Not only is the Holy Spirit acquainted with the inner reality of every cell in the body, more importantly, it is *au fait* with every nuance of human subjectivity, with all of its thoughts, memories and desires. God's Spirit knows us better than we know ourselves. Nothing is hidden from its penetrating, but benevolent gaze.

At the same time the Spirit also has an intimate knowledge of the infinite depths of God. We could say, in a rather anthropomorphic way, that the Spirit is familiar with the thoughts, memories and desires of God. Historically, they were manifested in the humanity of Christ, especially through his life, death and resurrection. Paul then goes on to say that God's Holy Spirit has been poured into the hearts of believers. In principle, therefore, graced individuals can, like Christ, know others, their bodies, minds and spirits, as God knows them, by means of the Spirit's gratuitously given revelation. Sometimes they will also have a sense of what God wants for the people they know in this intimate spiritual way. As Paul says, 'The spiritual man judges all things, but is himself to be judged by no one. 'For who has known the mind of the Lord so as to instruct Him?' But we have the mind of Christ' (1 Cor 2:14-16), e.g., when we receive words of knowledge.

Having looked at the meaning of the phrase 'word of knowledge,' we can examine its biblical roots. There is a divided opinion among scholars. One school of thought quotes what St. Paul said in 1 Cor 12:8, 'To one there is given through the Spirit... a message of knowledge by means of the... Spirit.' Commenting on this verse scripture scholars Carson, Kristemaker and Bittlinger,[3] say that the word of knowledge refers to an inspired ability to preach and teach the good news, i.e., 'the utterance of knowledge.' However, commenting on the same verse, Gordon D. Fee, an eminent Pentecostal scripture scholar, says in *God's Empowering Presence* that while the 'utterance of knowledge' can take the form of inspired teaching, it can also refer to 'a supernatural endowment of knowledge, factual information that could not otherwise have been known without the Spirit's aid, such as frequently occurs in the prophetic tradition.'[4] Catholic scripture scholar, George Montague concurs with Fee when he writes: 'In the history of the Christian interpretation of this gift two different meanings have been attached to it: one concerns an inspired knowledge of a fact, the other an inspired insight into the Christian mystery granted especially for the purpose of teaching.'[5] Writing about the utterance of knowledge Prospero Lambertini said that it was the result of infused knowledge, i.e., knowledge that is not acquired by personal effort or by instruction, but rather is produced directly in the mind. He added, 'Absolutely infused knowledge is that which no creature can acquire by natural strength, but is impressed on, and caused in the creature by God alone; and this is said to be absolutely and simply in the order of what is divine, and is above nature.'

Another school of thought believes that the word of knowledge is an aspect of the gift of prophecy which is mentioned in 1 Cor

12:10. Speaking about this gift, James Dunn echoes what we saw in a previous chapter when he says, 'For Paul prophecy is a word of revelation. It does not denote the delivery of a previously prepared sermon; it is not a word that can be summoned up to order, or a skill that can be learned; it is a spontaneous utterance, a revelation given in words to the prophet to be delivered as it is given (cf. 1 Cor 14:30).'[6] That definition is similar in many respects to Gordon D. Fee's definition of a word of knowledge. When all is said and done, it doesn't really matter whether words of knowledge are understood in terms of 1 Cor 12:8 or 1 Cor 12:10. I suspect that as forms of private revelation they overlap so much as to be almost inseparable.

Old and New Testament Examples

There are many instances of the word of knowledge in the Old Testament. We will refer to only three of many possible examples. The prophet Nathan knew about David's sin of adultery with Bathsheba, and he used the parable about the poor man and the lamb before confronting him by saying, 'You are that man' (2 Sam 12:1-12). Daniel had an inspired sense that Susanna was innocent of the accusations made by the two immoral old men and devised a test which exposed their guilt and the woman's innocence (Dan 13:44-49). When Saul was chosen as king, he hid himself. We are told that the people 'inquired further of the Lord, 'Has the man come here yet?' And the Lord said, (presumably through someone in the gathering uttering a prophetic word of knowledge) 'Yes, he has hidden himself among the baggage' (1 Sam 10:22).

In the New Testament we are told that Jesus seemed to be able to read people's hearts and to predict future events. For instance, he appeared to know all about Nathaniel although he had never met him before (Jn 1:48); and he was able to tell the Samaritan woman at the well that she hadn't one husband, but five (Jn 4:18). When asked to pay the tax, Jesus knew about the four drachma coin in the fish's mouth, which Peter would later retrieve (Mt 17:27). On another occasion, Jesus told the disciples that they would find a donkey in a certain place (Mk 11:2) and that they would meet with a man carrying a pitcher of water (Mk 14:13). During his scourging at the pillar the Roman soldiers taunted the blindfolded Jesus, by saying: 'Prophesy, who hit you?' This seemed to indicate that Jesus was known to have an ability to speak words of knowledge.

In the New Testament Church some of the believers were granted the word of knowledge. For example, Ananias and Saul met as a result of words of knowledge: 'The Lord told him, 'Go to the house of Judas on Straight Street and ask for a man from Tarsus named Saul, for he is praying. In a vision he has seen a man named Ananias come and place his hands on him to restore his sight' (Acts 9:11-12). St. Peter met with Cornelius, in much the same way when he and the centurion received words of knowledge (Acts 10:17-23).

Conclusion

In three places in the Bible the question is asked, 'who has known the mind of the Lord?' (cf. Is 40:13; Rom 11:34; & 1 Cor 2:16). Of course, speaking from a purely natural point of view the answer is, no one. However, if God so chooses, the Spirit can infuse a fragment of God's knowledge into the human mind. As a result, St. Paul attested in 1 Cor 2:16, 'we have the mind of Christ.' I suspect that many Christians are unfamiliar with the nature and exercise of the gift of the word of knowledge as an aspect of prophetic revelation. As this chapter has indicated the gift was one of the mysterious ways in which the prophetic gift was exercised in both the Old and the New Testaments. In contrast to the pagans, there was nothing occult about it. In the following chapter we will see that it can be used in a number of pastoral contexts to great effect.

NOTES

1. Francis Martin, 'Knowledge, word of' in *The New International Dictionary of Pentecostal and Charismatic Movements,* eds., Stanley M. Burgess, Eduard M. Van Der Maas(Grand Rapids: Zondervan, 2002), 823-825.
2. *Come Holy Spirit: Learning to Minister in Power* (London: Hodder & Stoughton, 1985), 99.
3. D. A. Carson, *Showing the Spirit: A Theological Exposition of 1 Corinthians 12-14* (Carlisle: Paternoster Press, 1987), 38; Simon Kistemaker *1 Corinthians* (Grand Rapids: Baker, 1994), 421; Arnold Bittlinger *Gifts and Graces: A Commentary on 1 Corinthians 12-14* (London: Hodder & Stoughton, 1967), 30-31.
4. (Peabody, Mass: Hendrickson, 1995), 167.
5. *The Holy Spirit,* (New York: Paulist Press, 1976), 151.
6. James D G Dunn, *Jesus and the Spirit* (London: SCM, 1978), 228.

TWELVE

CONTEMPORARY EXPERIENCE OF WORDS OF KNOWLEDGE

Many of us have heard of charismatic people like John Vianney, Padre Pio of Pietrelcina and the late Kathryn Kulhman who were blessed with 'words of knowledge' of different kinds, such as an ability to foretell future events, to read people's hearts, and to know what illnesses the Lord wanted to heal. In this chapter we will look at some examples of how this form of prophetic revelation was experienced by people in the relatively recent past.

SAINTS WHO RECEIVED WORDS OF KNOWLEDGE

In the year 1853, a group of young men set out from Lyons to go on pilgrimage to Ars. They were conscientious Christians; all except one, an old man who had joined the group, solely to please the young people. They reached the village at about three o'clock in the afternoon. 'Go to church, if you like,' said the unbeliever on leaving the carriage; 'as for me, I shall order dinner.' He walked a few yards, then stopped. 'No, on second thoughts, I will go with you,' he said, 'for you should not be that long!' So the whole group entered the church. Now at that very moment Fr. John Vianney, the Cure of Ars, came out of the sacristy and entered the chancel. He knelt down, stood up and turned round; his eyes were looking for someone in the direction of the holy water font, and finally he signalled to someone to come up. 'It is you he wants,' the youths told the astonished unbeliever. So he walked up, obviously feeling very embarrassed. As for us, we were chuckling inwardly, for we understood that the bird had been caught. The Cure shook his hand, saying: 'It is a long time since you were at confession?' 'My good Cure, it is something like thirty years, I believe.' 'Thirty years, my friend? Just think... It is thirty-three years; you were then at such a place...' 'You are right, Monsieur le Cure.' 'Ah, well, so we are going to confession now, are we not?' The old man said afterwards that he was so taken aback by the invitation that he dared not say no; but he added: 'I at once experienced a sensation of indefinable comfort.' The confession took twenty minutes, and made a new man of him.

I was very interested to note in Christopher O'Donnell's book, *Love in the Heart of the Church: The Mission of Therese of Lisieux*,[1] that when the cause for her canonisation was being processed, witnesses were asked, whether he or she was aware that Therese was sometimes enriched with heavenly gifts, such as apparitions, revelations, the gift of prophecy, reading hearts, rapture or ecstasy? It transpired that Therese had received some prophetic revelations during her short life. For instance, at the age of six or seven she had a fleeting glimpse of her father bent over with age, his face covered with a veil. Her sister Agnes testified that, 'she was convinced, not only of the reality of the vision, but also that this vision had a significance that would be manifested later, that it foretold some trial or misfortune.' In the event, St. Louis Martin developed dementia in the final years of his life. O'Donnell also provides other examples of prophetic activity in Therese's life.

Padre Pio had similar gifts. For example, Francesco Cavicchi and his wife visited the friar in June 1967. Francesco had already confessed three days before, but wanted to confess to Padre Pio anyway. He stood in line and when his turn was approaching, he got agitated. But Padre Pio calling him from the line said: 'Come forward, my son, I have been waiting for you for a long time.' He started the confession asking: 'How many days has it been since your last confession?' Francesco said that he couldn't remember. Padre Pio replied, 'You have a short memory, don't you. But let me ask you this. Do you remember the bombardment in Rimini many years back? Do you remember the air raid shelter? Do you remember the trolley bus? But why I'm asking you to go back in time? You cannot even remember what you did less than a week ago!' At that point, Francesco started recollecting that in November 1943, when he was 28 years old, he was travelling on the bus with about ten other people, including a middle aged monk. Then the bombs started falling. Francesco had difficulty getting off the bombed bus to reach the air-raid shelter and thought he was about to die. The monk helped him. The Capuchin once in the shelter began to recite the rosary and inspired calm and confidence in everyone. After the sirens gave the 'all clear' signal, the Capuchin monk was the first to leave. Suddenly Francesco asked: 'Were you the monk?' 'Well, who do you think it was?' asked the padre.

On many occasions, St Faustina Kowalska asserted that she had been able to see the condition of certain souls. In several entries, without naming names, she recounted how she was made to know that such a one was in danger of eternal damnation. She then proceeded to pray and sacrifice for that soul. Faustina reported that, not surprisingly, many of the sisters in her community would come to see her privately, asking for prayers.

MODERN CHRISTIANS AND THE WORD OF KNOWLEDGE

In the 20th century a number of well known charismatics exercised similar gifts. I suppose the person who was best known for this activity was the late Kathryn Kuhlman (1907-1976). She exercised a healing ministry for many years in the U.S.A. What made her unusual was the fact that she didn't pray for healing with the laying on of hands. Instead she would talk and pray until she received a special anointing of the Holy Spirit. Then inspired by words of knowledge she would say who was being healed of what ailment in specific areas of the auditorium. Speaking about her exercise of this remarkable gift Kathryn said: 'My mind is so surrendered to the Spirit, that I know the exact body being healed; the sickness, the affliction, and in some instances the very sin in their lives. And yet I do not pretend to tell you why or how.'[2] There are a number of inspiring books available which describe many of the miracles which occurred as a result of the prophetic ministry of this Protestant servant of God such as *I Believe in Miracles* and *God Can Do it Again*.

More recently, a new generation of prophets has appeared. Among the more notable is Shawn Bolz who seems to get extraordinarily accurate words of knowledge whereby he will receive very precise messages about people such as their names, birthdays, problems in their lives etc. He has written a book *Translating God: Hearing God's Voice For Yourself And The World Around You*. Another remarkable prophet is Heidi Baker Phd, who is a missioner in Africa. She has a remarkable gift of knowledge which leads to healing and miracle working. She has written a number of books such as, *Birthing the Miraculous: The Power of Personal Encounters with God to Change Your Life and the World.* Finally, Bill Johnson is widely recognised as someone, who, like Heidi Baker, is used by God to prophesy and to heal. He has written many books, one of which is entitled, *Releasing the Spirit of Prophecy: The Supernatural Power of Testimony.* Anyone who wants more information about any of these people will find that there are videos on Youtube which enable one to see and hear what they do and say.

In November 2014 I conducted a parish mission in Billings, Montana. While I was there I met a woman called Marti McCullough who told me an intriguing story which included a number of examples of words of knowledge. Before coming to Billings she and her husband had lived on the West coast of the United States. She recounts what happened. 'Five years ago, in prayer our Lord told me we needed to leave the Pacific coast. We had lived there for seventeen years or so. I went to my husband who is the head of our family and my rock and I told him to pray about it. He had a job he loved, our older children had moved out, married or were going to school near where we lived. He said that 'If it was God's will, doors will open, if it isn't they will close.' We just needed to move forward.

Every single door opened... At one point I went to visit a priest friend in Missouri... He asked me where I was moving. I replied that although my husband had applied for jobs all over the place, none had come through. He asked if I had prayed over a map. I shook my head, and said 'no' and he proceeded to get a map out and we prayed over it. He then said, 'You are going to Montana. Have you ever been to Montana?' My eyes were big as I said, 'Nope! We don't even have an application in Montana!' He then prayed again with me and said, 'You are going to

Billings. I hear that it is a nice town!' I laughed out loud. Then we headed out to a nearby Cathedral. As we were standing at the altar of St. Joseph, my husband called on my cell phone and said, 'Are you sitting down?' I whispered, 'No.' He said, 'Someone just called me and wanted to know if I was interested in a job in Billings, Montana...what do you think?' I whipped around and looked at the priest and burst into tears trying to say a stifled 'Yes! to my husband'.

The priest went on to say, 'I see a small grove of trees in the backyard, a giant rock and the word 'Hawthorn.' Sure enough, my husband didn't even know these details when he picked out our home and called me to get on a plane to come and look at his dream home. The small groves of trees were there, the rock and the street next to ours was Hawthorn. I prayed as I walked the property for our Lord to give me one more sign that this was the place he wanted us to be. I was leaving my children on the coast coming to a town where I didn't know anyone. I was bringing my father who had Alzheimer's with us so I could take care of him. It was such a huge act of faith! There on the pathway in the yard were yellow bricks and the writing on them was 'AP Green, Mexico, MO'. I smiled and shouted at the top of my lungs 'Thank you God! Thank you for providing for us in such a beautiful way! That company is where my father and my grandfather worked when my father was a young man in Missouri.'[3] It is a fascinating story. Marti's priest friend seemed to get a number of accurate words of knowledge which helped her and her husband to obey the Lord's word of guidance about moving from the West coast.

In January of 2015 I spent a month running a parish in Detroit.

While I was there, a woman I met invited me and a number of guests to a meal in her house. When I arrived I participated in one of the most memorable conversations I have ever had the good fortune to experience. From beginning to end my heart burned within me as I sensed the presence and power of the Lord in our midst. One woman shared how she and a number of her friends had begun to recite the rosary in her home on a regular basis. She said that as they did so a remarkable thing happened. Apparently, there was a wreath of dried flowers, herbs and leafy twigs somewhere in the room. As the friends said the rosary week after week they noticed that, inexplicably, all the dried plants became moist and alive looking. They have remained fresh like this ever since. Then another woman, who was English, said she wrote icons in her spare time. She recounted how she had painted one particular image of Christ's face. When the paint was being heat dried, however, something went wrong and the image became pockmarked. Sometime afterwards the artist asked a friend to photocopy the icon. When she looked at the image she could see that mysteriously there was no sign of the pockmarks. Then, Elizabeth, the woman who had invited us to the meal told her remarkable story which involved prophetic words of knowledge.

In April 2012 a young man called Tucker Cipriano murdered his father Bob with a baseball bat, and beat his mother Rose and brother, Salvatore, very nearly to death. Soon after the assaults, Elizabeth said that she had experienced a strange dream. She saw herself going into a room where there were a lot of young men dressed in khaki and saying the rosary. A few days later when Elizabeth went to pick up her son at his school, she found that the last class had been cancelled. All the boys were in the gym saying the rosary for the Cipriano family and they were dressed in khaki. On another occasion she heard an inner voice saying that she should go to the hospital where Rose and Salvatore Cipriano were fighting for their lives, in order to bless them with a relic of the true cross. In former times it had been used by Capuchin wonderworker, Venerable Solanus Casey (1870-1957) to bless people. When family members gave permission for the relic to be used to bless Rose and Salvatore, Elizabeth borrowed the relic from the Capuchins and went to the hospital. Firstly, she and a companion visited Rose's room where she was lying unconscious on life-support. Elizabeth blessed her with the relic while invoking the intercession of Solanus. Then she went to the room of Salvatore. Like his mother, he too was unconscious and failed to respond to anything that was said to him. However, shortly after he had been blessed by the relic, he raised his right hand and waved! As Elizabeth was leaving the room she heard an inner voice say to her, 'In three days time Salvatore's condition will improve.' Three complete days later she received an email to say that Salvatore had opened his eyes for the first time, having been addressed by name. By August 2013, Rose Cipriano had unexpectedly recovered 100% and her son Salvatore had greatly improved.

What I found striking about Elizabeth's testimony was the fact that on a number of occasions she had received private revelation from the Lord: in one case through a dream and on two other occasions by means of an inner voice. In all three cases the messages were confirmed by events, most notably in the miraculous recovery of Rose and Salvatore Cipriano. Elizabeth concluded her story with these words, 'I have taken the last two months to reflect on this beautiful work that God allowed to happen in my life. It has been very emotional, but most of all, I feel awe struck by the power of God, our Father. I was unable to talk about the situation for quite some time without crying. I know from being a witness to this that Fr. Solanus is in heaven with God.'

Conclusion

Dr. David C. Lewis of the Religious Experience Research Project, Nottingham University and the Alister Hardy Research Centre, Oxford attended a healing service in Sheffield City Hall in 1985. It was conducted by the late John Wimber. Both he and his assistant Blaine Cook were noted for their ability to receive words of knowledge. Having observed them closely, Dr. Lewis stated his professional opinion that the words of knowledge he had heard were not a matter of extra-sensory perception, clairvoyance, telepathy, spiritual mediumship, fraud or statistical probability.[4]

Judging by my own experience of exercising the gift of the word of knowledge I'd be inclined to say that it is one of the ways in which we can experience the transcendent holiness of God. German author Rudolf Otto wrote a book entitled, *The Idea of the Holy,* in which he said that any genuine religious experience of God, what he referred to as the numinous, is associated with a sense of mystery (*mysterium*) which is both awesome (*tremendum*) and fascinating (*fascinans*) at the same time. Anyone who is privileged to receive words of knowledge has a paradoxical sense of the transcendent awe inspiring holiness of God on the one hand, and of the immanent closeness and communication of the God of holiness on the other.

NOTES

1. (Dublin: Veritas, 1997), 195.
2. Kathryn Kuhlman, *I Believe in Miracles* (London: Lakeland, 1974), 199
3. *For a fuller account see https://charliej373.wordpress.com/2014/09/25/trust-to-the-god-of-abundance/ (Accessed 6/10/2015).*
4. Appendix A, 'Signs and Wonders in Sheffield: A Social Anthropologist's Analysis of Words of Knowledge, Manifestations of the Spirit, and the Effectiveness of Divine Healing' in John Wimber's *Power Healing* (London: Hodder & Stoughton, 1986), 252-273.

THIRTEEN

PROPHETIC UTTERANCES IN PRAYER MEETINGS

Vivien Snow, was one of the founders of the Catholic Charismatic Renewal in Wales. She was responsible for organising a number of national conferences. I visited her a few days before her untimely death on October 24th 2015. We had a long conversation, some of it about the early days of the Charismatic Renewal. When I returned home, I found that Vivien had sent the following email to a number of her friends and acquaintances. It read, 'It was a wonderful visit from Pat yesterday. We shared so much past, present and future. This is what I want to pass on. We talked about the early days of renewal in Wales and the quality of prayer, praise and charisms in the groups. We now have praise, which is good, but less effective. There is too much singing and too little of the anointed word. I was praying during the night, as I couldn't sleep, and the word came quite clearly, 'Rebuild on the old foundations.' 'Well,' I said to the Lord, 'we know that this has been your prophetic word for quite some time. The word came again, and then a third time. What the Lord was showing me was that we need to restore the early style of prayer, and to do so now. That is what nurtures the charisms, teaches and inspires.' I regard those words as Vivien's last will and testament to the Charismatic Renewal which she served in such a selfless way.

We all had to read sonnets at school. They are poems which express a single idea in fourteen lines. So the rules are strict, but in the hands of a master like William Shakespeare or George Herbert, the poet finds in the form, not bonds but wings. A prayer meeting is similar. It has an identifiable structure and dynamics, like a sonnet, within which the leader and participants can express the ever fresh inspirations of the Holy Spirit in an uninhibited way. So, ideally, good order and spontaneity go hand in hand. Order without spontaneity is lifeless, and spontaneity without order is chaotic. In this chapter, I will examine the form and dynamics of well conducted prayer meetings showing how they can foster receptivity to the gift of prophecy and its exercise. At this point we will begin by looking at the typical structure and dynamics of well run meetings.

Prayer as appreciation

A prayer meeting should normally begin with one or other of two forms of prayer. It could be a petition asking for God's mercy for faults and failings or invoking the Holy Spirit on the meeting. Once the prayer meeting has got under way, the members turn their attention to prayers of appreciation, i.e., thanksgiving, praise and adoration. We will look at each in turn.

A. Thanksgiving

In thanksgiving the people at the prayer meeting focus, in a grateful way, on the gifts of God. The psalmist says in Ps 100:4, 'Enter his gates with thanksgiving.' The word to 'thank' in English is taken from the Old English *thonc* which is a cognate with the German *dank,* meaning 'to think,' literally, 'to be mindful, to be aware of.' Appreciation as thanksgiving means that one is mindful and grateful for the gifts of God whether natural or supernatural. Like the leper who came back to thank Jesus for his healing, we thank God for the graces and blessings we have received. It is good for the prayer group leader to encourage those present to witness to God's goodness to them in the recent past, thereby providing people with good reasons for thanking God. They can respond in spontaneous words of thanksgiving, or the chorus of a hymn that expresses thanksgiving, or a full hymn/s of thanksgiving.

B. Praise

In the period of praise the people at the prayer meeting focus on the Giver of the gifts. The psalmist says in Ps 100:4, 'Enter his courts with praise.' The word 'praise' in English is derived from the Latin *pretiare* to prize, which is derived from *pretium* meaning price. Appreciation as praise acknowledges the value of the God of the gifts. The focus shifts from the gifts of God to the God of the gifts. The leader gives some reasons for doing so, indicates how it can be done in practical ways, while inviting the people to raise their minds, hearts and voices to the Lord.

The people present can contribute in different ways by quoting a suitable reading from the scriptures, e.g., part of a psalm of praise such as Ps 92:1-2: 'It is good to praise the Lord and make music to your name, O Most High, to proclaim your love in the morning and your faithfulness at night.' A number of years ago I attended a meeting in Belfast. The praise was fairly lacklustre. Then a woman saw an image of birds sitting on a wall. Although they had wings they never seemed to fly. Then the Lord said to her: 'Unless the birds use the wings of praise, I will not be able to bear them up on the wind of my Spirit.' As soon as they made the decision to praise, the Lord did the rest, until they were lifting the roof with anointed praises.

Praise hymns can also be used. When those who are in charge of the music have a menu of thanking, praising and adoration hymns made out, they are able to find an appropriate praise hymn quickly. If people want to nominate appropriate hymns they can say why they want them sung, e.g., by quoting a meaningful line.

Praying and singing in tongues also has an important role to play. When praise is offered in English, even the most articulate people can quickly run out of things to say even though they still want to praise. That is where the gift of praying and singing in tongues can be so helpful. Although the mind and imagination are at rest, the heart and lips can continue to praise the Lord. Thus tongues is a pre-rational, non-symbolic form of prayer, which enables the God within to pray to the God beyond. As the bible indicates on many occasions, praise should be loud and long. Sir 43:29-33 says: 'Where shall we find strength to praise him? For he is greater than all his works....When you praise the Lord, exalt him as much as you can; for he will surpass even that. When you exalt him, put forth all your strength, and do not grow weary, for you cannot praise him enough. Who has seen him and who can describe him? Or who can extol him as he is?'

C. Adoration

In the adoration phase of the prayer meeting, participants are led by the Spirit into an ever deeper appreciation of the mystery of God. Although the psalmist does not say, 'Enter the holy of holies with worship,' it is appropriate nevertheless. The word 'worship' in English is derived from the Old English *weorth,* meaning 'worth.' Appreciation as worship is a heartfelt awareness of the glory of the Lord. Ps 95:6 shows how the prayer of appreciation as thanksgiving and praise reaches its point of highest intensity in the form of adoration. 'Come, let us bow down in worship, let us kneel before the Lord our Maker.' Worship is commonly expressed in bodily gestures. There can be an anointing when the Lord's presence and glory are palpably present. It is then that the people are moved to adoration in the form of an awed, quieter acknowledgement of the inestimable worth of God whose majesty exceeds the narrow bounds of our human understanding. Appropriate worship hymns need to be sung at this time. They may melt into either a gentle singing in tongues or into silent adoration.

This is the time when words of wisdom about God's will, and words of knowledge about Christian truth can be received. The participants are also likely to receive inspirations, e.g., by means of a scripture text the Lord brings to mind, or a prompting to do something in the future such as sending an email to a friend. It is also the time when the Lord is likely to give individuals prophetic revelations. For example, a couple of days ago I was at a prayer meeting which was held in the context of a weekend workshop on the gifts of the Holy Spirit in 1 Cor 12:8-10. During a worshipful quiet time I saw an image of a rabbit and a mouse in a field. Then I got the impression that they were being told to run across the field. Needless to say, the rabbit effortlessly out-distanced the little mouse, even though the mouse was running as fast as he possibly could. The Lord was standing at the end of the field. When the rabbit arrived he was disappointed when the Lord virtually ignored him and moved out to meet the mouse. I felt he was saying, 'Don't compare yourself with the rabbit. You gave of your very best with the lesser gift of speed you have received, but he did not. So I am more pleased with you than him.' The implication is that we all receive gifts, some lesser, others greater, but what really matters is how conscientiously we use them for the good of the body of Christ, and that there should be no competitive envy or jealousy as a result of invidious comparisons. As St Paul said in Rom 12:1-2, 'I urge you, brothers, in view of God's mercy, to offer your bodies as living sacrifices, holy and pleasing to God - this is your spiritual act of worship.'

Having attended hundreds of prayer meetings, I think it would be true to say that the commonest way in which prophetic words are uttered is as follows. During the quiet times that follow the period of prayer and praise, a person may say something like this, 'My people, I say... such and such to you.' Then the message follows, and it may end with the words, 'thus says the Lord.' I have always been uneasy with this form of delivery. Firstly, it is formulaic. Secondly, it strikes me as being a little presumptuous. A person speaks as if he or she is definitely the Lord's spokesperson. Given the fact that we can all be mistaken and subject to illusions and false inspirations, surely, it would be better to say something like the following, 'It seems to me that the Lord may be saying this to us.' Then the message would follow and concluded in a tentative way with words like the following, 'I offer these words for your discernment.' I have found that when a prophetic message is genuine, it evokes an answering amen in the hearts of the listeners, who recognise that the Lord has truly spoken.

Genuine prophetic utterances are memorable. I can still recall some striking prophecies that I heard many years ago. Back in the 70's and early 80's I was a member of a prayer group in the Servite

Priory, in Benburb, Northern Ireland. That was the place where I first experienced the gift of prophecy. When I reflect back on those meetings, one of them stands out as being special. It took place either at the end of 1980 or early in the following year. From the moment the prayer meeting started I had a sense that it was going to be blessed in a special way. And so it was. At one point a woman who was present said that she had experienced a vision of a lady; she said it was Mary the mother of Jesus, holding a child in her hands at the height of her head. Shortly afterwards her prophetic word was fulfilled in a strange way. The door where we were meeting, suddenly opened and a distraught woman rushed in. She said, 'a priest downstairs told me to come to your meeting. My baby is dying in hospital. I urgently need prayers.' That request made sense of the anticipatory vision granted to the woman who had spoken a little earlier. We urged the visitor to calm down and we promised to pray for her and her baby. While we were interceding on her behalf, another woman stood up and gave an utterance, as opposed to a prayer in tongues. Then the leader asked for silence so that we could wait upon the Lord to give someone an interpretation (as opposed to a translation). The interpretation can come in many ways such as a verse from scripture, an image, a vision, or a word of knowledge. On that occasion, however, the interpretation came in the form of a prophetic utterance in English which said that the baby would be healed, but not immediately, and that in the meantime the mother would face adversity but that she was not to lose heart. Following the prayer, the utterance in tongues and the prophetic word, the woman left the prayer meeting and went home. Some time afterwards we heard that the baby had recovered when her doctors discovered that she was allergic to milk. But before that happened the mother had been involved in a car accident which injured her leg, but not too badly. It appeared that the prophecy had been fulfilled.

Later in that same meeting we reached stage three when we shared what the Lord was saying to us either during the week or at that very moment. I can remember that at one point, the woman who had given the utterance in tongues did so again in a powerful and insistent way. As before, we waited for an interpretation. While we did get one, I can't now remember what it said. When the meeting ended, a nun approached me. She said, 'I am Sr, Marie Slevin, Cardinal Thomas O'Fee's secretary. This is the first time I have ever attended a Charismatic prayer meeting.' Having welcomed her, she went on to say, 'You know when the woman stood up and spoke in a foreign language during the meeting, were you aware of what she was saying?' I explained, that no, I didn't know what she was saying, nor did the woman herself, because she was speaking in tongues. 'That is why we waited for an interpretation' I explained. 'But I know what she was saying,' responded the visitor. 'I was a missionary for many years in West Africa, and she was speaking a good deal of the time in Swahili.' I was really taken aback. Although I had heard of rare occasions when a person spoke a foreign language - it is known as *xenoglossia* in the Greek of the New Testament - this was the first time I had experienced it. 'What did the woman say?' I enquired. 'Actually she was reciting the Litany of Loreto,' the nun replied, 'But she kept repeating one phrase, 'Mary is queen of peace'.'

Shortly after that meeting, I received an invitation to attend a Charismatic Leaders Meeting in Rome, during May, 1981. I was unable to go, but a fellow leader, who had witnessed all that had occurred during our memorable prayer meeting, went in my place. The Rome meeting she attended took place a relatively short time before the apparitions began in Medjugorje. Sr. Briege McKenna, a well known Irish nun was also present at the gathering. Afterwards she told how during those days of prayer she had met a group of priests from the Mostar diocese in Yugoslavia. One of the priests asked Sr. Briege to pray with him for the youth of his region who were succumbing to the propaganda of the communists and losing their faith. Sr. Briege explained what happened during that period of prayer. 'As I prayed, what I saw interiorly was this Croatian priest sitting in the main celebrant's chair in front, and he was looking into the body of the church, and it was packed with young people. And from behind him on the altar there were streams of water, like rivers flowing, and the young people were cupping it and drinking it, and after they would drink it they would go out and bring others in. I said to him, 'You know Father you don't have to worry, because many young people will come to your church.' I shared this with him… I told him that I saw a white church with two huge steeples. And when I said this, almost immediately, Father Emile Tardif, who is a Sacred Heart Priest, a missionary... walked over and got this prophetic word. He could not have heard what I had just said because I was speaking to another priest who was translating for the Croatian Friar. But Fr. Tardif walked over and said, 'You know, Father, Our Lady is going to visit your church.'

Soon afterwards those prophetic messages were fulfilled when the apparitions in Medjugorge began. What was significant for those of us who had attended the anointed prayer meeting in Benburb, was the fact that during the apparitions, our Lady of

Medjugorje identified herself as 'The Queen of Peace,' the very title that had been revealed to us in a prophetic manner in Northern Ireland during the worst of the Troubles. Ever since then the visionaries have claimed to have received a succession of messages from Our Lady. If these private revelations are truly coming from God through Our Blessed Mother, they are prophetic in the way that messages to other visionaries were, such as Margaret Mary Alacoque (1647-1690), Catherine Laboure (1806-1876), John Bosco (1815-1888), Bernadette Soubirous (1844-1879), Faustina Kowalska (1905-1939). Whereas in the past, it seemed as if only exceptionally holy people received prophetic utterances, nowadays they seem to be more common and widespread.

SHARING

Sharing forms an important part of the prayer meeting. During the worship time the Lord may speak a revelatory word to the meeting, either in the form of a prophecy, vision, picture or word of knowledge. Scripture assures us, 'A king's secret it is prudent to keep, but the works of God are to be declared and made known' (Tob 12:7). Sharing can take two other basic forms. Firstly there is testimony, when a person shares how God has acted in a major event in the person's life such as a conversion experience, baptism in the Spirit, a healing etc. If the prayer group leader is familiar with the people attending the meeting s/he could invite a person to give such a testimony while proposing guidelines about how to do it. It should follow the ABC of good communication by being Audible, Brief and Christ centered. Secondly, there is witness when people tell those attending the prayer meeting how the Lord has revealed the divine presence, word, and will during the week as they prayed and reflected, while describing how they tried to respond in a practical way.

TEACHING

Teaching is an important aspect of any well run prayer meeting. As St Paul said: 'Let the word of Christ dwell in you richly, teach and admonish one another in all wisdom' (Col 3:16). Pope John Paul II has said in his Apostolic Exhortation *Catechesis in Our Time* that prayer groups should provide systematic, programmed teaching about the Christian life. 'It aims,' John Paul says in par. 20, 'at developing understanding of the mystery of Jesus in the light of God's word, so that the whole of a person's humanity is impregnated by the word.' Given the importance of the gift of prophecy, prayer group leaders would be well advised to provide good teaching on the subject. It is interesting to note that there were at least three Old Testament groups of prophets consisting of men who followed the teachings of Samuel, Elijah, and Elisha. For example in 2 Kings 6:1-2, we read, 'The company of the prophets said to Elisha, 'Look, the place where we meet with you is too small for us. Let us go to the Jordan, where each of us can get a pole; and let us build a place there for us to live." Evidently it was there that followers were taught by their mentor.

INTERCESSION AND PETITIONS

By and large, prayers of supplication are offered near the end of the prayer meeting. Prayers of petition are offered for one's own personal intentions. Experience teaches that vague and repeated petitions such as 'for a special intention, Lord hear us' are not only fairly meaningless, they tend to have a deadening effect on the meeting. To avoid a long list of petitions, the leader could ask people to think of their personal intentions in silence and then to gather them up in a general prayer of petition. Prayers of intercession are offered for the intentions of others. Par 45-46 of the *General Instruction of the Roman Missal* has this to say about it: 'In the general intercessions or prayer of the faithful, the people, exercising their priestly function, intercede for all humanity. It is appropriate that this prayer be offered for the Church, civil authorities, those oppressed by various needs, all young people, and for the salvation of the world.' The topic of prophetic intercession will be examined in chapters seventeen and eighteen.

Conclusion

When Paul said in 1 Cor 14:1, 'Follow the way of love and eagerly desire spiritual gifts, especially the gift of prophecy' it is not exactly clear to whom his words were addressed, to individual believers, or the Christian community. I suspect it is the latter. In par 12 of *The Dogmatic Constitution on the Church,* Vat II said, 'Extraordinary gifts are not to be sought after, nor are the fruits of apostolic labour to be presumptuously expected from their use.' Undoubtedly, prophecy is one of the extraordinary gifts referred to. I think those words apply to individuals who rashly ask for a particular gift. But surely, given what Paul says in 1 Cor 14:1; 39. 'earnestly desire the spiritual gifts,' the words of the Council Fathers were addressed to communities but not individuals. They can ask that God would equip their members with whatever gifts are needed in the body of Christ. As par. 12 of *The Dogmatic Constitution on the Church* says, 'They are to be received with thanksgiving and consolation for they are perfectly suited to and useful for the needs of the Church.'

FOURTEEN

FOSTERING THE GIFT OF PROPHECY

In the previous chapter, we looked at the way in which the gift of prophecy can be received and exercised, especially during worship times. There is a need in prayer groups, and by extension in all Christian groups, to foster the gift of prophecy by means of good teaching and example. This can be done by focusing on the nature of the gift, the motives we have for exercising it, and the means we have of being receptive to prophetic revelation on the one hand and of expressing it verbally on the other.

MOTIVES FOR DESIRING PROPHETIC REVELATION

In previous chapters we have already adverted to the nature of prophecy and the motives we have for receiving and expressing prophetic revelation.

Firstly, we were created in order to enjoy intimate fellowship with the Blessed Trinity. The prophet Moses epitomised that sense of intimacy. We are told that God talked with him, in an unmediated way, face to face. In Jer 31:33-34 the Lord promised that in the future all people could enjoy that depth of relationship, 'This is the covenant I will make with the house of Israel after that time,' declares the Lord. 'I will put my law in their minds and write it on their hearts. I will be their God, and they will be my people.

No longer will a man teach his neighbour, or a man his brother, saying, 'Know the Lord,' because they will all know me, from the least of them to the greatest.' That promise was fulfilled with the sending of the Holy Spirit, which not only leads us into the truth about God, it can reveal the word and the will of God to us. As 1 Jn 2:27 assures us, 'the anointing which you received from Him abides in you, and you have no need for anyone to teach you, but as His anointing teaches you about all things.' When a person receives a revelatory word of a prophetic kind there is a profound, and awesome sense of being in living contact with the One who lives in unapproachable light.

Secondly, in 1 Cor 14:3 St Paul said, 'everyone who prophesies speaks to men for their edification, exhortation and comfort.' Notice that Paul says that prophetic utterances have three functions:

- In a very positive way they have the ability to build up the community in oneness of mind and heart. Speaking about himself, St. Paul said, 'By the grace God has given me, I laid a foundation as a wise builder, and someone else is building on it. But each one should build with care' (1 Cor 3:10). Prophecy has a role to play both in laying the foundation and the building up of loving Christian communities.
- Prophecy exhorts by speaking a word of encouragement to the Church. It might be that the Lord says to the community that the members should not be afraid, because God is with them giving them strength and upholding them in the midst of whatever difficult circumstances they have to contend with.

- Finally, Paul says that prophecy comforts. There is an interesting distinction made in counselling between consoling and comforting. When a person seeks to console another, he or she tries to help the person feel better about something negative, e.g., a bereavement. When a person seeks to comfort, instead of trying to console the other person, he or she tries to help the man or woman to tap into their Spirit given strength in order to bear with the negative situation with courage and endurance. In like manner, prophecy seeks to strengthen people. As Paul said in 2 Cor 1:3-5, 'Praise be to the God and Father of our Lord Jesus Christ, the Father of compassion and the God of all comfort, who comforts us in all our troubles [e.g. by means of a prophetic utterance], so that we can comfort those in any trouble with the comfort we ourselves have received from God.' Notice that, unlike the Old Testament, there is nothing forbidding in what Paul says in 1 Cor 14:3 about prophecy. No wonder Archbishop Rino Fisichella says, 'In the New Testament any kind of fear, judgment, and condemnation has completely disappeared. Instead the prophet is the one who infuses courage and brings a message of salvation.'[1]

Thirdly, because prophecy sometimes is concerned with the future, (see point 2 in the section on the nature of prophecy), it can help Christians to discern the signs of the times while providing a vision, albeit of a general, unspecific kind, which provides Christian leaders and their people with a sense of God's providential purposes.

Fourthly, Paul says rightly in 1 Cor 14:24-25 that the prophetic word, as the sword of the Spirit, can be instrumental in bringing about conversion. As he observed, 'if an unbeliever or someone who does not understand comes in while everybody is prophesying, he will be convinced by all that he is a sinner and will be judged by all, and the secrets of his heart will be laid bare. So he will fall down and worship God, exclaiming, 'God is really among you!'

Fifthly, in 1 Cor 14:31, Paul added another motive for desiring revelations of a prophetic kind when he said, 'you can all prophesy in turn so that everyone may be instructed.' While members of the Christian community are instructed principally by means of teaching and preaching, prophecy can also convey God's here and now word, in an anointed and relevant way, while providing the power to carry it out (cf. Is 55:11; Phil 2:13).

Sixthly, prophetic utterances in the form of words of knowledge are immensely helpful in all kinds of ministry situations such as praying for inner and physical healing, engaging in intercession, or reading of hearts. Revelatory knowledge of a prophetic kind, not only discloses the will of God, it evokes the expectant faith that is necessary for moving metaphorical mountains of difficulty. That subject will be explored in chapters nineteen and twenty.

MEANS OF RECEIVING AND SHARING PROPHETIC REVELATIONS

How can prayer group leaders encourage and prepare those attending meetings to be open and receptive to the gift of prophecy? Firstly, as mentioned already, they need to offer sound teaching on the nature of prophecy. Secondly, they need to encourage the members to earnestly desire this wonderful gift and to express that desire in the form of personal petitions and communal intercession which are offered with expectant faith. Thirdly, the members should be encouraged not to be self-absorbed and parochial in their interests. Like John Wesley they should regard the wide world as their parish. If they have magnanimity of heart, their compassion will open them to receive a prophetic word that will help them to read the signs of the times. Fourthly, the prayer meeting leader needs to explain that the most likely time to receive a prophetic revelation is during the worship phase of the prayer meeting, especially the silence that often follows a period of adoration in the form of speaking and singing in tongues. In recent times I have begun to urge those present at prayer meetings to sit upright in their seats with their feet firmly planted on the floor and their hands resting lightly on their knees. I urge them to be absolutely still and silent in the belief that a quiet body leads to a quiet mind. Then I advise them to say interiorly, 'speak Lord, your son or daughter is listening.' Then they wait, like good Quakers, for the Lord to speak in one way or another. We have described, in chapter sixteen, some of the many different ways in which the Lord can reveal his word, e.g., by means of a vision, a picture, a spontaneous thought etc.

Whenever a person receives a prophetic revelation, whether praying on their own or in a group, a number of questions need to be asked. Firstly, who is it for? me personally, or for another person, or for a group? Secondly, is the word associated interiorly with feelings of consolation or desolation? If the word comes in a peaceful, hopeful way, it is a sign that it probably is from the Lord. Thirdly, is the word I have received one that will be edifying, encouraging and comforting? Fourthly, is the utterance Christ centered? In Rev 10:10 we read, 'Worship God! For the testimony of Jesus is the spirit of prophecy.' George Montague comments, 'the spirit of prophecy is proven to be authentic by witnessing to Jesus.'[2] Speaking about the same verse Jack Deere observes, 'Prophecy is meant to testify to the awesomeness of Jesus, not to the prophetic ministry. The greatest prophets want people to behold the glory of Jesus.'[3] As the mighty prophet John the Baptist said, 'He must become greater; I must become less' (Jn 3:30).

A. A PROPHECY FOR ONESELF

If one receives a word of personal prophecy, it is good to write it down as exactly as possible so it won't be forgotten. During my adult life I have received a few such prophetic messages. I have given examples in *Guided by God.*[4] Recently, when I was praying with others I saw an image of cactus in the desert. When I asked the Lord what its significance was, I felt God was saying, 'a time of great spiritual aridity and testing is coming upon the world. Though you will be in the midst of this desiccated, desert experience, I will keep you refreshed by the waters of my Spirit just like the cactus.'

B. A PROPHECY FOR SOMEONE ELSE

If one receives a word for someone else, it is important to pray for guidance about how to share it with the other person. For example, about a year or two ago I was visiting a foreign city. One morning when I was praying, I felt that the Lord was telling me to talk to the local lay leader of a Charismatic community to tell him that the Lord seemed to want him to retire from his secular job in order to devote his life to full time ministry in the belief that Divine providence would see to it that he, his wife and children would have enough to live on. When I approached him to share this message, I did so in a tentative way by saying, 'I got the impression in prayer that the Lord wanted me to share this word with you, of course, I may have been mistaken.' When he heard what I had to say, the leader became emotional and responded, 'That is remarkable. I spent time this morning in prayer, asking God whether I should go into full time Church ministry or not. You have given me God's answer.' I firmly believe, that a prophetic word is only intended to confirm something that the Lord has already prompted in the person's heart. A prophecy should not override their personal freedom.

Recently, an Italian woman came to see me, accompanied by two friends. She was emotional and asked for prayer, without being specific about what she wanted from the Lord. As I prayed for her, I saw an image of Our Lady who had a young person nestling under her mantle. I asked the woman if she had any needy young relative. She burst into tears and said, 'As you were praying, I was thinking of my nephew who is suffering from leukaemia.' 'Well,' I said, 'Our Lady is saying that she is caring for your nephew. I cannot say he will be healed, but he will be blessed. As the Marian prayer says, 'never was it known that anyone who fled to your protection, or sought your intercession was left unaided.'

C. A PROPHETIC WORD FOR A GROUP

One may also receive a word that has implications for a number of people. Let me offer an extended personal example. Many years ago my mother and two of my siblings visited Wales. While there, my mother decided that they should visit her brother who was a doctor in Anglesey. When she arrived unannounced at his house, she was disappointed to find that he wasn't there. When my mother got back from the holiday she rang me and told me about the abortive visit. Then she said, 'Pat I was disappointed that your uncle wasn't at home. I fear I will not have an opportunity of seeing him again because he has a heart problem and may not live much longer.' As soon as she said those words, a thought came spontaneously into my mind, yes you are right you will not see your brother again, not because he will die but because you haven't much longer to live yourself. What surprised me about this prophetic realisation was the fact that my mother seemed to be in relatively good health at the time. Soon after that telephone conversation I told a woman friend about my premonition.

A few weeks afterwards I was attending my annual retreat in Mill Hill, London. During one of the talks the door opened. I looked over at the priest who was standing there. Wordlessly, he pointed at me, and made a gesture to indicate that I was wanted on the phone. As I left the room and walked down the corridor I was apprehensive, fearing the worst. When I lifted the phone my younger brother was on the other end. When I heard his first syllable I knew that he was going to tell me something really bad. 'Pat' he said, 'I have sad news for you, mammy died suddenly and unexpectedly a short time ago. By the way it presents us with a problem, our brother John and his family are on a camping holiday in Europe and we have no way of contacting him to tell him about mammy's death.'

When I put the phone down, I was in a state of shock, and headed straight to the chapel. I knelt down in front of the blessed sacrament and prayed. Almost immediately a scripture text from that day's Divine Office came to mind, 'Naked I came from my mother's womb, and naked I will depart. The Lord gave and the

Lord has taken away; may the name of the Lord be praised' (Job 1:2). I had an immediate sense that I should not cling to my mother. So in a very solemn way I said to God the Father, 'Lord you gave my mother to me as a gift. I thank you for all the ways in which she blessed my life. Now I solemnly offer her back to you. May you have mercy upon her and bring her into your kingdom. From now on Lord you will be my only real parent.'

As soon as I said those words, I felt a deep down sense of spiritual peace, although at a more emotional level I still felt a great sense of loss and sadness. Then I thought about the problem of contacting my brother. As the eldest in the family, I was faced with a real dilemma. If we couldn't contact John and his wife should we wait until he returned from his holiday in about twelve days time, or should we go ahead with the funeral in the usual Irish way, with the removal to the Church a day or two after mother's death followed by the funeral mass and burial the next day. I was feeling a powerful sense of connection with God the Father, so I told him about my dilemma and asked for guidance. When no response seemed to be forthcoming, I asked myself, what my mother would have wanted. I felt that she would have desired for John to be at the funeral, not for her sake but for his. Then I recalled a scripture which says, 'If you, then, though you are evil, know how to give good gifts to your children, how much more will your Father in heaven give good gifts to those who ask him!' (Mt 7:11-12). Instantly, I had a firm and clear inner sense that we were to go ahead with the funeral in the normal way, and that God would bring my brother home from wherever he was, if needs be, as a result of some kind of providential mishap.

When I got back to Dublin, I told my brother and sister that we should proceed in the usual way with the funeral. I assured them that the Lord would see to it that our brother would be there. They agreed with the decision to go ahead with the funeral while being very sceptical about my prediction that our brother would return. Of course we rang anyone who might know where he intended going, but no one had any contact information. By the time we brought our mother's remains to the church there was no news about our brother's whereabouts. Much later that evening we were chatting together, as bereaved family members tend to do, when the phone rang. A friend of my brother's, a man we had contacted in London earlier that day, was on the other end. 'You won't believe this' he said, 'but your brother and his family arrived here a few hours ago. Apparently, your niece got into trouble in a swimming pool. Although she was rescued and is O.K. your sister in law was so upset that she insisted on returning to Ireland. I have told John about your mother's death and the funeral arrangements. He has already headed off for Holyhead in the hope that he will catch the ferry and get to the funeral.' When I put down the phone I just knew that he would arrive as God had assured me. The following morning I processed on to the altar. There was no sign of my brother. I began the mass, and as soon as I did, a side door of the church opened and in walked my brother and sister in law to take their place beside our other relatives. God's prophetic word to me and my family had been fulfilled to the letter.

D. A PROPHETIC WORD FOR THE WIDER COMMUNITY

Needless to say God can use a person to speak a prophetic a word to a group or even the wider Church. For example, in Nov 2013 there was a Catholic, international prophetic consultation in Bethlehem, Israel. One of the significant things that happened during the week was the fact that the electricity failed for a time. The delegates saw this power failure in symbolic terms as a sign of a lack of spiritual power in the Charismatic Renewal. Apparently those present praised the Lord in the dark. Then someone said, 'The Lord just reminded me of what happened on the Duquesne weekend in 1967 [the beginning of the Catholic Charismatic Renewal]. During that weekend the plumbing at the retreat centre broke, and it looked like the retreat was over. So they all began praying for water. The Lord answered their prayer and the plumbing was fixed – but he answered in a way far beyond what they had expected. Floods of living water, the Holy Spirit, came pouring down from heaven... and so began the Catholic Charismatic Renewal. It was the 'early rain.' Now we're at a different time. The fact that we've lost electric power today has prophetic significance. Just as back then they prayed for water and the Lord gave water from heaven, so now we have to pray for power, and the Lord is going to give us power from on high. We have to lean into this moment, pay attention to what the Holy Spirit is telling us symbolically and ask for power with great confidence.'

Following this word Patti Mansfield, who had been one of the students on the Duquesne retreat, stood up and said, 'I want to confirm that, and add a couple of things. When the plumbing broke, David Mangan [another student] decided to pray by thanking the Lord in advance for the water he was going to give us. So the Lord is calling us now to thank him with expectant faith for giving us power – power from on high for the Charismatic Renewal and the whole Church, power to preach the gospel to the ends of the earth, power for the breaking down of walls of division among all Christians, and power for the removing of the veil from our Jewish brothers and sisters that they would come to know Jesus the Messiah.'

A little later during the consultation two more prophecies were delivered. 'My people, you have taken off your shoes in my holy presence. One shoe is the shoe of pride. The other is fear and insecurity. There is no place for pride, because all that you do is totally dependent on me. And there is no place for fear and insecurity, because all that you do is totally dependent on me. When you go forth, you will go forth in power. You will not need to be afraid, because it is my power.' Another word was, 'I give you a new faith, faith that is deep. Today I break all your bondages. I cut all your chains. Today I let go of your past, I free you, I build a new city in your midst, today the doors are opened. And I see a huge crowd, multitudes. Dear brothers and sisters, the Renewal shall not be the same, if we learn to hold on to the Lord and let go of ourselves. The Lord Jesus is in front. He called us and he knows what he's doing. We have done it our own way for a long time. He says, now he rises up with victory.' Surely, those words have relevance not only for those who heard them, but for all believers.

The role of leaders in facilitating prophecy

A good prayer group leader has a number of tasks to perform, with regard to the gifts of the Spirit in general, and the charism of prophecy in particular.

Firstly, he or she should encourage the exercise the gifts while being careful not to 'quench the Spirit' (1 Thess 5:19). This is particularly true where prophecy is concerned. In my experience, whereas false prophecies are unusual, non-prophecies are common enough. A false prophecy is one which emanates either from one's own ego or from the illusions and false inspirations of the evil one. An obvious criterion for gauging the status of a prophecy is to ask, does it lead to or from relationship with Christ? Furthermore, is it in accordance with the teaching of scripture and the Church? If the leader thinks that a prophecy is false, he or she should say so. I can remember attending an international, ecumenical conference many years ago. A Pentecostal minister from Brazil had uttered many powerful prophetic words during the week. But on one occasion, while he was still speaking, the chairman, Rev Tom Smail, hit the table with his fist and said, 'Stop immediately, that is a false prophecy.' Although we were shocked by this dramatic intervention, in our hearts we were all saying 'amen' because it did sound off key. Rather than being false, many of the utterances we hear are non-prophecies, e.g., a pious sentiment expressed in a prophetic way. In all likelihood, non prophecies probably emanate from the speaker's imagination, intelligence, learning or previous experience. It is probably better to allow them, in the hope that a genuine prophecy will be uttered. At the end of the sharing period the leader can summarise by saying, 'I think that what the Lord has been saying is such and such.' In some prayer meetings, a secretary is appointed to take note of genuine words from the Lord. Subsequently, they are circulated to the members for their prayerful reflection during the week.

Secondly, it is important to foster and affirm the gifts, especially the gift of prophecy. In the nineteen seventies I was fortunate to be a member of an ecumenical service committee in Northern Ireland. We had regular meetings, many of them in the Christian Renewal Centre, in Rostrevor, county Down. I can remember that at one such meeting we decided to engage in an interesting exercise. After a period of prayer we were asked to do two things. Firstly, each person present was urged to identify what gifts of the Spirit the Lord had given to him or her for the edification of the Church. Secondly, each person was asked to say what gifts, in their opinion, had been given to them by the Lord. It was fascinating to hear what the members of the group had to say about each other, and how it differed from what they had said about themselves. For example, as far as I can remember I said that I felt that the Lord had given me the gifts of teaching, and preaching. But when those present got to say what gifts they thought I possessed, one after the other they told me that, while it was true that I was a preacher and teacher, they thought that my outstanding gift was that of prophecy. They felt that God had blessed me with a sense of vision, an ability to read the signs of the times, and to speak God's challenging word to the Christian community. All this came as a complete surprise to me, because up to that point I didn't see myself in that way. As Brutus said to Cassius in Shakespeare's *Julius Caesar,* 'The eye sees not itself but by reflection, by some other things... And since you know you cannot see yourself so well as by reflection, I, your glass, will modestly discover to yourself that of yourself which you yet know not of.'[4] That meeting turned out to be a landmark one for me, insofar as I began to acknowledge that my colleagues were probably right, and that by the grace of God I had been granted the gift of prophecy as a way of serving the Christian community in love.

Conclusion

It would probably be true to say that the Church owes a debt of gratitude to the Charismatic Movement because it's prayer groups have helped to foster and exercise the gifts of the Spirit, including the gift of prophecy. Sad to say, however, prophecy is often notable by its absence at Charismatic prayer meetings and conferences. Furthermore, Pope Francis has rightly insisted in par. 130 of *The Joy of the Gospel*, that the gifts of the Spirit, including prophecy, are not the peculiar preserve of a particular movement, but rather, are given to the entire church for its edification. '[Charisms] are not an inheritance,' he said, 'safely secured and entrusted to a small group for safekeeping; rather they are gifts of the Spirit integrated into the body of the Church.'

NOTES

1. 'Prophecy' in *Dictionary of Fundamental Theology*, eds., R. Latourelle & R. Fisichella (New York: Crossroad, 1995), 795.
2. *The Holy Spirit: Growth of a Biblical Tradition* (New York: Paulist Press, 1976), 325.
3. *Surprised by the Voice of God* (Grand Rapids: Zondervan, 1996), 207.
4. Pat Collins, C.M., *Guided by God*, op. cit., 262-263.

FIFTEEN

CONTEMPLATIVE PRAYER AND PROPHECY

As was noted earlier in the book, Moses was the great man of prayer in the Old Testament. He used to enter the tent of meeting which would be overshadowed by the presence of the Lord. Once inside, Moses would pour out his thoughts feelings, and desires to the Lord. Then in Ex 33:11 we read, 'The Lord would speak to Moses face to face, as one speaks to a friend.' In a messianic prophecy, God spoke about Jesus when he prophesied through Moses, 'I will raise up for them a prophet like you from among their brothers; I will put my words in his mouth, and he will tell them everything I command him' (Deut 18:18).

As St. Peter confirmed in Acts 3:22, Jesus was the new Moses. Although he did not enter the tent of meeting in the same way as Moses, he did so in another symbolic manner. Like all Jewish men Jesus wore a shawl called a *tallit*. The word literally means 'little tent.' So, as a devout Jew, Jesus could enter his own tent of meeting by pulling his prayer shawl over his head. Meantime the tabernacle of his heart was overshadowed by the Holy Spirit. There he would talk to his Father and listen to him. No doubt when Jesus prayed he poured out his thoughts, feelings and desires to the Father. In the course of his prayer, the Father reciprocated by pouring out his thoughts, feelings, and desires, to Jesus. He testified, 'What I speak, I speak just as the Father has told me' (Jn 12:50). The Father also told Jesus what to do. He testified, 'Very truly, I tell you, the Son can do nothing on his own, but only whatever the Father does, the Son does likewise' (Jn 5:19). Pope Benedict XVI observed in *Jesus of Nazareth*, 'What was true of Moses only in a fragmentary form has now been fully realised in the person of Jesus: He lives before the face of God, not just as a friend, but as a Son; he lives in the most intimate unity with the Father.'[1]

Can we modern Christians pray like Jesus? Jesus said, 'anyone who has faith in me will do what I have been doing.' (Jn 14:12). Par 521. of the *Catechism of the Catholic Church* says something similar, 'Christ enables us to live in him all that he himself lived, and he lives it in us.' The word *all* is striking in that statement. Surely it includes the notion of praying in the contemplative way that Jesus prayed.

Lectio Divina

When it comes to prayer, the Catholic Church encourages its members to engage in regular periods of *lectio divina* (i.e. divine reading), as a traditional, yet fruitful way of reading and praying the scriptures (cf. pars 86-87 of *On the Word of God in the Life and Mission of the Church*). In par. 152 of *The Joy of the Gospel* Pope Francis wrote, 'There is one particular way of listening to what the Lord wishes to tell us in his word and of letting ourselves be transformed by the Spirit. It is what we call *lectio divina*.' By the Spirit's help, this way of praying enables the word upon the page, to become a living word that is spoken to the heart. Guigo II, a Carthusian, sometimes known as the Angelic (d. 1188 AD), described the method in these succinct words: 'Reading is the careful study of the Scripture, concentrating all one's powers on it. Meditation is the busy application of the mind to seek with the help of one's own reason for knowledge of the hidden truth.

Prayer is the heart's devoted turning to God to drive away evil and obtain what is good. Contemplation is when the mind is in some sort lifted up to God and held above itself, so that it tastes the joys of everlasting sweetness... Reading seeks for the sweetness of a blessed life, meditation perceives it, prayer asks for it, contemplation tastes it. Reading, as it were, puts food whole into the mouth, meditation chews it and breaks it up, prayer extracts its flavour, contemplation is the sweetness itself which gladdens and refreshes. Reading works on the outside, meditation on the path: prayer asks what we long for, contemplation gives us delight in the sweetness which we have found... The first degree is proper to beginners, the second to proficients, the third to devotees, the fourth to the blessed.'[2] *Lectio Divina* consists of a number of steps:

- Firstly one begins with a petitionary prayer when we request divine guidance, e.g., 'I ask the God of our Lord Jesus Christ, the glorious Father, to give me the Spirit of wisdom and revelation, so that I may know him, his word and will' (cf. Eph 1:17-18).
- Secondly, one goes on to read a chosen text slowly and with attention. It could be a liturgical reading for that day or the following Sunday.
- Thirdly, one reflects on the text while keeping two questions in mind. What did the inspired author intend to say? In this connection it can be helpful to read footnotes in a study Bible or a commentary on the passage. Then one asks, what relevance does the reading have nowadays?
- Fourthly, once one's reflections have stirred up thoughts, feelings and desires, one stops reflecting and begins to talk to the Lord about them. This phase of prayer can go on for quite a time.

Contemplative prayer

Lectio divina is a two way activity. As we have already noted, I petition, read, reflect and pray. Once that has been done it is time to listen in a contemplative way. Before talking about this activity in specific terms, it is worthwhile dwelling for a moment on the meaning of contemplation. As is often the case, the etymology of the word is helpful. It is derived from the Latin *contemplationem*, meaning 'to gaze attentively, to observe.' Embedded in the English word, is the Latin, *templum* or temple, i.e., a piece of consecrated ground in front of an altar where the auguries i.e., those involved in divination, sought to discover the will of God. We will have cause to refer to this notion shortly.

There have been many helpful definitions of contemplation, e.g., St. Francis de Sales wrote:

> 'Contemplation is simply the mind's loving, single-minded, permanent attention to the things of God.'[3]

St. Vincent de Paul, a contemporary of Francis said to some Daughters of Charity,

> 'The other sort of prayer is contemplation. In this the soul, in the presence of God, does nothing else but receive from Him what He bestows. She is without action, and God himself inspires her, without any effort on the soul's part, with all that she can desire, and with far more. Have you ever experienced this sort of prayer? I am sure you have often been astonished that, without doing anything on your part, God Himself has replenished your soul and granted you knowledge you never had before.'[4]

Contemplation has the following two characteristics. It is other directed and self-forgetful. It escapes the gravitational pull of self-absorption, and excessive self-reference by bracketing out distracting needs, memories, thoughts, images and feelings in order to pay undivided attention to the Other. Contemplation is also intuitive, i.e., the spiritual faculty of knowing directly without the use of rational, analytical processes.

During a time of contemplative attention, the Person, word and will of God can be revealed in an experiential way to the heart. As the Lord promises in Jer 33:3-4, 'Call to me and I will answer you and tell you great and unsearchable things you do not know.' Likewise, in Isa 48:6-8 we read, 'From now on I will tell you of new things, of hidden things unknown to you. They are created now, and not long ago; you have not heard of them before today. So you cannot say, 'Yes, I knew of them.' In Jn 6:45 Jesus said, 'It is written in the Prophets: 'They will all be taught by God.' When Jesus said this he was probably referring to Is 54:13 which says, 'All your sons will be taught by the Lord.' While this messianic text points to Jesus as the One who, *par excellence*, teaches on God's behalf, it also implies that believers will be taught directly by means of divine inspirations, revelations and promptings (cf. Jer 31:34). I want to focus in particular on this inspirational and revelatory aspect of *lectio divina*, not only because it is important, but also because many books and articles on the subject fail to talk about what it actually involves in a practical way. This phase of prayer needs two interrelated forms of discipline.

A. Physical stillness

To begin with there is a need for physical stillness. As par. 66 of Pope Benedict's, *On the Word of God in the Life and Mission of the*

Church says, 'The word of God, can only be spoken and heard in silence, outward and inward.' A word about physical silence and stillness. Sometimes I engage in what is known as belly breathing in order to quieten my body. It involves slow and deep inhalation through the nose, usually to a count of ten, followed by slow and complete exhalation for a similar count. I usually repeat the process for a couple of minutes. When I reach this phase of *lectio divina*, I try to sit with my back straight and my arms either folded or resting gently on my knees. Once I have assumed my prayer pose I try to remain completely still during the contemplative period of my prayer, without moving a muscle. This usually lasts for ten to twenty minutes. As I mentioned in a preceding chapter, I find that if my body is quiet, my mind also tends to become quiet.

B. Inner stillness

We live in an excessively extroverted culture where people, as T.S. Eliot pointed out 'are distracted from distraction by distraction.'[5] As a result men and women in the age of social media find it hard to concentrate for more than a few seconds. Our minds and imaginations are like demented wasps darting from one place to another. It is a terrible pity because the ability to pay sustained attention lies at the heart of contemplation. Writing about prayer, *The Catholic Encyclopaedia* says, 'attention is of the very essence of prayer... As soon as this attention ceases, prayer ceases.'[6] No wonder, therefore, the psalmist says, 'Be still before the Lord and wait patiently for him' (Ps 37:7). We need to develop the ability to still our minds and imaginations in order to focus on the presence of God.

i. THE CLOUD OF UNKNOWING

The Gospel description of the transfiguration of Jesus is instructive. At first the apostles, Peter, James and John could see the radiant Jesus in the company of Moses and Elijah. However, as Peter was speaking, 'a bright cloud covered them' (Mt 17:5). Down the ages, contemplatives have understood the reference to the cloud in symbolic terms as a way of going beyond the mediating role of concepts and images. That transition is well described by the anonymous author of a medieval book entitled, *The Cloud of Unknowing*. He wrote, 'For God can well be loved, but he cannot be thought. By love he can be grasped and held, but by thought, neither grasped nor held. And therefore, though it may be good at times to think specifically of the kindness and excellence of God, and though this may be a light and a part of contemplation, all the same, in the work of contemplation itself, it must be cast down and covered with a cloud of forgetting. And you must step above it stoutly but deftly, with a devout and delightful stirring of love, and struggle to pierce that darkness above you; and beat on that thick cloud of unknowing with a sharp dart of longing love, and do not give up, whatever happens.'[7]

ii. DARKNESS IN THE HOLY OF HOLIES

If anyone visited the Herodian temple, in the time of Jesus, he or she would have had to pass through a number of courts to reach the holy of holies. I see them as symbols of the different stages in *lectio divina*. The holy of holies was the most sacred space in the temple. When Pompey conquered Jerusalem in 63 BC, he looked into the sacred space and was amazed to find that it was empty. In symbolic terms this seems to imply that in the holy of holies there is nothing present that would aid the imagination. John

McKenzie says in his *Dictionary of the Bible* that it was also totally dark in the holy of Holies. In symbolic terms is seems to imply that the intellect had nothing that it could think about. That notion appeals to me because the God who is mysteriously present to us is ultimately incomprehensible. As article two of the constitutions of the fourth Lateran Council stated, 'between creator and creature there can be noted no similarity so great that a greater dissimilarity cannot be seen between them.' In other words, while images and concepts may be reliable intimations of the mystery of God, if the truth be told, God is incomprehensibly greater than anything they can encapsulate. So during the contemplative phase of *lectio divina,* one could say that the soul is in a state of dynamic passivity. Dynamic in the sense that it yearns to know the Person, word and will of the Lord, and passive in the sense that it is inactive from an imaginative or conceptual point of view. As Hab 2:1 puts it, 'I will stand at my watch and station myself on the ramparts; I will look to see what he will say to me.' Dynamic passivity of this kind was well described by St. Gregory of Nyssa when he wrote, 'What then does it mean in Exodus 20:21 when it says that Moses entered the darkness and then saw God in it?... As the mind... approaches more nearly to contemplation, it sees more clearly what of the divine nature is unknowable. For leaving behind everything that is observed, not only what sense comprehends but also what the intelligence thinks it sees, it keeps on penetrating deeper until by the soul's yearning for understanding it gains access to the invisible and the incomprehensible, and there it sees God. This is the true knowledge of what is sought; this is the seeing that consist in not seeing, because that which is sought transcends all knowledge, being separated on all sides by incomprehensibility as by a kind of darkness... When therefore, Moses grew in knowledge, he declared that he had seen God in the darkness, that is, that he had then come to know that what is divine is beyond all knowledge and comprehension, for the text says, Moses approached the dark cloud where God was. What God? He who made darkness his hiding place.'[8]

I can say in passing that some forms of contemplation, such as that described by St Gregory of Nyssa and Centering Prayer, seem to me to be too ineffable. The latter is a modern version of John Cassian's approach to contemplation. From the 1970s onwards it has been adapted and advocated by people such as M. Basil Pennington and Thomas Keating, monks from St. Joseph's Abbey in Spencer, Massachusetts. Spiritually speaking its approach is apophatic, i.e., a type of prayer that realises that, 'God's nature is incorporeal, un-compounded, simple, and cannot be seen by human eyes nor conceived adequately by a human mind.'[9] Well known 20th century theologian, Karl Rahner, S.J., believed that from the beginning, Christendom has been influenced by this kind of Platonic predilection for wordless and imageless forms of faith. He thought that it did so at the expense of a more authentically Christian approach to prayer which was more prophetic and kerygmatic in nature.[10] While I think that it is good, during the contemplative stage of *lectio divina,* to clear one's mind of personal images and concepts, it is done, not in order to enter some kind of nirvana, but in order to be receptive to the presence of God and to images and concepts that can be spontaneously revealed by God.

So, when I reach the contemplative stage of *lectio divina,* I will sometimes pray quietly in tongues within myself. I have found that it is a dynamic form of prayer in the sense that it enables me to express my yearning for God, while at the same time it is passive in the sense that it does not involve images or concepts originating from my own mind. As St Paul observed, 'if I pray in a tongue, my spirit prays, but my mind is unfruitful' (1 Cor 14:14). Like many others I have found that praying in tongues is rather like a farmer ploughing his field in readiness to receive the seed. As I pray in the spirit, my soul is prepared to receive the seed of God's revelation.

CONCLUSION

I am writing this paragraph during the Christmas season. I am reminded of a lovely scripture verse which was used in years gone by in the liturgy. It is from Wis 18:14-15, and reads, 'When peaceful silence lay over all, and night had run the half of her swift course, down from the heavens, from the royal throne, leapt your all-powerful Word like a pitiless warrior into the heart of a land doomed to destruction. Carrying your unambiguous command like a sharp sword.' These verses are redolent with symbolism. In contemplative prayer we enter a zone of exterior and inner silence, where the rational mind and the imagination are darkened as the person sighs for God to send his revelatory word, like a two edged sword, into the heart. He or she waits with bated breath, like Mary and Joseph who longed with great expectancy for the coming of the Messiah on the first Christmas Day.

NOTES

1. *Jesus of Nazareth* (London: Bloomsbury, 2007), 6.
2. *The Companion to the Catechism of the Catholic Church* (San Francisco: Ignatius Press, 1994), 922.
3. *Treatise on the Love of God,* Vol. 1, Book 6, chap. 3, (Rockford, Ill.: Tan, 1975), 275.
4. St. Vincent de Paul, 'Conference on Prayer, May 31, 1648', *The Conferences of St Vincent de Paul to the Daughters of Charity,* (London: Collins Liturgical Publications, 1979), 374.
5. *The Four Quartets,* Burnt Norton.
6. Wynne, J. (1911). "Prayer." In *The Catholic Encyclopedia.* (New York: Robert Appleton Company). Retrieved March 19, 2018 from New Advent: http://www.newadvent.org/cathen/12345b.htm.
7. *The Cloud of Unknowing and other Works* (London: Penguin Classics. 2001), 27-28
8. *Life of Moses,* par. 164.
9. John Cassian, 'Tenth Conference on Prayer', in *The Fire and the Cloud: An Anthology of Catholic Spirituality,* ed. David A. Fleming (London: Geoffrey Chapman, 1978), 30.
10. Karl Rahner, *Visions and Prophecies,* (London: Burns & Oats, 1963), 20.

SIXTEEN

WAYS IN WHICH PROPHECY CAN BE RECEIVED DURING CONTEMPLATION

In Jn 5:2-11 we read about the still waters of the pool of Bethesda in Jerusalem. It is said that if they were touched by an angel, the first person into the water would be healed. As has already been mentioned, the word angel means 'a messenger of God.' I imagine that my soul is like a pool of water waiting for the touch of a heavenly prompting, inspiration or revelation from the living God. Recently, a Dutch man sent me a beautiful image by Korean artist Yongsung Kim which captures what I had in mind. It is a picture looking upward from under the surface of a pool of water. Above it is an image of Jesus who is standing on the water while bending down and touching its surface. Circular ripples spread out from where his finger tip has entered the water. For me it is a striking image that captures those wonderful moments in contemplative prayer when the Lord, by his Spirit, touches the soul in a numinous and revelatory way. Here are a number of ways in which it can happen.

1. A SENSE OF PRESENCE

During the contemplative phase of *lectio divina,* the Lord can reveal the divine presence. Instead of merely believing that the Lord is present, there is a heartfelt awareness of that presence. There is a sense of connection to the mystery of the One in whom we live and move and have our being (cf. Acts 17:28). We may be moved by an awareness of some outstanding attribute of the Lord such as love, forgiveness, understanding, acceptance, affirmation, benevolence, power, etc.

2. The Alive and Active Word of God

Not surprisingly, it sometimes happens during this phase of prayer that an aspect of the text which was the basis of the *lectio divina* comes alive with new meaning and relevance. As was noted at the end of the preceding chapter, there is a lovely verse in Wis 18:14-16 which is a wonderful image of a prophetic word of a revelatory kind being spoken into a person's heart. John Cassian described this phenomenon when he wrote, 'There are times when a person understands God's Scriptures with the clarity with which a surgeon understands the body when he opens up the marrow and the veins. These are the times when our experience seems to show us the meaning by practical proofs before we understand it intellectually.'[1] There will be other occasions when one can feel prompted to look at a specific book, chapter and verse. For instance, on June 21st 2015, I was praying about the state of the priesthood in Ireland. At one point I felt the Lord directed me to read Jer 5:31, which says, 'The prophets prophesy lies, the priests rule by their own authority, and my people love it this way. But what will you do in the end?' Occasionally, the Lord may prompt me to cut the Bible, to put my finger on the page, and read what the verse says, as the Lord's living, alive word for now. Recently at the Lord's prompting I cut the scripture at Mal 2:7 and read, 'It is the duty of priests to teach the true knowledge of God. People should go to them to learn My will, because they are the messengers of the Lord Almighty. But now you priests have turned away from the right path. Your teaching has led many to do wrong.'

3. A PROMPTING

One can get a prompting in contemplation to do something, e.g., to pray for someone, to phone a friend, to take an evangelistic initiative etc. Some time ago I was asked to pray for a woman's nose in the Slovak Republic. Having said a healing prayer I was prompted to say, 'you should smell a rose as soon as you can.' When she turned around she found that unexpectedly there was a rose nearby on the ground which she was then able to smell.

4. AN IMAGE/VISION

Sometimes a static image, or a video-like vision will come to mind, with or without words. If it doesn't make sense, it is good to ask the Lord for clarification. Recently, when praying with others I had an image of an egg. It didn't make much sense to me. I asked God for clarification and felt led to read Lk 11:11-13, in which our Lord says, 'Which of you fathers, if your son asks for... an egg, will give him a scorpion? If you then, though you are evil, know how to give good gifts to your children, how much more will your Father in heaven give the Holy Spirit to those who ask him!' Having read those words I felt that the Lord was urging me to trust wholeheartedly in Him.

On July 2nd 2015, I was praying in silence with other people. At one point during our contemplation I saw a vision of a red bricked garden wall. I entered the gate and saw that the garden was full of trees laden with fruit. Not only were there trees such as apple and pear, there were also lemon and orange trees. There was a great choice of fruit. I picked a lemon, cut it in two and squeezed the juice into a glass of cold water which I was able to take from a tap in the wall nearby. Although it was bitter to taste I found that is was refreshing to drink. Then I was led to read Is

5:20, 'Woe to those who call evil good and good evil, who put darkness for light and light for darkness, who put bitter for sweet and sweet for bitter.' I felt that the Lord was disapproving of priests and lay people who try to sweeten the demanding sayings of scripture in order to make them more palatable to people of our day. However, although those sayings may be bitter to worldly people, nevertheless they are refreshing and life giving to true believers.

When one is in a state of dynamic passivity during contemplative prayer, the Lord can give one a prophetic revelation for oneself or for others. A number of years ago I attended Mass in St Peter's Basilica in Rome. While I was praying there, a strange image came into my mind. I saw St. Peter's in a state of ruin. Half of the main dome over the altar had obviously collapsed so that I could see the sky. Parts of the walls had also collapsed. There were bushes growing in the sanctuary. It looked as if the Basilica had been abandoned for some time. I had no idea what had happened to bring this about.

In this connection I was surprised to find sometime afterwards that, well known visionary, Bl. Catherine Emmerich (1774-1824) prophesied on Sept 10th, 1820, 'I saw the Church of St Peter: it has been destroyed but for the Sanctuary and the main altar. St Michael came down into the Church, clad in his suit of armour, and he paused, threatening with his sword a number of unworthy pastors who wanted to enter. That part of the Church which had been destroyed was promptly fenced in with light timber so that the Divine office might be celebrated as it should. Then, from all over the world came priests and laymen and they rebuilt the stone walls, since the wreckers had been unable to move the heavy foundation stones. And then I saw that the Church was being promptly rebuilt and She was more magnificent than ever before.'[2]

Cardinal Henry Edward Manning (1808-1892) gave four lectures in 1861. Among other things he said, 'The apostasy of the city of Rome from the vicar of Christ and its destruction by Antichrist may be thoughts very new to many Catholics, that I think it well to recite the text of theologians of greatest repute. First Malvenda, who writes expressly on the subject, states as the opinion of Ribera, Gaspar Melus, Biegas, Suarrez, Bellarmine and Bosius [noted theologians in centuries gone by] that Rome shall apostatise from the Faith, drive away the Vicar of Christ and return to its ancient paganism. ...Then the Church shall be scattered, driven into the wilderness, and shall be for a time, as it was in the beginning, invisible; hidden in catacombs, in dens, in mountains, in lurking places; for a time it shall be swept, as it were from the face of the earth. Such is the universal testimony of the Fathers of the early Church.'[3]

Erika Holzach (1903-1987) was a Protestant woman who became a Catholic and joined a community that had been founded by well known theologian Hans Urs Von Bathasar and his collaborator Adrienne Von Speyr. Holzach had been a secretary to professor Feiner, who was a theological expert who attended Vatican II. Following Holzach's death, Von Balthasar wrote a book about her and her experiences of private revelation.[4] In it he recounted how there was one passage in Holzach's notes which reads: 'There will be a brief persecution of Christians under Islam.' But Our Lady 'through her intercession, will shorten the catastrophe.' Was this a prophetic intimation of an attack on Rome by Muslim Jihadists? Time will tell.

5. A WORD OF KNOWLEDGE

It often happens that if I'm engaged in *lectio divina* before running a healing service, the Lord will give me words of knowledge. It is the God given ability of one person to know what the Lord is currently doing or intends to do in the life of another person. It can also be defined as knowing the secrets of another person's heart. Recently, this happened in Birmingham, England. During my time of contemplation before the service, the Lord let me know that a woman suffering from bulimia would attend the service. Although I was tempted to think that she would be young, the Spirit led me to believe that she would in fact be middle-aged. She was making herself sick in order to keep her weight down, because she was sensitive about her size. I mentioned this problem during the service and said, 'if there is any woman like that who is present, see me afterwards.' Sure enough a woman approached me and admitted that she was suffering from bulimia. She told me that she was fifty two and worried about her weight. While I was talking to her, I was inspired to ask her whether she had suffered sexual abuse in the past, only to find that she had. When our conversation came to an end I prayed with her that she might be healed. What was striking about that incident was the accuracy of the word of knowledge.

6. A PROPHETIC WORD

On the 1st of October 2015 I attended our weekly prayer meeting in the course of which I received an image accompanied with prophetic words. I saw a rope on a boat. It was linked in a looped way around the edge of the boat. The sea was quite choppy. There were people in the water swimming towards the boat. The rope was there to help rescue them. I had a thought that if we were to bring them on board we would be in danger of sinking. But, the Lord said – 'Believe Me, you are not going to sink. I am with you. Battle through the storm. I am not going to stop the storm but I will be there with you. Rely on Me. You will not sink.' I felt that the Lord was saying through the prophecy, that if Christians sometimes feel overwhelmed by the sheer volume of human need that impinges on them, they are not to be afraid to respond with generosity and compassion, God will be there to help them, as he did when he multiplied the fives loaves and two fish.

LIGHT IN DARKNESS

As I have engaged in regular *lectio divina* over the years, I have, by the grace of God, experienced the presence, promptings, inspirations and revelations of the Lord, especially during the contemplative phase. In this connection I was interested to see that St. Thomas Aquinas wrote, 'The prophet must first be lifted up and inspired by the Holy Spirit to attend to God [i.e. in contemplation]; then the prophecy is completed by revelation, the removal of the veils of *darkness and ignorance* [my italics] so that the prophet can see what God is revealing. Bodily eyes need physical light to reveal things and the mind needs a mental light, the revelation being proportionate to the light which causes it. . . Since prophecy involves knowledge beyond the power of natural reason it needs light beyond the power of natural reason to make it knowable: 'when I sit in darkness the Lord will be my light' (Mic 7:8).'[5] Arguably, the kind of prophetic revelation that can be received during the contemplative stage of *lectio divina* may be an example of what theologians refer to as infused contemplation, i.e., a supernatural gift by which a person's mind and will become totally centered on God. Under this influence the intellect receives special insights into things of the spirit. Lastly, we need to keep in mind the words of Sts. Paul and John respectively: 'do not treat prophecies with contempt. Test everything. Hold on to the good,' and 'Dear friends, do not believe every spirit, but test the spirits to see whether they are from God, because many false prophets have gone out into the world' (1 Jn 4:1-2).

Conclusion

One does well to remember that the process of *lectio divina* is not fully concluded until it leads the praying person/s to make a practical resolution which will help him or her to express in action what the Lord has revealed. Ideally, the resolution should be single, precise and possible. As St. Thomas Aquinas said, one primary purpose of prayer is to give to others the fruit of contemplation. He wrote in his *Summa Theologica*, 'the contemplative life is, absolutely speaking, more perfect than the active life, because the latter is taken up with bodily actions: yet that form of active life in which a person, by preaching and teaching, delivers to others the fruits of his or her contemplation, is more perfect than the life that stops at contemplation, because such a life is built on an abundance of contemplation, and consequently such was the life chosen by Christ.'[6]

NOTES

1. John Cassian, 'Tenth Conference on Prayer,' *The Fire and the Cloud*, ed. David Flemming, S.J. (London: Geoffrey Chapman, 1978), 38.
2. *http://www.catholicrevelations.org/PR/bl%20anna%20maria%20katarina%20emmerick.htm (Accessed 25/10/2015).*
3. *The Present Crisis of the Holy See* (London: Burns and Lambert, 1861), 88-90.
4. Von Balthasar, *Erika* (Einsiedeln-Trier: Johannes Verlag, 1988).
5. *Summa Theologiae: A Concise Translation*, ed. Timothy McDermott (London: Methuen, 1989), 444-5.
6. *ST, III*, 40, 3, as 2.

SEVENTEEN

PROPHETIC INTERCESSION IN THE BIBLE

While the word prayer in English embraces all kinds of interrelated activities, above all else it is a form of supplication whereby one asks God for favours of one kind or another. It can take two forms, petition where one asks God for something for oneself, and intercession where one acts as a go-between by asking for something for others. One could argue that supplicatory prayer is the fundamental religious act because it expresses a sense of utter dependence on God. Closely related to this creature feeling is a trusting reliance on the providence of God. It is an acknowledgement that God has a benevolent plan for our lives (cf. Jer 29:11). It also believes that God provides for us and the whole world, in a non-magical way, so that we can fulfil the divine plan. In this chapter we are going to focus on intercessory prayer of a prophetic kind in particular.

OLD TESTAMENT PROPHETS AND INTERCESSION

All of the prophets were intercessors and needless to say, their prayers were deeply influenced by the things that God had revealed to them by the Spirit. As Jer 27:18 says, 'If they are prophets and have the word of the Lord, let them plead with the Lord Almighty.' We can illustrate this point by looking at some of the many Old Testament prophets to see how their revelatory insight led to intercessory prayer.

In Gen 18:16-33, God revealed to Abraham that he was going to punish Sodom and Gomorrah for their immoral behaviour. When he received this prophetic knowledge, Abraham acted as a mediator between God and people by pleading with Yahweh on Sodom's and Gomorrah's behalf. He implored the Lord not to destroy the city if even ten just people lived there. But apparently, only Lot and his family were faithful. They were urged to leave the city which later on was destroyed.

Moses was another great model of intercession on behalf of the people. Jethro, his father in law, encapsulated the purpose of his role when he said: 'You should represent the people before God and bring their cases before God' (Ex 18:19). On four separate occasions he interceded on behalf of the people to save them from God's anger. He stood between the people of Israel and God's wrath at the rebellion of Korah (cf. Num 16:20-22), pleaded for mercy for his sister Miriam in her pride and rebellion (cf. Num 12:9-14), and sought on behalf of the people of Israel to protect them from Pharaoh's army at the Red Sea. Par. 2574 of *The Catechism of the Catholic Church* cites Moses as the greatest intercessor of the Old Testament, the one on whom Jesus would later model his intercessory role.

Like his mother Hannah, Samuel was a person of prayer. As he said himself, 'God forbid that I should sin against the Lord in ceasing to pray for you' (1 Sam 12:23). God revealed to the prophet that he was sorry that he had allowed Saul to become the king on account of his subsequent infidelity. This revelatory knowledge led Samuel to engage in intense intercessory prayer on the king's behalf. However, the king failed to repent, so Samuel said to him, 'You have rejected the word of the Lord, and the Lord has rejected you as king over Israel!' As Samuel turned to leave, Saul caught hold of the hem of his robe, and it tore. Samuel said to him, 'The Lord has torn the kingdom of Israel from you today and has given it to one of your neighbours — to one better than you'(1 Sam 15:26-29).

Isaiah was not only a great prophet, he was also an intercessor. In one place we are told that Sennacherib's invading army, 'spoke about the God of Jerusalem as they did about the gods of the other peoples of the world — the work of men's hands. King Hezekiah and the prophet Isaiah son of Amoz cried out in prayer to heaven about this. And the Lord sent an angel, who annihilated all the fighting men and the leaders and officers in the camp of the Assyrian king. So he withdrew to his own land in disgrace. And when he went into the temple of his god, some of his sons cut him down with the sword' (2 Chron 32:19-21).

The prophet Jeremiah was another outstanding intercessor. We are told in a number of texts that he felt called to represent the cause of his ungrateful people before the Lord. In Jer 42:2 the people approached the prophet and asked him to pray to God on their behalf: 'Let your God show us where we should go and what we should do.' Jeremiah replied: 'very well I am going to pray to the Lord your God as you request and whatever the Lord answers, I will tell you.'

Two Old Testament images of intercession

When we read the Old Testament two images recur in relation to intercession. The first is that of standing in the gap, or the breach. In Ps 106:23 we read, 'had not Moses, his chosen one, stood in the breach before him to keep his wrath from destroying them.' In

Ezek 22:30, the Lord says: 'I have been looking for someone among them...to man the breach in front of me, to defend the country.' As the book of Nehemiah illustrates so graphically, a breach in the walls of a city is the place of greatest danger and vulnerability. The intercessor stands in that place of weakness, where the winds of adversity blow, where the jackal of unbridled instinct cries and where the enemy of our souls can try to enter under the cloak of darkness. Many years ago I received a personal prophetic word which said, 'Stand in the breach, and intercede for yourself and for my people. Stand in the breach and listen to my word. Then call my people to the breach to rebuild the walls of Jerusalem.'[1]

The second image of intercession is that of the watchman. In Ezek 33:7 we read, 'Son of man, I have made you a watchman for the house of Israel; so hear the word I speak and give them warning from me.' Many years ago I attended an international conference which was hosted by Cardinal Suenens in his residence in Malines in Belgium. Towards the end of the proceedings he referred to the fact that in some respects the Church resembled Jerusalem at the time of Nehemiah. The walls of its spirituality have been breached, so that the enemy, in the form of the Trojan Horse of worldliness, can be insinuated into its midst by the Devil, in order to secretly disgorge his malevolent and disruptive influences. Then the Archbishop read the following passage from Isa 62:6-7, 'I have posted watchmen on your walls, O Jerusalem; they will never be silent day or night. You who call on the Lord, give yourselves no rest, and give him no rest till he establishes Jerusalem and makes her the praise of the earth.' Having read the passage, Suenens said, 'As you return home, remember to pray for the restoration of church unity and for the revival and renewal of all those who have been baptised into Christ.' When Jeremiah did just this, he received the following prophetic words from the Lord. Perhaps they are also being spoken to the Church of today, 'I will bring back your health and heal your injuries,' says the Lord, 'because other people forced you away. They said about you, 'No one cares about Jerusalem!'' This is what the Lord said: 'I will soon make the tents of Jacob's people as they used to be, and I will have pity on Israel and the king's palace will stand in its proper place' (Jer 30:17-18). Surely, the prophets of the Old Testament are our role models. They listened to the Lord and prayed in accordance with the divine will.

Jesus our Intercessor

The ministry of intercession in the New Testament centres around two great advocates, namely Jesus the Son of God and the Holy Spirit. We will look at each in turn. Before doing so we can make three introductory points about Jesus' intercessory role. Firstly, it is clear in the gospels that Jesus admired and modelled his ministry on that of Moses. Secondly, Jesus' intercessory prayer was motivated by compassion.[2] Thirdly, as Jesus himself testified, his prayer, like all his activities, was guided by divine revelation. He bore witness to the prophetic origin of his intercessory prayer when he said, 'I tell you the truth, the Son can do nothing by himself; he can do only what he sees his Father doing, because whatever the Father does the Son also does' (Jn 5:19-20). Fourthly, as intercessor, Jesus is an advocate. The word has a legal background. It refers to a lawyer who acts on a client's behalf, by expertly and effectively pleading his or her cause. Jesus is our advocate our definitive mediator before the Father. There are a number of examples of his intercessory prayer in the Gospels. We will look at three of them.

As his passion drew near, Jesus anticipated that, although they were full of good intentions, Peter and the apostles would have to cope with strong temptation and disillusionment. In Luke 22:31-32 he declared in a prophetic way, 'Simon, Simon, Satan has asked to sift you as wheat. But I have prayed for you, Simon, that your faith may not fail.' Jesus spoke with the kind of understanding that is rooted in loving intimacy, but he did so without any hint of judgment or condemnation. His prayer was suffused with the confidence that it would be heard by the Father because he knew that he was praying in the Spirit in accordance with the benevolent will of God.

The second example is to be found in Jn 17:20-21. It occurred at the last supper when Jesus prayed his high priestly prayer on behalf of the apostles and all those, down the ages, who would believe in him. He said: 'My prayer is not for them alone. I pray also for those who will believe in me through their message, that all of them may be one, Father, just as you are in me and I am in you. May they also be in us so that the world may believe that you have sent me.' It is obvious from this prayer that Jesus had a passion for unity, a yearning that all those who believed in him would be so united in mind and heart that they would not only be a credible witness to the communion that exists in the Trinity, but also of its presence in their community. As he said: 'For where two or three come together in my name, there am I with them' (Mt 18:20).

The third example of the intercessory prayer of Jesus took place on the cross. In Is 53:12 we read prophetic words that referred to the messiah to come: 'For he bore the sin of many, and made intercession for the transgressors' (Isa 53:12). That intercession reached a high point when Jesus prayed while we were still his enemies through sin: 'Father, forgive them, for they do not know what they are doing' (Lk 23:34).

Following his death, resurrection and ascension into heaven, Jesus' role as advocate continued. This is made clear in three texts. In 1 Jn 2:1 we read: 'we have one who speaks to the Father in our defence - Jesus Christ, the Righteous One.' Heb 7:25 adds that Jesus: 'is able to save completely those who come to God through him, because he always lives to intercede for them.' In Rm 8:34 St. Paul asks the rhetorical question: 'Who is he that condemns? Christ Jesus, who died-- more than that, who was raised to life-- is at the right hand of God and is also interceding for us.' Clearly the answer is an emphatic no. 'For those who are in Christ Jesus,' declares St Paul, 'there is now no condemnation' (Rm 8:1). What a consoling thought. No matter how cut off, miserable and misunderstood we may feel, there is always One who prays for us, night and day, 'with loud cries and tears' (Heb 5:7), before the Father in heaven. Mary, and the saints are intimately associated with the compassionate intercessory prayer of the glorified Lord.

The Spirit as Intercessor

During his ministry Jesus promised that he would send the Holy Spirit to be our go-between-God. 'I will ask the Father,' he said, 'and he will give you another Advocate to be with you always, the Spirit of truth' (Jn 14:16). Acting in and through our compassionate concerns the Spirit bears witness to the intercession of the heavenly Jesus. So whenever we pay empathic attention to the sufferings of others with feelings of tenderness, protectiveness, understanding etc., we can become aware of another Presence which sanctifies and transforms our natural emotions in such a way that we share in Christ's concern for others. In this way our hearts become a point of intersection between the travail of the body of Christ on earth, and the intercessory travail of the risen Lord in heaven, through the action of the Holy Spirit.

When people are interceding on behalf of others they will often be able to express their longings in articulate ways in the form of remembered, written and vocal prayers. But there will be times when the pre-conceptual longings of our hearts cannot be put into words. As St Paul said in a memorable passage in Rm 8:26-27, 'In the same way, the Spirit helps us in our weakness. We do not know what we ought to pray for, but the Spirit himself intercedes for us with groans that words cannot express. And he who searches our hearts knows the mind of the Spirit, because the Spirit intercedes for the saints in accordance with God's will.' Sometimes these inarticulate longings can only be expressed in the form of tears, groans and sighs. One is reminded in this regard of the travail of Jesus at the tomb of Lazarus. John says that he not only wept, 'He was deeply moved in spirit and troubled' (Jn 11:33). Those who have received the gift of praying or singing in tongues - which is a form of pre-conceptual prayer expressed in unintelligible words - can intercede with the lips even when their understanding is shrouded in a cloud of unknowing. They know and believe that the Spirit within them is praying to the God beyond, in accordance with the mind and heart of the risen Jesus. When St. Paul wanted to describe this form of prayer, he compared it to the travail of childbirth. It is an apt image. Compassionate intercession is a painful movement of the spiritual womb which longs to give birth to new life in others. As St. Paul says: 'We know that the whole creation has been groaning as in the pains of childbirth right up to the present time. Not only so, but we ourselves, who have the first fruits of the Spirit, groan inwardly' (Rm 8:22-23).

The Virgin mother of God, spouse of the Spirit and our heavenly mother, is referred to in Catholic spirituality as 'our gracious advocate.' In the *Memorare* we say, 'Remember, O most gracious Virgin Mary, that never was it known that anyone who fled to thy protection, implored thy help, or sought your intercession was left unaided.' In the light of the maternal characteristic of intercessory prayer, it doesn't surprise me, that women I have known over the years seem to have had a particularly deep insight into the nature, purposes and dynamics of compassionate intercession in the Spirit.

CONCLUSION

It is not really surprising to find that many of the Old and New Testaments prophets were also intercessors. There was a reciprocal relationship between their prayers and the revelatory insights they were receiving. They would ask for and receive divine guidance, and that guidance found expression in requests to God for many graces. It is interesting to see that on one occasion God said, ' Jeremiah, don't pray for these people! I, the Lord, would refuse to listen. Do you see what the people of Judah are doing in their towns and in the streets of Jerusalem? Children gather firewood, their fathers build fires, and their mothers mix dough to bake bread for the goddess they call the Queen of Heaven. They even offer wine sacrifices to other gods, just to insult me. But they are not only insulting me; they are also insulting themselves by doing these shameful things' (Jer 26:16-20). Prophetic intercession is very demanding because it has to be rooted in a deep compassion that invites the praying person to give empathic expression to the pain and needs of the people.

NOTES

1. Cf. Pat Collins, C.M., 'Mending the Breaches: A Parable for Today' in *Word and Spirit* (Dublin: Columba, 2011), 12-21.
2. 'The Compassion of God' in *Spirituality for the Twenty First Century*, (Dublin: Columba, 1999), 134-149.

EIGHTEEN

PERSONAL AND GROUP INTERCESSION OF A PROPHETIC KIND

Many years ago I attended a charismatic conference in the Royal Dublin Society in Ballsbridge. At one point a priest spoke about the troubles in Northern Ireland. When he had finished he recalled something that John Paul II had said during his visit to Ireland in 1979. 'I ask you for a great, intense and growing prayer for all the people of Ireland, for the Church in Ireland, for all the Church which owes so much to Ireland. Pray that Ireland may not fail in the test. Pray as Jesus taught us to pray: 'Lead us not into temptation, but deliver us from evil.'[1] Then he invited the large audience of over two thousand people to spend some time in prayer for the healing of our nation. At one point people began to sing quietly in tongues. They did so spontaneously in a minor key. It was quite haunting to hear a large crowd singing a lament in perfect harmony. It seemed to express the inexpressible sadness and prophetic longings of the people in unintelligible words, to a melody that was taking spontaneous shape as they sang it. The whole experience sent shivers up and down my spine. Not only was it beautiful in a strange and poignant way, I had a profound impression that the Spirit was anointing our compassionate, but inarticulate desires, and that God was doing immeasurably more than we could ask or think, according to his power that was at work within us (cf. Eph 3:20).

Intercession and spiritual warfare

Because the evil one knows that intercession is so effective in advancing God's cause, it is not surprising that he attacks the intercessors in one way or another through such things as misfortune, ill-health, false inspirations, temptations etc. Sometimes he will do this as an angel of light, i.e., under the appearance of an apparent good (cf. 2 Cor 11:14), e.g., excessive and imprudent zeal. One way or another he will try to undermine their authority. Intercessors need to become aware of these possibilities and to pray for protection against them. In Eph 6:16 Paul assures us that 'the shield of faith puts out all the fiery darts of the evil one.' In other words, if the person under attack nestles in the Lord through faith, e.g., by means of praise, instead of trying to wrestle with the evil one, he or she will be freed from the harmful effects of such things as illusions, false inspiration and temptations.

Discernment of spirits also enables intercessors to become aware of what to pray against in external situations of need. So if intercessors are praying about some situation, such as a war in another country, they need to recognise that the murderous, lying spirit of the Accuser may well be at work. In this context the following New Testament text is particularly helpful. It states, 'For though we live in the world, we do not wage war as the world does. The weapons we fight with are not the weapons of the world. On the contrary, they have divine power to demolish strongholds. We demolish arguments and every pretension that sets itself up against the knowledge of God, and we take captive every thought to make it obedient to Christ' (2 Cor 10:3-5). With this assurance in mind, it is advisable to pray a deliverance prayer, one that opposes the oppressive power of whatever evil spirits may be at work in the situation which the intercessors are concerned about, in order to deliver the people from oppression. Intercessors can silently command them, in the name of Jesus Christ, to yield to the liberating power of God. As St Paul testified in 1 Cor 4:20, 'The kingdom of God is not a matter of talk but of power,' i.e., in the Holy Spirit.

It is a striking fact that when Jesus was led into the wilderness to be tempted by the evil spirit, he fasted for forty days. In all probability this kind of mortification not only heightened his awareness of the presence and malign intentions of the devil he would have to contend with throughout his ministry, it also helped him to recognise his false inspirations and to reject them. It is not surprising, therefore, that when the apostles asked Jesus why they hadn't been able to expel an evil spirit from an epileptic boy, Jesus replied: 'This kind can only come out through prayer and fasting' (Mk 9:29). In par. 26 of a document published by the Congregation for the Doctrine of the Faith entitled, *Some Aspects of Christian Meditation*, we read: 'The Christian fast signifies, above all, an exercise of penitence and sacrifice; but, already for the Fathers, it also had the aim of rendering people more open to the encounter with God and making a Christian more capable of self-control and at the same time more attentive to those in need.' Realising this to be true many people who engage in intercessory prayer become involved in discreet and prudent fasting. Some live on bread and water on a designated day, others abstain from all food for part of a day, or for a few days. Many of those who fast in these ways find that they are not only more alert and perceptive from a spiritual point of view, their physical hunger acts as a symbol of their radical need for God's help. As the *Magnificat* says: 'He fills the hungry with good things' (Lk 1:53).

Interceding as an Individual

In Eph 6:18 St Paul says, 'pray in the Spirit on all occasions with all kinds of prayers and requests. With this in mind, be alert and always keep on praying for all the saints. A similar point is made in 1 Tim 2:1-3 where Paul says, 'I urge, then, first of all, that requests, prayers, intercession and thanksgiving be made for everyone— for kings and all those in authority, that we may live peaceful and quiet lives in all godliness and holiness.' In my experience there are two ways of interceding as an individual; non prophetic and prophetic. Non charismatic intercession is the norm. It can occur in a number of ways, as a spontaneous prayer which is evoked by conscious awareness of some kind of need in the worldwide Church or society, e.g., for victims of an earthquake. It could be the result of a response to some situation of need one has experienced oneself, e.g., a colleague at work who is a victim of alcoholism; or because someone has asked you to pray about some urgent need, e.g., a marriage that is on the rocks. Personal prayers of intercession may be very brief, e.g., short aspirations. They may be offered during a designated part of a person's regular prayer time, e.g., the final ten minutes. People may occasionally devote all of their personal prayer time to intercessory prayer. Whether regular or irregular, short or long, it is important that intercessors tell God how they feel about the situation and what it is that they desire. If at all possible they should try to tune in to God's feelings and desires about the situation. During quiet moments like these, intercessors can get an inspired sense of God's presence and purposes in a manner that assures them that God will respond to their intercessions in one way or another.

St John illustrates the potential efficacy of intercessory prayer by saying it can bring about repentance in the lives of sinners. He writes in 1 Jn 5:16, 'If you see your brother or sister committing what is not a mortal sin, you will ask, and God will give life to such a one - to those whose sin is not mortal.' The reference, here, to mortal sin, is not to 'ordinary' grave sins but to some extremely deadly sin such as the sin against the Holy Spirit or deliberate and knowing apostasy. For example, in Heb 6:4-6 we read: 'It is impossible for those who have once been enlightened, who have tasted the heavenly gift, who have shared in the Holy Spirit, who have tasted the goodness of the word of God and the powers of the coming age, if they fall away, to be brought back to repentance, because to their loss they are crucifying the Son of God all over again and subjecting him to public disgrace.' The inspired author speaks here about intercessory prayer, he hasn't intercessions in general in mind, but rather prayer for a non-schismatic member of the community who has fallen into some kind of public sin e.g., robbery or sexual promiscuity. If the community, pray with the kind of expectant faith already mentioned, 1 John 5:16 promises that the prodigal will eventually come to his or her senses, and will repent.

Here is an example of prophetic intercession on one's own. Jennifer le Clair, who lives in Florida, went for a time to do missionary work in South America. She described how she was led to prophetic intercession when she was praying on her own. 'The turning point for me,' she explained, 'was during a mission trip to Nicaragua. I woke up feeling severely depressed for no apparent reason. I felt down and out, like giving up, throwing in the towel, calling it quits and running home to pull the covers over my head. It felt like my best friend had just died. I sat there for about 20 minutes trying to figure out what was wrong with me and crying out to God to help me escape these oppressive feelings. As I persisted, I heard that still small voice in my spirit saying, 'Despondent. This is how the people of this nation feel. Pray. Despondence is a feeling of extreme discouragement, dejection or depression.' Jennifer went on to describe what happened when she received that revelation, 'Once the Lord gave me that insight, I joined with others in a circle to pray against the oppression with the weapons of our warfare, which are not carnal but mighty through God to the pulling down of strongholds' (2 Cor. 10:4).

Recently I met a man in Dublin who is very much involved with promoting the Divine Mercy devotion which originated with Sr. Faustina Kowalska (1905-1938). He prays a lot. He told me that, a short time before our conversation, he had a vivid dream about a large fire. When he recalled it, after waking up, he had a sense that many people were going to die in a large blaze. So he prayed fervently for the salvation of their souls. A couple of days later his wife told him about a terrible fire in a nightclub in Bucharest in Romania, 30th October 2015. It had killed over thirty people. He felt that his prophetic dream had been a prompt from God to intercede for those who were going to die.

Group Intercession

The members of the New Springtime Community in Dublin, to which I belong, believe that effective evangelisation has to be backed up by a good deal of intercessory prayer. The community has drawn up the following guidelines for group intercession.

1. Appoint someone to take responsibility for leading the intercessory session by keeping the guidelines in mind, which

suggest when to move from one point to another, and ending the meeting within a specified time limit. Ideally, each member of the group should have a prayer partner who intercedes for them on a regular basis between meetings.

2. Make a conscious act of faith in the presence and power of God.

3. Ask the Holy Spirit to fill you and to guide your time of intercession by means of a spirit of wisdom and revelation. Speaking about this kind of prayer Johannes Facius says in his book *God's Prophetic Agenda*, 'We need spiritual revelation and divine light to be able to see what God sees in the whole situation. We need to come away from looking at things from a physical perspective and instead see them from a heavenly position.'[2]

4. Spend some time in worship by thanking, praising and adoring the Lord. As Ps 144:2 assures us, 'He is my loving God and my fortress, my stronghold and my deliverer, my shield, in whom I take refuge.'

5. Speaking about communal intercession pars. 45-46 of the *General Instruction of the Roman Missal* say, 'In the general intercessions or prayer of the faithful, the people, exercising their priestly function, intercede for all humanity. It is appropriate that this prayer be included in all Masses celebrated with a congregation, so that petitions will be offered:

- For the Church,
- Civil authorities,
- Those oppressed by various needs,
- All young people
- The salvation of the world.

6. In Eph 6:18 we read, 'Pray in the Spirit on all occasions with all kinds of prayers and requests. With this in mind, be alert and always keep on praying for all the saints.' As was mentioned earlier in chapter seventeen; in Is 62:6-7 we are told that intercessory prayer should be persistent and insistent, 'I have posted watchmen on your walls, O Jerusalem; they will never be silent day or night. You who call on the Lord, give yourselves no rest.' In chapter nine we took note of Pope John Paul's prophetic sense that we are living at a time of immense danger and are involved in the final confrontation between the realms of light and darkness. That awareness can give rise to a lot of intercession.

7. At this point blank your mind, pray in tongues for a while and ask the Spirit to guide your prayer by means of the charisms of revelation such as inspired thoughts, intuitions, a vision, word of knowledge, prophetic utterance or scripture reading. As Gal 5:18 says 'be guided by the Spirit.' One could refer to this kind of prayer as prophetic intercession.

8. If no charismatic guidance seems to be forthcoming, intercede in an agnostic way by praying and singing in tongues, in the belief that the Spirit within is praying to God beyond. As Phil 2:13 assures us, 'God is at work within you to will and to do God's good purpose.'

9. As the time of intercession comes to an end, thank God in the belief that the Almighty is doing immeasurably more than you can ask or think through the power of the Spirit at work within you (cf. Eph 3:20).

An Example of Prophetic Intercession

On Sept 14th 2014 the members of the New Springtime

Community attended their annual vision day in Glendalough, county Wicklow. Mindful of what Paul wrote in Eph 1:17, 'I keep asking that the God of our Lord Jesus Christ, the glorious Father, may give you the Spirit of wisdom and revelation,' one part of the day was devoted to prayer for divine guidance. During a period of silent listening I inwardly heard the words, 'Speak to Eli.' They took me completely by surprise and didn't make sense at first. Then I recalled that Eli, the priest, was the one who had told the boy Samuel, that if he felt called again, he should say, 'speak, Lord, your servant is listening.' So I decided to read what came after that verse and was surprised to find that in actual fact Samuel got a word which was for Eli. Because it was negative Samuel was reluctant to speak it, but Eli urged him to do so. So Samuel told him about God's dissatisfaction on account of his failure to administer a stern rebuke to his priestly sons Hophni and Phinehas who had scandalised the people (cf. 1 Sam 2:23). Apparently, he had only gently chided them for their illicit behaviour, such as appropriating the best portion of the temple sacrifices for themselves, and having sexual relations with the sanctuary's serving women. Although the character of Eli was sincere and devout, he seemed to have been lacking in firmness because of human respect.

When I reflected on the fact that Eli had failed to deal with the abusive behaviour of his priestly sons, I was reminded of the way in which some Irish bishops and religious superiors had also failed to deal adequately with the sinful crimes of their colleagues. When Pope Benedict wrote his letter to the Irish Church in 2010 he said among other things, 'I have been deeply disturbed by the information which has come to light regarding the abuse of children and vulnerable young people by members of the Church in Ireland, particularly by priests and religious. I can only share in the dismay and the sense of betrayal that so many of you have experienced on learning of these sinful and criminal acts and the way Church authorities in Ireland dealt with them.' Later, addressing the bishops he said, 'It cannot be denied that some of you and your predecessors failed, at times grievously, to apply the long-established norms of canon law to the crime of child abuse. Serious mistakes were made in responding to allegations.' He added that there was, 'a misplaced concern for the reputation of the Church and the avoidance of scandal.'

As I prayerfully recalled these points, I thought at first, that perhaps the Lord was asking me and the members of The New Springtime Community to speak to Eli by focusing on one particular line in our mission statement which reads, 'we will contribute to the formation of clergy – with a view to facilitating effective evangelisation in their parishes.' However, I got the distinct impression that this was not what the Lord was saying. I felt instead that he was saying to me, 'you do not know who Eli is or what to say to him, but I will reveal it to you in my own good time. So do nothing other than to wait for my guidance.'

About two weeks later, during my daily prayer time, I was focusing on some point I cannot now remember. However, right in the middle of it I thought I heard the Lord say to me, 'I want to talk a little more about the message for Eli. Immediately, a vague memory of a particular paragraph in the letter of Pope Benedict to the Irish Church came to mind. Since then I have found that is says in par. 14, 'I propose that a nationwide Mission be held for all bishops, priests and religious. It is my hope that, by drawing on the expertise of experienced preachers and retreat-givers from Ireland and from elsewhere, and by exploring anew the conciliar documents, the liturgical rites of ordination and profession, and recent pontifical teaching, you will come to a more profound appreciation of your respective vocations, so as to rediscover the roots of your faith in Jesus Christ and to drink deeply from the springs of living water that he offers you through his Church.' The inner voice seemed to say, 'tell Eli, that I want this to be done.' Then I asked, 'But Lord, who is Eli?' Then I got a distinct impression that he was saying that it was a particular bishop in Ireland, whose name I will not mention. I also had a sense that no word of rebuke was involved for that bishop but only a word of guidance. As this second time of inspiration came to an end I was given to understand that until the nationwide Mission had been completed, the work of the new evangelisation would not be truly effective.

Following that sequence of prophetic words I contacted the bishop the Lord had designated and with a good deal of apprehension told him about the word the Lord wanted to speak to him about the national mission. I wondered how he would react. In the event he was open, honest, and said that he had been thinking on similar lines. He promised that he would think about what I had said and encouraged me to keep in contact with him. At this time of writing I have had a number of conversations with the bishop, but as yet, nothing has been decided.[3]

It is worth mentioning that ever since hearing the words, 'speak to Eli' I have received a number of messages from the Lord about priests. Here are a few examples. On Wed April 8th 2015 when I was thinking and praying about my dialogue with the bishop, I felt that the Lord wanted me to read Mal 2:3-10. I had no preconceived idea of what it would say. This is what I read, 'For the lips of a priest ought to preserve knowledge, and from his mouth men should seek instruction - because he is the messenger of the Lord Almighty. But you have turned from the way and by your teaching have caused many to stumble; you have violated the covenant with Levi,' says the Lord Almighty. 'So I have caused you to be despised and humiliated before all the people, because you have not followed my ways but have shown partiality in matters of the law.' Have we not all one Father? Did not one God create us? Why do we profane the covenant of our fathers by breaking faith with one another?' In the *English Standard Bible* a note says, 'Since the priests failed to guard the purity of the temple, the Lord threatened to punish them in a manner that fits their crime, because they 'despised' (1:6) and failed to give honour to the Lord's name they will be despised before all the people... Because they presumed to bless the people of God, as if Israel's sacrifices had been accepted and atonement made, God will now curse their blessings.' As Matthew Henry puts it, 'Nothing profanes the name of God more than the misconduct of those whose business is to do honour to it.' I found that the reading from the prophet Malachy was surprisingly pertinent. In late October 2016, I was once again praying about the national mission called for by Pope Benedict. At one point I recalled what God the Father had said at the transfiguration of Jesus, 'Listen to him.' I replied, 'I am trying to listen Father, what does Jesus want to say?' Soon afterwards I felt that he wanted me to read Ezek 13:14. 'I will tear down the wall you have covered with whitewash and will level it to the ground so that its foundation will be laid bare. When it falls, you will be destroyed in it; and you will know that I am the Lord.' I was stuck as a result of reading it within its context that it was part of Ezekiel's diatribe against false prophets. Once again I felt that the Lord was rebuking bishops and priests who were saying things to please and appease their people instead of courageously proclaiming the unadulterated word of God. Pope Francis spoke about this danger when he addressed a mixed congregation of priests and lay people on June 15th 2015 'When Jesus warns the people to watch out for the 'pseudo-prophets.' He went on to add, 'By their fruits, you will know them'... they do wonders, they do great things but do not have their hearts open to listen to the Word of God, they fear the silence of the Word of God and these are the 'pseudo-Christians', the 'pseudo-pastors'. It is true, they do good things, it's true, but they lack the rock, i.e., the rock of the love and the Word of God. Without it, they cannot prophecy or build on a solid foundation based on God: only on themselves.'

CONCLUSION

Pope Francis said in par. 281 of *Evangelii Gaudium*, 'One form of prayer moves us particularly to take up the task of evangelisation and to seek the good of others: it is the prayer of intercession.' It has been said that in non charismatic intercession we bring the people's burdens to the Lord, but that in prophetic intercession we are enabled to tune in to the burdens of the Lord. Prophetic intercession is not coming to the Lord with a prayer list but coming to the Lord to get a prayer list. As we have noted in other chapters, God can reveal the divine will to us in many different ways. Once we have received such guidance we can pray with great confidence.

NOTES

1 *The Pope in Ireland: Addresses and Homilies,* (Dublin: Veritas, 1989), 78.
2. *'To See as God Sees' in* (Lancaster: Sovereign World Ltd., 2009)
3. See Pat Collins, C.M., 'A Letter to the Irish Bishops,' in *The Furrow* (Jan 2018): 28-31.

NINETEEN

PROPHETIC MINISTRY

The notion of prophetic ministry may be new to many people. Quite simply, it refers to any form of ministry such as counselling, spiritual direction, exorcising evil spirits, or healing that is conducted with the aid of a prophetic word of revelation.

St. Thomas Aquinas contextualises the focus of this chapter by making a very interesting point on the relationship of ministry to the gift of prophecy. As was noted in chapter seven, he says that there are three kinds of interrelated charismatic gifts. Firstly, there is prophetic revelation, then there is prophetic utterance and finally, there are deeds of power which bear witness to the truth of what was revealed and proclaimed. Thomas wrote, 'The knowledge a prophet receives [by means of revelation] from God must be communicated to others through... utterance, and that utterance [by means of proclamation] must be confirmed as believable by the working of miracles: God confirming the message with attendant signs [by means of demonstration].'[1] In his commentary on 1 Cor 12:7-11, Thomas said, 'But matters pertaining to the teaching of salvation cannot be confirmed or proved by reason, because they transcend human reason, as Sir 3:23 says: 'Matters too great for human wisdom have been shown.' They are confirmed or proved by a divine sign;... But God's sign is based in one way, on something God alone can do... the Apostle here distinguishes two kinds. For he says first: to another is given the gift of healing, i.e., through which he can heal someone's infirmity, by one and the same Spirit. 'Heal me, O Lord, and I will be healed' (Jer 17:14). For by these, one is persuaded not only on account of the greatness of the deed, but also on account of the benefit. Secondly, he says: 'To another the working of miracles,' by which a person is persuaded solely by the greatness of the deed.'[2]

When a Christian receives prophetic revelation, e.g., in the form of a word of knowledge, that very living, alive, and active word of God can evoke the gift of mountain moving faith which is required to perform a deed of power such as a healing or a miracle.[3] The charism of this kind of expectant faith (cf. 1 Cor 12:9) can be defined in the following way. It is a special grace which is given to some people in order to perform a deed of service. It is given in particular situations. Rooted in the discernment of the will of God, by means of a revelation from God. Knowledge of God and God's will leads to the heartfelt conviction, and trustful expectation that God is beginning to act in the present and will continue to act in the future. God's mercy and love are mainly manifested in a deed of power such as a healing, exorcism or miracle. Such deeds of power are intimations and anticipations in the present of the Second Coming of Jesus.

Jesus spoke on a number of occasions about this unusual kind of unhesitating trust. In Mk 11:12-14 we are told how he cursed a fig tree. Then in Mk 11:20-23 we are informed that: 'In the morning, as they went along, they saw the fig tree withered from the roots. Peter remembered and said to Jesus, 'Rabbi, look! The fig tree you cursed has withered!' 'Have faith in God,' Jesus responded. 'I tell you the truth, if anyone says to this mountain, 'Go, throw yourself into the sea,' and does not doubt in his heart but believes that what he says will happen, it will be done for him.' In Lk 17:6 we read, 'If you have faith as small as a mustard seed, you can say to this mulberry tree, 'Be uprooted and planted in the sea,' and it will obey you.' No wonder Jesus could say in Jn 14:12, 'I tell you the truth, anyone who has faith in me will do what I have been doing. He will do even greater things than these, because I am going to the Father.'[4]

A person cannot make an act of will in order to have the kind of faith Jesus spoke about. It is evoked by a revelatory word from the Lord. As Paul said in Rm 10:17, 'Faith comes from hearing the message, and the message is heard through the word of Christ.' While Paul was referring principally to the proclamation of the kerygma, i.e., the basic Christian message, his point can be extended to any word that comes from God, such as a revealed word of knowledge or prophecy. They disclose the existential will of God in the here and now, thereby authorising the recipient of the revelation to utter a prayer of command with expectant faith. As the author of 1 Jn 5:14-15 assured his readers, 'This is the confidence we have in approaching God: that if we ask anything according to his will, he hears us. And if we know that he hears us - whatever we ask - we know that we have what we asked of him.' Apparently the phrase 'we have what we asked him' in Greek, is in the continuous present. Literally it means, 'you already have what you asked for, i.e., a first instalment, and will go on receiving it.'

A person with hesitant trust accepts God's promises at a notional level, believing them to be true in his or her mind. However, when faced by a particular problem such as an illness, he or she may not be quite sure whether God is going to act, right now, in these particular circumstances. So the person has to pray a prayer of petition in the *hope* that God may do something in the *future, if* what is asked is in accordance with the divine will, e.g., 'Lord I know that nothing is impossible to you. I ask you, if it is your will, to heal this person whom you love.' This is praying with hope. But Jesus never said, 'Your hope has made you well!'

However, a person with expectant faith not only accepts that the promises of God are true at a notional level; as a result of a word of knowledge or a prophetic word in a particular situation of need, he or she has no lingering doubts about God's intentions and confidently believes that the Lord has begun to act and will continue to do so. Often such a person prays a declaratory prayer of command rather than a prayer of petition (cf. Mk 11:23; Lk 17:6). Instead of having to see evidence in order to believe, this kind of confident faith believes in order to see evidence of change. At moments like these, secular, sequential time in which we experience chronic problems, gives way to sacred time, the eternal now of God in which God's power is manifested. There are a number of situations where prophetic revelation leads to a power encounter.

Reading of Hearts

As was mentioned in an earlier chapter, there is a type of prophetic word of knowledge which is sometimes referred to as the reading of hearts. When one reads the biographies of saintly people there is evidence that they received this gift on numerous occasions. I know a priest who conducted a retreat a few years ago. He told me about a particular man who came to confess his sins in the sacrament of reconciliation. He had a distinct sense that he hadn't told him everything. When he had confessed, the priest asked, 'Is that everything?' 'Yes,' he replied, 'there is no more to tell.' The confessor responded, 'are you really sure?' 'Yes,' he retorted. 'Surely, you have forgotten something' the priest said, while going on to mention a disordered relationship in the man's life. The penitent was really taken aback, 'How on earth, did you know about that, what you have said is true. I was ashamed to mention that problem.' Following this disclosure, a very fruitful conversation ensued. When the priest gave the man absolution, he got another prophetic word which prompted him to say that he was going to open the Bible at random and put his finger on the page in the belief that it would be on a verse about healing. He told the man that he was going to do this to illustrate the fact that the Lord was empowering him to pray effectively for healing. Then, with his eyes shut, the priest opened the Bible at random and put his finger on the page. It was over a verse in Hos 6:1, 'Come, let us return to the Lord. He has torn us to pieces but he will heal us; he has injured us but he will bind up our wounds.' 'There you are,' said the priest to the man, 'Didn't I tell you my finger would land on a verse about healing, and so it has. This indicates that the Lord wants you to pray for others in order that they experience healing.' He found out years later, that the man had indeed been instrumental in the healing of a few people.

When I reflected on that ministerial incident I could see that the prophetic revelation the priest had received had evoked certain faith in him and led to effective ministry. So, occasionally when I'm about to meet with someone who comes to me for ministry, e.g., administering the sacrament of reconciliation, counselling or spiritual direction, I'll sometimes pray to the Lord before the person visits and I ask, 'Lord, is there anything you want to tell me about this person before he or she arrives?' There have been occasions when the Lord has told me things about my clients which turned out to be a vital key to effective ministry.

GUIDANCE IN PRAYER FOR INNER HEALING

Those who pray for inner healing are sometimes led by a 'word of knowledge' to focus on a repressed memory. I must say that I have found this gift can be a great help when ministering to needy people in different situations. Let me give a few examples.

I can remember an occasion many years ago when a relatively young man asked to have a chat with me. He told me that he was married and that at night time he couldn't sleep unless the bedroom light was left on. Not surprisingly, his wife would have preferred to turn it off. He also mentioned that if his wife was away from home overnight, he had to have someone else in the room, and the light had to be left on. I really smiled when he told me that his mother in law was often the substitute. She would sleep in a separate bed while the light remained on. Not surprisingly, he asked if I could help him. From a psychological point of view, it sounded as if he had been traumatised in some way or another in the past. As a result he was afraid to sleep in the dark on his own. So I asked him if he could remember any scary incident which might be the root cause of his problem. He said that he couldn't remember any such experience. Then I said that we would both go silent and pray for guidance. During the period of quiet, I saw an image of an old woman laid out dead in a bed. I guessed that it was the man's grandmother. So I asked, 'did your grandmother die when you were around eight or nine years of age?' After a long pause he said, 'Yes, I am just now recalling how she was laid out upstairs in a bedroom. My mother brought me up to the room, stood at the door and said, 'go over and kiss your grandmother goodbye.' So I walked over to the bed on my own and kissed nana on the forehead. I was shocked when I sensed how cold she was and rushed immediately out of the bedroom.' I commented, 'I think that your repressed memory of that fearful incident, is the cause of your current phobia. You associate bedrooms with death. The fact that God revealed your problem is a sure sign that it is the Lord's will to help you. I'll pray now in the expectation that you will recover.' I did pray with him, and as far as I can recall he had no sleeping problems afterwards.

GUIDANCE IN DELIVERANCE PRAYER

Surely it is significant that when Jesus sent the disciples out to preach the good news to the whole world, he said that the first sign of power they would be given was the power to drive out evil spirits (cf. Mk 16:17). The curse and penalty of sin came into the world as a result of the devil's envious temptation of Adam and Eve. When Jesus died on the cross, he defeated Satan. As Col 2:15 tells us, 'He disarmed the principalities and powers and made a public example of them, triumphing over them .' So when Christians evangelise, not only do they proclaim that Jesus, by his death, has lifted the curse of sin, and is removing its penalty, he also wants to deliver us from the oppression of the evil one. The Church says that there are two ways of doing this. Firstly, there is the solemn rite of exorcism which can only be performed by a priest appointed by the bishop. It is a sacramental which is administered to people, who over time, have forfeited their freedom to a demonic power. Secondly, there is deliverance prayer which can be offered by any believing Christian in order to free others from oppressive or obsessive spirits. Neal Lezano has influenced many Catholics who are interested in the deliverance ministry by means of his excellent books, *Unbound: A Practical Guide to Deliverance,* and *Resisting the Devil: A Catholic Perspective on Deliverance.*[5] In both he proposes five keys, or steps in the dynamic of deliverance, namely, repentance and faith; forgiveness; renunciation, authority and blessing. Like others engaged in the deliverance ministry I have found that it can be hard at times to identify the vulnerabilities that left the person open to the influence of the evil one. That is where a prophetic revelation from the Lord can enable the one praying to identify an entry point. Once the problem has been diagnosed in this charismatic way, the one ministering can pray in an accurate, focused way with the assurance that God's word will not return to God empty without achieving its purpose.

GUIDANCE AT HEALING SERVICES

As the ministry of people like Kathryn Kuhlman, John Wimber Damian Stayne and others have shown, words of knowledge are sometimes granted to those praying for physical cures, particularly at healing services. Let me give a number of examples:

Many years ago I conducted a number of workshops, on different aspects of healing, in a parish in Singapore. As far as I can remember we had a number of well attended healing services in the large parish church. I can recall that at one of those services I got a word of knowledge about a man who was suffering from a serious liver disease. Having mentioned the condition I saw a man in the congregation raise his hand to indicate that he was the one in question. I said a prayer from the altar and moved on.

When the service was over, the man came into the sacristy and said that he was indeed suffering from a serious liver complaint. I can't remember what it was exactly. He asked for a personal prayer, so I laid hands and prayed with him. When I got back from Singapore, I received an email from the man. He recounted, that soon after my departure, he had gone to a hospital for a scheduled appointment. He described how his liver had been checked and how the doctor had expressed great surprise because he could find no sign of disease, and couldn't explain why it had disappeared. But the man who sent the email said that he knew why his liver was normal, God had healed him. Not only was I delighted, I could see the intimate connection there had been between the prophetic word and effective healing. God's living word carries out what it says.

In 2005 I joined Damian Stayne of the *Cor et Lumen Christi* community to conduct a Miracle Rally in the Friend's Meeting House in Euston, London. It was two days after the London bombings of July 7th. Before we started I can recall asking Damien whether he relied on words of knowledge when he was praying for healing. As far as I remember he said that normally he didn't. However, when we got to the time when he was ministering to the hundreds of people who were present, I heard him speak a word of knowledge. He said there was a woman present who was not at peace with her sister and that they hadn't talked with one another for many years. He said that the Lord was urging the woman to make her peace with her sibling by means of heartfelt forgiveness. Then he moved on.

Eventually, in his usual style, he began to mention different ailments such as cancer, arthritis and so on. He would ask people who had one or other of the ailments he had mentioned to put up their hand or stand. Then he would utter a prayer command and tell the illness to go. At one point he addressed people at the front of the congregation who were in wheelchairs. He urged them to stand up. I was amazed when I noticed one stout lady lift herself out of her wheelchair and stand. The following day when Damian asked people who had been healed the previous day to come forward and share their story with the rest of us, I noticed that the lady I had seen getting out of her wheelchair was walking to the stage, climbing the steps and coming toward the microphone where Damian wanted to interview her. The woman explained that the word of knowledge about a person who had been alienated from her sister for years was meant for her. 'I think,' she said, 'that we hadn't talked for about thirty years. I knew God was speaking to me, and I made a decision to forgive my sister from my heart. Then when we were told to get out of our wheelchairs and stand, I knew that the word was for me. Although I hadn't been able to walk for sixteen years I felt I would be able to stand, and with God's help I did.'

A few weeks later Damian rang me to say there was a happy addendum to the story. The woman who had been healed searched for her sister, and with the help of the Salvation Army found where she was living. She headed North on a train and eventually found her sister's house. When she knocked at the door, her sister opened it, but at first didn't recognise who her visitor was. Then the truth dawned on her, and she exclaimed, 'My God, you are my sister.' Instead of being resentful she was delighted to see her long lost family member and gave her a warm hug. That was the completion of the healing that had begun with an accurate word of knowledge about the need to forgive.

A number of years ago I was a speaker at a conference in Wales. I was due to give a talk on the gifts of the Holy Spirit, one of which is the word of knowledge i.e., an inspired intuition about some unknown fact. Before going out on stage, I asked the Lord if he wished to give me such a word so that I would be able to illustrate the section of my talk which dealt with the charism of prophecy with a concrete example. With that, the image of a woman came to mind. It seemed as if something was wrong with one of her eyes and that it was causing her a good deal of pain. In the course of my talk sometime later, I referred to this mental image. When the talk was over a woman came forward. She said that the moment I mentioned the symptoms, she knew that she was the person in question. Apparently, two assailants had attacked her a year before. They had beaten her up and hit her in the face. The sight in one eye had been temporarily damaged and the other eye was causing her a lot of pain. A number of us gathered round and prayed for her. Because of the word of knowledge we were convinced that we were praying within the will of God and that the Spirit was acting. Well, a few hours later the painful eye was restored, the pain was gone, never to return. Not only that, the traumatic effects of the attack, such as panicky fear and apprehension, melted away over a period of a few hours, so that the woman was filled with an inner sense of peace.

MINISTERING WITHIN ONE'S MEASURE OF FAITH

In Rom 12:6, St Paul wrote, 'We have different gifts, according to the grace given us. If a man's gift is prophesying, let him use it in proportion to his faith.' It would have to be said that the precise meaning of this verse is hard to establish. Scholars maintain that it can be translated in different ways and that it is open to a number of interpretations.[6] I don't want to rehearse all those difficulties here. To begin, it is worth noting, that once again Paul highlights the importance of prophecy. It seems to me that there are three ways to interpret what Paul had in mind when he talked about prophesying 'in proportion to one's faith,'[7] one objective and two subjective.

Firstly, Paul may be saying that when the charism of prophecy is exercised it needs to be measured against the faith, i.e., the entire Gospel message, to make sure that it does not contradict it in any way. In this context it is significant that Paul doesn't say 'in proportion to *his* faith.' Secondly, the word faith can be understood in a more subjective sense as a reference to saving faith as firm trust in the Person of Jesus and the saving merits of his death and resurrection. Thirdly, others understand the phrase in terms of charismatic faith, which is the faith that moves mountains (1 Cor 13:2). I suspect that one can legitimately understand the phrase, 'in proportion to the faith,' in all three senses. However, as someone who has occasionally exercised the prophetic gift in ministry situations, I lean toward the third understanding. One can only engage in deeds of power such as deliverance, healing and miracle working, if they are rooted in a prophetic revelation which has manifested the here and now will of God. Otherwise one could be ministering in a vain and presumptuous way that would fail to be effective. Jesus talked about the difference between notional belief and heartfelt faith when he said, 'I tell you the truth, if anyone says to this mountain, 'Go, throw yourself into the sea,' *and does not doubt in his heart* [my italics] but believes that what he says will happen, it will be done for him' (Mk 11:23-24).

CONCLUSION

Thanks to the internet, and Youtube, one can see the charism of prophecy being exercised in ministry situations. Let me cite three examples that have inspired me. When I was a young priest I was very much influenced by the ministry of Kathryn Kulhman. She healed people as a result of words of knowledge during large miracle services. Although she died in 1976, there are inspiring videos on Youtube which record what she said and did. The late John Wimber was gifted with revelation of a prophetic kind. There are videos on Youtube which not only enable us to hear his teaching on words of knowledge and prophecy, they also show him exercising those gifts as a prelude to effective ministry together with his collaborator Blaine Cook. Todd White is a street evangelist who relies on words of knowledge to guide him in healing people and thereby revealing the love of Jesus to them. Videos in which he is interviewed and shown in action are well worth watching because they build faith.

NOTES

1. St Thomas Aquinas, *Summa Theologiae: A Concise Translation*, ed. Timothy McDermott (London: Methuen, 1991), 451
2. *http://dhspriory.org/thomas/SS1Cor.htm#122 (Accessed 15/10/2015).*
3. Cf. Pat Collins, C.M., *Expectant Faith and The Power of God* (Dublin: Columba, 1998).
4. Cf. Pat Collins, C.M., 'Claiming the Promises of Scripture,' in *Word and Spirit* (Dublin: Columba, 2011), 104-125.
5. *Unbound* (Grand Rapids: Chosen Books, 2003); *Resisting the Devil* (Huntington: Our Sunday Visitor, 2009).
6. Dr. Paul Kariuki Njiru has written a long commentary on this verse in his book, *Charisms and the Holy Spirit's Activity in the Body of Christ: An Exegetical-Theological Study of 1 Cor 12:4-11 & Rom 12:6-8* (Rome: Gregorian University, 2002), 245-260.
7. Cf. Joseph Fitzmyer, S.J., *Romans: A New Translation with Introduction and Commentary* (New Haven: Yale University Press, 1998), 647.

TWENTY

Prophetic Leadership

Over the years I have come to admire the gift of leadership in the secular and religious spheres. In politics I admire people like Angela Merkel and Nicola Sturgeon and in the Christian world I admire Pope Francis and Anglican archbishop Justin Welby. As Prov 11:14 says, 'Without wise leadership, a nation falls' and, by extension, so do all kinds of companies, groups, associations and communities. Not surprisingly therefore, a great deal has been written about the subject of leadership. Let me mention a few examples.

Some secular ideas on leadership

Max Weber (1864-1920) was a founder of the science of sociology. In one of his books, *The Sociology of Religion* he included a chapter on prophets.[1] He said that they are people endowed with charisma which he described as, 'a certain quality of an individual personality, by virtue of which he is set apart from ordinary men and treated as endowed with supernatural, superhuman, or at least specifically exceptional powers or qualities.'[2] I smiled wryly when I read his observation that the prophet declares new revelations because of his or her charisma, whereas a priest serves a sacred tradition. It is no accident, he said, that almost no prophet has come from the priesthood! He maintained that there were two kinds of prophet, exemplary and ethical. The former, leads by example, rather like the ecstatic prophets in the Old Testament, whereas others preach the will of God rather like the major and minor prophets of the Old and New Testaments. Regardless of whether a prophet is predominantly ethical or exemplary in character, he or she receives prophetic revelation, a fact that is recognised by the prophet and those that he or she influences. He said that people who possessed charisma were often regarded as leaders. Their authority and legitimacy depended on their being accepted as genuine messengers of God. However, he felt that there is a tendency in communities to ritualise the charism of prophecy and to institutionalise it in a way that lacks an on-going prophetic dimension.

Now we move from the sociology of religion to the realm of psychology. Millions of people have taken the Myers-Briggs Type Indicator Test which is based on Carl Jung's theory of personality. It not only indicates which of sixteen personality types each person belongs to, it also highlights the characteristic strengths and weaknesses which are associated with each personality type. Furthermore, the test can also describe the typical leadership style which is associated with each of the personality types. While they will not be described here, there are many good books which can be consulted for enlightenment.[3]

The Disc Personality Test has also been used by millions of people. The four letters in the word disc have the following significance:

D is for dominance and refers to people who place a lot of emphasis on accomplishing results and success in a confident way.

I is for influence and refers to people who place a lot of emphasis on such things as openness, relationships and influencing or persuading others.
S is for steadiness, and refers to people who place a lot of emphasis on cooperation, sincerity, and dependability.
C is for conscientiousness, for people who put a lot of emphasis on quality, accuracy, expertise, and competency.

The test highlights eight leadership styles[4] :

1. *Pioneering*. They can be courageous, passionate leaders who inspire others to take chances on new directions. They might be impulsive, overconfident leaders who use their charm to gain support for impractical ideas.
2. *Energising*. Energising leaders can be upbeat, eager, and willing to take chances on colourful new ideas. They can also be scattered, erratic leaders who see little need for consistency.
3. *Affirming*. At their best, they can be supportive leaders who work to create a respectful, positive environment. At their worst, they can be indirect, conflict-averse leaders who fail to hold others accountable.
4. *Inclusive*. Inclusive leaders can be sincere, accommodating people who collaborate with others to make decisions where everyone wins. Sometimes they can be passive, overly trusting leaders who let others take advantage of their supportive, patient nature.
5. *Humble*. They can be modest, fair-minded leaders who provide reliable outcomes through steadiness and consistency. They can also be rigid, overly cautious and afraid to move beyond the status quo.
6. *Deliberate*. Deliberate leaders can be conscientious, disciplined people who provide high-quality outcomes through careful

analysis and planning. They can also be risk-averse, perfectionist leaders who pay little attention to the human element.

7. *Resolute*. They can be questioning, independent leaders who aren't afraid to challenge the status quo to get better results. They can also be cynical, insensitive leaders who seem intent on putting a negative spin on everything.
8. *Commanding*. Commanding leaders can be powerful and decisive, enlisting others to work quickly toward ambitious goals. Or they can be forceful, egotistical leaders who push others at the expense of morale.

Allied to this secular notion of leadership are the related subjects of management and administration, strategy and tactics. Managers in businesses and organisations co-ordinate the efforts of people to accomplish explicit goals and objectives by using available resources in an efficient and effective way. Administrators handle the day-to-day practicalities of an organisation. They formulate a strategy which deals with the larger, overall plan that can contain several tactics. Tactics are the plans, tasks, or procedures that can be carried out as part of a larger strategy. While all leaders are good at formulating strategy they are not necessarily managers and administrators. Conversely, not all managers and administrators are leaders.

Good leaders differentiate between needs and priorities. The president of an American steel company went to a New York consultant. 'I'll pay you any price,' he said, ' if you will tell me how to get more things done without undue stress.' The consultant replied: 'At night spend five minutes analysing what you need to do the following day. 'Write them down on a sheet of paper, but place them in their order of importance. Then tackle the first item as soon as you get to the office. Stick to it until it is finished. Then move to the number two and so on. Test this method as long as you like, and then send me what you think it is worth.' Sometime later the consultant received a note from the company president. Enclosed was a cheque for $25,000 with the words, 'For the most helpful advice I ever received.'

Evidently the New York consultant knew about the *Pareto Principle*, or the 80/20 rule. It states that if a person has listed ten goals in their order of importance, and tackles the top two, 80% of his or her effectiveness will be derived from them. Only twenty per cent of his or her effectiveness will be derived from the other eight! People who fail to discriminate between top priorities and lesser needs, can end up using a lot of energy achieving very little. Leaders know that time management is really worth-while. It increases efficiency, while protecting the person from the tyranny of having to respond to an endless succession of needs. In the name of worthwhile priorities leaders say 'no' with a good conscience. Instead of reacting to needs, leaders are proactive in pursuing their priorities.

In Mk 1:35-38 there is evidence that as a prophetic leader Jesus distinguished between pastoral needs and evangelical priorities. On one occasion we are told how he declined to return to a village to heal people (i.e. pastoral needs). He replied, 'Let us go somewhere else - to the nearby villages - so I can preach there also. That is why I have come' (i.e. evangelical priorities). Arguably he was able to distinguish between evangelical priorities and pastoral needs as a result of prophetic insight received in prayer.

RELIGIOUS PERSPECTIVES ON LEADERSHIP

There are also many studies which look at the topic of leadership from a more Christian point of view. Some of them are biblical in approach. The prophets were referred to as seers, people to whom divine revelations were granted in visions, sometimes with implicit or explicit reference to future events. For instance, in 1 Chron 29:29 we read, 'the events of King David's reign, from beginning to end, are written in the records of Samuel the seer, the records of Nathan the prophet and the records of Gad the seer.' Prophets tune in to the providential purposes of God. As was mentioned earlier in the book the word providence includes two interrelated notions, firstly, foresight in the form of intimations of God's plan, and secondly, confidence that God will provide natural and supernatural help to carry out the plan. Through prophetic revelation, therefore, seers can tune into to the providential purposes of God.

Clearly, there were great leaders in both the Old and New Testaments such as Moses, Joshua, David, Job, Daniel, Jesus, Paul and Barnabas who were seers in that sense. Like many others I admire the prophet Nehemiah as a remarkable Old Testament leader for a number of reasons.[5] Firstly, he was a man of passion. Although he had never been in Jerusalem he was deeply disturbed when he heard that the holy city was de-populated, its walls had been breached and its gates destroyed (cf. Neh 1:2-3). This awareness evoked within him a strong desire to do something practical about the situation. Secondly, he was a man of vision. Following a time of prayer he had a divinely inspired plan for the restoration of the city (cf. Neh 1:4-10). Thirdly, he was a man of action. Having received permission from King Artaxerxes I to implement his plan to repair the walls of Jerusalem (cf. Neh 2:5) he made a discreet survey of the city to see exactly what would be needed (cf. Neh 2:11-16) and recruited many people to help him. Fourthly, Nehemiah made arrangements to protect the city and the workmen from the attacks of enemies who wanted to disrupt the work.

The contemporary Church desperately needs leaders like Nehemiah, men and women of passion, and practicality. But most of all they need a vision of a renewed Church, not a vision that is based on purely human thinking, but one which is inspired by the Holy Spirit. As the Psalmist warned, 'Unless the Lord builds the house, the builders labour in vain. Unless the Lord watches over the city, the guards stand watch in vain' (Ps 127:1). Sad to say, nowadays there seem to be very few leaders who have a prophetic vision of what the Church of the future might be like.

In the New Testament, Jesus was the outstanding leader. As the *Living Bible* translation says, 'Keep your eyes on Jesus, our leader and instructor' (Heb 12:2). At the heart of Jesus' notion of leadership was a paradox. 'The kings of the Gentiles,' he said, 'lord it over them; and those in authority over them are called benefactors. But not so with you; rather the greatest among you must become like the youngest, and the leader like one who serves. For who is greater, the one who is at the table or the one who serves? Is it not the one at the table? But I am among you as one who serves' (Lk 22:25-27). It is not surprising therefore, that it has been said that, 'Christian leadership is a dynamic relational process in which people, under the influence of the Holy Spirit, partner to achieve a common goal - it is serving others by leading and leading others by serving.'[6]

As a leader, Jesus had a clear God given vision. It found expression in the words, 'The kingdom of God is near' (Mk 1:15). Related to a vision statement is a mission statement, which describes the core purpose and focus of a person or group. It normally remains unchanged. A mission is different from a vision in so far as the former is the cause and the latter is the effect; a mission is something to be accomplished whereas a vision is something that informs and energises the mission. Jesus gave expression to his mission shortly after he was filled with the Spirit as a result of being baptised in the Jordan. Soon afterwards he said in his native synagogue in Nazareth, 'The Spirit of the Lord is on me, because he has anointed me to preach good news to the poor. He has sent me to proclaim freedom for the prisoners and recovery of sight for the blind, to release the oppressed, to proclaim the year of the Lord's favour' (Lk 4:18-19). The phrase, 'he sent me to bring good news to the poor' was the essence of his mission statement. He would accomplish it firstly, by lifting the curse of sin through the outpouring of the free gift of God's unconditional mercy, and secondly, he would remove the penalty of sin by healing sickness and suffering.

Conclusion

Many people mistakenly quote a saying attributed to St. Thomas Aquinas, which says, 'Grace builds on nature.' What he actually said was that 'Grace perfects nature.' This is so where Christian leadership is concerned. The Lord may have given an individual many natural leadership gifts such as good judgement, decisiveness, magnanimity, an ability to inspire and motivate people, courage etc. But from a biblical point of view God can choose such a person and endow him or her with graces such as wisdom, knowledge, God given vision, firm faith etc., which enable the person to be a good Christian leader. In my experience the gift of prophetic leadership is one of the most needed and precious in the Christian community.

NOTES

1. Max Weber, *The Sociology of Religion* (Boston: Beacon Press, 1964).
2. Max Weber, *'The Nature of Charismatic Authority and its Routinization, in Theory of Social and Economic Organization'* (New York: Free Press, 1964).
3. Cf. David Keirsey, 'Leading and Intelligence,' in *Please Understand Me II: Temperament, Character, Intelligence* (Del Mar: Prometheus Nemesis, 1998); Sandra Hirsh & Jean Kummerow, *Life Types* (New York: Warner Books, 1989).
4. Cf. Zigarmi, Fowler & Lyles, *Achieve Leadership Genius* (New Jersey, FT Press, 2007).
5. Cf. Gene A. Getz, *Nehemiah: Becoming a Disciplined Leader* (Nashville: Broadman & Holman, 1995).
6. The Christian Leadership Centre of Andrews University,USA

TWENTY ONE

VISION AND PROPHETIC MINISTRY

In Rom 12:6-8, St Paul said, 'We have different gifts, according to the grace given us... if it is leadership, let him govern diligently.' As a member of a religious order I have learned a lot about good and bad leadership. When Vatican II ended in 1965, religious congregations engaged in the arduous but exciting task of renewing themselves in the light of the conciliar documents. Over a period of time my congregation wrote our new *Constitutions* so that the *Common Rules*, which were written by St. Vincent de Paul, could be updated in order to be in tune with modern circumstances while remaining true to their core values. I can remember how, in our Anglo-Irish province, we engaged in two very interesting exercises. Firstly, we wrote a charism statement which expressed our vision. Secondly, we wrote a mission statement that expressed our aims, the values that informed them, and action steps we would take to realise them.

Every four years or so we meet for what is known as a provincial assembly, when we plan what we are going to do in the future, not only in the light of our charism and mission statements, but also in the light of the urgent, unmet needs of the time. Usually, after consultation with the members of our Anglo-Irish communities, a preparatory commission writes an agenda for the gathering. When we meet we pray together, e.g., the *Divine Office*, we listen to position papers, discuss them, and finally formulate lines of action. While all of that is laudable, what has struck me, time and time again, is the virtual absence of a prophetic dimension. Invariably, we fail to spend time listening for God's prophetic word. It always strikes me as a terrible pity, because, as a result, we are not fully attuned to divine providence. What I see happening in my own religious order is replicated in dioceses, parishes, church organisations, movements etc. There is leadership yes, but, more often than not, the prophetic dimension is notable by its absence.

Happily, there are exceptions. At this point I want to describe a contemporary example of prophetic leadership. When I was living in Detroit I heard Fr. Mark Montminy of St. Marie's in Manchester, New Hampshire, tell the story of how his struggling inner-city parish had been transformed from being a dispirited, introspective community to being a more outgoing, and evangelising one.[1] Mark himself had undergone a spiritual awakening when he experienced the power of the kerygma as a result of attending a *Cursillo* weekend and sometime later he was baptised in the Holy Spirit as a result of attending a Life in the Spirit Seminar. He said that when he arrived in St. Marie's parish, the pastoral council, like so many others, was reacting to urgent needs while neglecting pastoral and evangelical priorities. They were preoccupied with administrative issues such as the purchase of new boilers, reducing the parish debt, fixing a leak in the church roof and the like.

Prophetic leadership in the parish

As a good leader, Fr. Mark met with the parish pastoral council and invited them to pray for an outpouring of the Spirit and to dream prayerfully with him about the future of the parish. For the next five months each meeting began with an hour of prayer and afterwards by sharing dreams of what the parish could look like in five and ten years time. Fr. Montminy put the primary emphasis on the need to discover a God given vision for the parish and its future. Eventually, the parishioners expressed that vision in these words, 'Today, in the midst of a disintegrating society marked by alienation, loneliness and despair, we feel a particular urgency to rekindle and magnify the power of our Beacon; for only the Light of Christ can overcome the darkness of this present age and only His Love can bring us fullness of life. As we continue our journey with God, we will keep our eyes on the cross of Christ, our ears attentive to His Word, and our hearts docile to His Spirit. In that same Spirit we offer what follows as a means through which God's plan for our community is fulfilled.'

Too often when people decide to plan for the future in church circles, a quick prayer is said at the beginning of the meeting and then the participants get down to the serious work of discussing possibilities and setting goals. The danger is that, instead of being guided by the Spirit, as Paul advocates in Gal 5:18, they are merely guided by their own natural thinking and knowledge. In his Papal Message for the World Youth Day on July 24th 2007, Pope Benedict XVI endorsed the prophetic kind of approach, which had been used in St Marie's, when he said, 'Apostolic and missionary fruitfulness is not principally due to programs and pastoral methods that are cleverly drawn up and efficient, but is the result of the community's constant prayer.'

Encouraged by Fr. Mark, St. Marie's parish pastoral council also organised a meeting where any and every parishioner, who so wished, could speak about their hopes for the future. Following this process the pastoral council attempted to compose a mission statement in collaboration with every existing committee, society and organisation in the parish. Finally, they published the following mission statement. 'That all who join St. Marie Parish may come to know Jesus Christ in a more personal way, to accept Him as their Lord and Saviour, and to be His Light in the world, proclaiming the Good News in word and deed. We will do this:

- By providing a Eucharistic liturgy marked by living faith, prophetic preaching and inspiring music, in the midst of a welcoming environment.
- By emphasising the power of prayer - both in community and in the silence of hearts as a source of strength and nourishment for our spiritual journey.
- By offering catechetical programs which will lead people to a deepened understanding of our faith.
- By promoting social justice as a community through financial means and personal sacrifice and through community programmes.
- By being an evangelising community who reach out with the Gospel to families, friends and co-workers, and who welcome in our midst all those who seek Jesus; the Way, the Truth and the Life.'

It strikes me that this is not only a really inspiring mission statement, it is one that has been prompted by the Lord.

Although Fr. Mark Montminy was clearly a gifted leader in his parish, the prophetic element was shared by the community and expressed through the parish pastoral council together with the parish priest. In the meantime two other inspiring books about parish renewal have been published. The first was written by Fr. Michael White and Tom Corcoran. It is entitled, *Rebuilt: Awakening the Faithful, Reaching the Lost, and Making Church Matter.*[2] It describes how the parish of the Nativity in Baltimore, USA, was transformed to become missionary as a result of prophetic leadership. Another book by Fr James Mallon, entitled, *Divine Renovation: Bringing Your Parish from Maintenance to Mission*[3] tells a similarly inspiring story of transformation as a result of prophetic leadership.

Prophetic leadership in a lay community

In mid June 2008 four members of the Alpha board in Ireland suggested that interested people be invited to join them on four successive Sunday nights to pray for a Spirit filled revival in the Church. When the four weeks had passed the meetings continued by common agreement. Sometime later, eighteen or so participants acknowledged that they were becoming a community with a common sense of purpose. As a result they wrote a mission statement. It began by stating their guiding vision in these words, 'With the help of the Holy Spirit, we will engage in evangelisation ourselves, as well as teaching, training and equipping others who also desire to evangelise those who have not yet developed an intimate personal relationship with Jesus as their Lord and Saviour.' After that, they spelled out what they intended to do.[4] In May 2009 the members were led by the Spirit to call themselves the New Springtime Community and to choose the buttercup as their logo. Sometime later a team of four was elected to lead the community for three years when there would be another election. That group elects a leader from among their number subject to the approval of the community.

In 2011 the members agreed that they would commit their energies primarily, though not exclusively, to one or other of three interconnected streams; Evangelising; Formation; and Intercessory Prayer. When the community was founded the members sought and experienced God's guidance at each and every step, some of it prophetic in nature. Each week the community spends time in prayer and praise together followed by a time of complete silence when the members pay attention to the inspirations and revelations of God in whatever way they come. Each year the community has a vision day when the members go away to pray and plan together. They always ask for a spirit 'of wisdom and revelation' (Eph 1:17). A vital aspect of those days is the period of time when the members prayerfully wait upon the Lord in the expectation that they will receive guidance in a prophetic way. I have always been impressed and full of gratitude for the ways in which the Lord has revealed the divine Person, word and will to the community members in pictures, visions, scripture texts, and prophetic utterances.

Pope Francis as a prophetic leader

In the chapter on reading the signs of the times it was suggested that Pope Francis has a prophetic gift. Many secular magazines such as *Time* and *Forbes* have acknowledge that he is an exemplary Christian leader. They write articles that highlight his leadership qualities. For instance, writing in *Forbes*, Geoff Loftus said in an article entitled, 'Three Leadership Lessons From Pope Francis,' that, firstly, the Pope remains focused. His message, over and over again, to different audiences, is much the same: Show mercy to the poor and disadvantaged. Secondly, he models what he says by his behaviour. When he's not on the road or meeting with foreign dignitaries, he eats his meals in a cafeteria. When he meets strangers, he introduces himself, offering his hand and says, 'I am Pope Francis.' Thirdly, he takes responsibility for his own actions even in tiny matters. He is responsible for what he hopes for himself, making the people he leads responsible for measuring up.[5]

In the course of a homily he gave on Dec 15th 2013, Pope Francis said that a prophet is someone who is aware of past, present and future. He went on to explain, 'About the past: the prophet is aware of the promise and has in his heart the promise of God, he lives, remembers and repeats it. Then he looks at the present, at his people and feels the power of the Spirit to say a word to help them to their feet and to continue the journey towards the future. A prophet is a man of three times: the promise of the past, contemplation of the present; the courage to show the way towards the future. And the Lord always has guarded his people by means of the prophets, in difficult times, in times when the people were discouraged or destroyed.' He went on to say that in times of crisis, 'the intervention of the prophet is necessary. And the prophet is not always welcome, many times he is rejected. Jesus says as much to the Pharisees that their fathers had killed the prophets, because they said unpleasant things: they told the truth, they remembered the promise! And when prophecy is lacking the people of God recognise that something is missing: the life of the Lord is missing.' When there is no prophecy power becomes legality, legalism takes over... When there is no prophecy in the people of God, the void it leaves is filled by clericalism... But when legalism reigns, the Word of

God is absent and the people of God who believe, cry in their heart, because the Lord is absent: they need prophecy.'[6] I think that many people would agree that Pope Francis practices what he preaches where prophecy is concerned.

It is clear that Francis has an antipathy to clericalism. On one occasion he explained, 'When a priest leads a diocese or a parish, he has to listen to his community, to make mature decisions and lead the community accordingly. In contrast, when the priest imposes himself, when in some way he says, 'I am the boss here,' he falls into clericalism.'[7] On Monday, 22 December 2014, Pope Francis led a 15 point examination of conscience for bishops, priests and religious who worked for the Roman Curia. Among other things it was trying to counter a stultifying clericalism of a worldly and legalistic kind. At the time Pope Francis made it clear that the examination of conscience could be extended to include anyone who exercised a position of responsibility or leadership in the Church whether clerical or lay.[8] Briefly put, he asked the following questions. Do I:

1. Feel superior to those who work for me?
2. Demonstrate an imbalance between work and other areas of life?
3. Substitute formality for true human intimacy?
4. Rely too much on plans and not enough on intuition and improvisation?
5. Spend too little time breaking silos and building bridges?
6. Fail to regularly acknowledge the debt I owe to my mentors and to others?
7. Take too much satisfaction in my perks and privileges?

8. Isolate myself from direct contact with parishioners and volunteers?
9. Denigrate the motives and accomplishments of others?
10. Exhibit or encourage undue deference and servility?
11. Put my own success ahead of the success of others?
12. Fail to cultivate a fun and joy-filled work environment?
13. Exhibit selfishness when it comes to sharing rewards and praise?
14. Encourage parochialism rather than community?
15. Behave in ways that seem egocentric to those around me?

On Jan 27th 2015, Pope Francis gave a homily in Santa Martha on the subject of discovering and doing God's will. Although the secular articles on his leadership qualities do not mention this point, I suspect that it is the key to his approach. In the course of his discourse he said to all believers in general, and to those exercising leadership in particular, 'Do I pray that the Lord gives me the desire to do his will, or do I look for compromises because I'm afraid of God's will? Another thing: praying to know God's will for me and my life, concerning a decision that I must take now... there is the need to pray to know God's will, then to pray for the desire to do it, and finally when we have these things, we pray 'for the third time, to follow it. To carry out that will, which is not my own, it is God's will. And all this is not easy.' As the Pope has pointed out on other occasions, sometimes the Lord's will is revealed in a prophetic way. I think that many people would agree that at times Francis seems to exercise prophetic leadership because he is not only listening to God, the Lord is revealing the divine will to him in unexpected but prophetic ways which can be quite challenging.

Prophecy and persecution

In Deut 11:26-28, Moses spoke about two ways of living when he said, 'See, I am setting before you today a blessing and a curse - the blessing if you obey the commands of the Lord your God that I am giving you today; the curse if you disobey the commands of the Lord your God and turn from the way that I command you today by following other gods.' These words were mirrored in Jer 21:8, where we read, 'Tell the people, 'This is what the Lord says: See, I am setting before you the way of life and the way of death.' Jesus also spoke of two paths when he said, 'Enter through the narrow gate. For wide is the gate and broad is the road that leads to destruction, and many enter through it. But small is the gate and narrow the road that leads to life, and only a few find it' (Mt 7:13-14). An early Christian document from the first century called the *Didache* began with the line, 'There are two ways, one of life and one of death, and there is a great difference between the two.'

All of us are moulded, often in unconscious ways, by the beliefs, values, attitudes, and mores of the secular culture in which we live. All too often it is at variance with the beliefs, values, attitudes and mores of Christianity. Prophetic leaders, speak the truth in love on God's behalf. They are not motivated by a desire to please people. St. Paul expressed this God centred attitude of the true prophet when he said, 'Am I now seeking human approval, or God's approval? Or am I trying to please people? If I were still pleasing people, I would not be a servant of Christ' (Gal 1:10). That is why St. Paul could also say things like, 'Do not conform any longer to the pattern of this world, but be transformed by the renewing of your mind. Then you will be able to test and approve what God's will is - his good, pleasing and perfect will' (Rm 12:2).

In doing this prophetic people will often evoke a negative response from believers and unbelievers alike, people who don't wish to change their ethical behaviour to do with topics such as sinful relationships, social justice, sexual morality, abortion, euthanasia and ecology. Instead they will resist the call to change and ridicule the messengers of God.

Jesus warned that this is what prophetic leaders can expect when he said, 'Blessed are you when people insult you, persecute you and falsely say all kinds of evil against you because of me. Rejoice and be glad, because great is your reward in heaven, for in the same way they persecuted the prophets who were before you' (Mt 5:11-12). He knew this from personal experience. For example, in Mk 6:1-5 we read, 'Jesus left there and went to his home town, accompanied by his disciples. When the Sabbath came, he began to teach in the synagogue, and many who heard him were amazed. 'Where did this man get these things?' they asked. 'What's this wisdom that has been given him, that he even does miracles! Isn't this the carpenter? Isn't this Mary's son and the brother of James, Joseph, Judas and Simon? Aren't his sisters here with us?' And they took offence at him. Jesus said to them, 'Only in his hometown, among his relatives and in his own house is a prophet without honour.' In Mk 6:3 we read about Jesus' family, 'Is not this the carpenter, the son of Mary and brother of James and Joses and Judas and Simon? And are not his sisters here with us?'

According to *The Infancy Gospel of James* (140-160 A.D. approx) Joseph was a widower who had at least six children when he married Mary the mother of Jesus.[9] It would seem that the legal siblings of Jesus did not accept that he was a prophet. Indeed in

Mark 3:20-2 we are told that, 'Then he went home, and the crowd gathered again, so that they could not even eat. And when his family heard it, they went out to seize him, for they were saying, 'He is out of his mind.' Is it any wonder therefore, that Jesus warned in Jn 15:18-22, 'if the world hates you, keep in mind that it hated me first. If you belonged to the world, it would love you as its own. As it is, you do not belong to the world, but I have chosen you out of the world. That is why the world hates you. Remember the words I spoke to you: 'No servant is greater than his master.' If they persecuted me, they will persecute you also. If they obeyed my teaching, they will obey yours also. They will treat you this way because of my name.' So if you feel called to be a prophet, remember what Sir 2:1-2 says, 'My child, if you aspire to serve the Lord, prepare yourself for an ordeal. Be sincere of heart, be steadfast, and do not be alarmed.' Is it any surprise that St James advised, 'Take as an example of hardship and patience, brothers and sisters, the prophets who spoke in the name of the Lord' (Jm 5:10). Evidently, prophets are not popular!

Conclusion

This book has not only tried to describe the nature of the prophetic gift, it has also argued that it needs to be restored to the everyday life of the Church, in order that it may be attuned to the will of God and act in the power of the Holy Spirit. We conclude with a fitting quotation from Pope Benedict XVI, 'It seems clear to me that—considering the entire life of the Church, which is the time when Christ comes to us in Spirit and which is determined by this very pneumatological Christology - the prophetic element, as an element of hope and appeal, cannot naturally be lacking or allowed to fade away. Through charisms, God reserves for himself the right to intervene directly in the Church to awaken it, warn it, promote it and sanctify it. I believe that this prophetic-charismatic history traverses the whole time of the Church. It is always there especially at the most critical times of transition.'[10]

NOTES

1. Mark Montminy, 'The Story of an Evangelising Parish,' in *John Paul II and the New Evangelisation*, ed. Ralph Martin & Peter Williamson (Cincinnati: Servant Books, 2006), 236.
2. (Ann Arbor: Ave Maria Press, 2013).
3. (Mystic, CN: Twenty-Third Publications, 2014)
4. *http://www.newspringtime.ie/mission-statement (Accessed 15/11/2015).*
5. *http://www.forbes.com/sites/geoffloftus/2015/09/30/3-leadership-lessons-from-pope-francis/ (Accessed 15/11/2015).*
6. *http://www.asianews.it/news-en/Pope:-When-Church-lacks-prophecy-the-vacuum-is-filled-by-legalism-and-therefore-clericalism-29823.html (Accessed 6/1/2016).*
7. Jorge Mario Bergoglio & Abraham Skorka, *On Heaven and Earth: Pope Francis on Faith, Family, and the Church in the Twenty-First Century* (New York: Image, 2013)
8. *http://www.americamagazine.org/content/dispatches/pope-francis-gives-roman-curia-15-point-examination-conscience (Accessed 27/10/2015).*
9. Robert F. Hock, *The Infancy Gospels of James and Thomas* (Santa Rosa: Polebridge Press, 1995). This apocryphal Gospel, though written in the late second century, is attributed to James the Just, a son of Joseph who succeeded Peter as the leader of the Jerusalem church. The Christian historian Eusebius (265-340 AD) suggested that the bothers and sisters of Jesus were his first cousins, the children of Joseph's brother Clopas (cf. Lk 24:18) and his wife Mary (cf.Jn 19:25).
10. Joseph Ratzinger in 'Foreword,' to Niels Christian Hvidt, *Christian Prophecy: The Post-Biblical Tradition* (Oxford: Oxford University Press, 2007), viii.

EPILOGUE

I have travelled around the British Isles for about fifty years on my different motorbikes. At night time the headlamp is not as bright as those of a car. Whereas it does light up the road immediately around my bike, its beam only lights the road ahead in a progressively less effective way until nothing can be seen at all. I mention this because the headlamp on a motorbike is a bit like the gift of prophecy. While it reveals the truth about the present time quite clearly, it only throws an ever vaguer, less clear light on the future. Hence the title of this book, *Prophecy: Truth for Today, Light for Tomorrow.* That connection between present and future was referred to in Cardinal John Henry Newman's famous hymn which prays, 'Lead, kindly Light, amid the encircling gloom... I do not ask to see the distant scene; one step enough for me.'

WINTER OF DISCONTENT

It seems to me that believing Christians are entering a time of darkness, beginning in the Church and then in the secular world. As Church statistics of all kinds indicate, we are living at a period of mass apostasy from the Christian faith. Commenting on this situation St. John Paul II, said in par. 9, of *Ecclesia in Europa,* in our continent there, 'is an attempt to promote a vision of man apart from God and apart from Christ. This sort of thinking has led to man being considered as the absolute centre of reality, a view which makes him occupy - falsely - the place of God and which forgets that it is not man who creates God, but rather God who creates man. Forgetfulness of God leads to the abandonment of man. It is therefore no wonder that in this context a vast field has opened for the unrestrained development of nihilism in philosophy, of relativism in values and morality, and of pragmatism – and even a cynical hedonism – in daily life.'

As we noted in the chapter entitled, 'Five Recent Popes and the Signs of the Times,' John Paul II believed that absence from God inevitably leads to absence from one's deepest self. Such alienation has disastrous results. Carl Jung, a noted 20th century psychologist concurred with this view. He believed that if the self is unable to experience the divine, the personality becomes confused, neurotic and out of touch with its shadow side, i.e., the rejected, inferior, vulnerable aspect. Everyone has a shadow. The less it is embodied in the individual's conscious life, the blacker and denser it is. From the unconscious it poisons consciousness with negative, thoughts, feelings and attitudes. Jung believed that just as an individual can have a personal shadow, so a whole society can have a collective one. From the collective unconscious it can poison the consciousness of a group or nation with negative feelings, attitudes and prejudices. These people can then go on to project their shadow on to others, seeing and hating in them, what they have failed to acknowledge or accept in themselves. This is what happened in Nazi Germany. Having lost touch with their own collective shadow, many Germans projected it from their unconscious minds on to the Jews, gypsies, handicapped people etc. As a result millions of innocent men, women and children were murdered in the *Shoah*, or Holocaust.

Like Jung, theologian, Bernard Lonergan, S.J., believed that a lack of transcendence would lead to personal and social corruption and consequently cultural decline. He wrote, 'Corrupt minds have a flair for picking the mistaken solution and insisting that it alone is intelligent, reasonable, good. Imperceptibly the corruption spreads from the harsh sphere of material advantage and power to the mass media, the stylish journals, the literary movements, the education process, the reigning philosophies. *A civilisation in decline digs its own grave with relentless consistency.*'[1] When I was younger I felt that the USSR was a corrupt society in Lonergan's sense, and was convinced that eventually it would collapse due to the fact that it was built on the sand of a false, Godless philosophy. That collapse occurred suddenly in 1991.

In March of 2018 I attended a European Charismatic Leader's consultation in Assisi on the subject of prophecy. During one of our prayer times together I received what appeared to be a prophetic message which I recognise, in retrospect, had a certain affinity with some others which were recounted in previous chapters. It went as follows, 'Lower the flags all over Europe. Weep and mourn for the people, because I have died in their hearts. They have walked away from me in large numbers. They no longer acknowledge my sovereignty or keep my commandments. Warn the people, that in departing from me, they have departed from their true selves and from my blessings. Now they are on their own. Warn them, that their apostasy even frustrates the natural world, as they no longer mediate with me on its behalf. It is going to shake. There will be great storms, much rain will fall, rivers will overflow, crops will fail, many lives will be lost. The chaos in nature, will only be a reflection of the greater chaos in the hearts of many people. It too will break forth in destructive ways. Pray against the coming of this time of tribulation. Although your prayers will not be able to prevent it, they may lessen its severity. Times of chastisement and humbling are coming. You too will suffer with the many.' It would seem therefore, that if this is truly an inspired word from the Lord, the outworking of God's benevolent providence will be painful but purposeful.

Because of the silent apostasy of millions in Europe and elsewhere, it is my belief that, having lost contact with the living God, many people have also lost touch with their deepest humanity in the way that Pope John Paul, Jung and Lonergan have described. As a consequence, their unacknowledged selves have grown darker and more threatening. As this kind of alienation increases it could lead to a socio-political unrest. Recently, I was interested to see that, speaking about the economic crash in 2008, Mervyn King, a former governor of the Bank of England, said in *The End of Alchemy : Banking, the Global Economy and the Future of Money,* 'The crisis was not a failure of individual policy makers or bankers but of a system, and the ideas that underpinned it... There was a general misunderstanding of how the world economy worked.' A little later he predicted, 'Another crisis is certain, and the failure… to tackle the disequilibrium in the world economy makes it likely that it will come sooner rather than later.'[2] If there is another world wide economic crisis, it could be a catalyst that leads to all kind of unwelcome consequences.

For example, dating back to the 1970s there have been a number of prophecies which indicated that a time would come when money would lose its value, and when there would be a widespread lack of food. For example, in January 1976 the following prophetic word was spoken at a meeting of the National Service Committee of the Catholic Charismatic Renewal in the USA. 'Son of man, do you see that city going bankrupt? Are you willing to see all your cities going bankrupt? Are you willing to see the bankruptcy of the whole economic system you rely upon now, so that all money is worthless and cannot support you? 'Son of man, do you see the crime and lawlessness in your city streets, and towns and institutions? Are you willing to see no law, no order, no protection for you except the protection which I myself give you? 'Son of man, do you see the country which you love? Are you willing to see no country, no country to call your own except those I give you as my body? 'Son of man, do you see those churches you can go to so easily now? Are you ready to see them with bars across the doors? Are you ready to depend only one me and not on all the institutions of schools and parishes that you are working so hard to foster? 'Son of man, I call you to be ready for that. The structures are falling and changing. It is not for you to know the details now, but do not rely on them as you have been. I want you to make a deeper commitment to one another. I want you to trust one another, to build an interdependence that is based on my Spirit. This is an absolute necessity for those who would base their lives on me and not on the structures of a pagan world. 'I have spoken, and it will take place. My word will go forth to my people. They may hear and they may not, and I will respond accordingly. But this is my word. 'Look about you Son of man. When you see it all shut down, when you see everything removed which has been taken for granted, and when you are prepared to live without these things then you will know what I am making ready.'

In recent years I can recall writing a chapter in one of my books entitled, 'Sharing During Times of Economic Need,' which had something like this scenario in mind. Among other things I suggested that parishes should prepare for such an exigency by collecting non perishable food while they still could, for distribution during the time of crisis. I cited an example I had seen in Detroit during the downturn of the car industry. 'In the parish where I was living, the local conference of the St. Vincent de Paul Society was doing great work. Besides helping people to pay electricity and water bills and many other good works, they had a food pantry. In reality it was an area in the pastor's house where donated foodstuffs were stored. Each weekend there was a collection of non perishable food items that parishioners brought to the church in order to help the needy members of the community who were struggling to make ends meet. If any particular foodstuff was running low a request was placed in the parish newsletter. So much food came in each weekend, it overflowed on to a corridor. Then people, such as unemployed parents of large families, could call to the priest's house and discreetly request supplies. I must say that I found the whole enterprise most edifying. It was a good example of Christian faith expressed through love (cf. Gal 5:6).'[3] While it goes without saying that we have to proclaim the *kerygma* i.e., core Christian message, what will give it credibility in the years to come, is the fact that the believers live the *kerygma* by means of charitable deeds and action for justice.[4]

In November 2017, a number of Catholic Newspapers reported how Monsignor Mauro Longhi, a friend of the late St John Paul II, recounted in the course of a lecture how the Pope had told him during a hiking trip that he used to receive private revelation in visionary form. He said that on one occasion the Pontiff said as a result of a vision, 'Tell this to those whom you will meet in the church of the third millennium. I see the church afflicted by a deadly scourge. Deeper, more painful and more deadly than those of this millennium. It's called Islamism. They will invade Europe. I saw the hordes coming from the West to the East. They will invade Europe, Europe will be like a cellar, old relics, shadowy, cobwebs. Family heirlooms. You, the church of the third millennium, will have to contain the invasion. Not with armies - armies will not suffice - but with your faith, lived with integrity.'

As people experience painful upheaval in the world it may lead many of them, like the prodigal son, to come to their senses and to humbly seek the meaning of life. As Pope John Paul said in 1976, this dynamic which will effect believers as well as unbelievers, 'lies within the plans of Divine providence. It is therefore in God's plan, and it must be a trial which the Church must take up, and face courageously.'[5] You may remember that in chapter nine I referred to Joseph Ratzinger's view that the affliction of the Church and then of society could be a *felix culpa*, i.e., a happy fault, which could lead many, people to, 'find themselves unspeakably lonely... Then they will discover the little flock of believers as something wholly new. They will discover it as a hope that is meant for them, an answer for which they have always been searching in secret.' When, as a result of suffering and profound disillusionment, many people seek the Lord, the time will have come for the minority who have remained faithful to engage in a great evangelistic outreach, one that, hopefully, will lead to the new Springtime for Christianity which has been spoken about by popes John Paul II, Benedict XVI, and Francis.

As the latter said in par. 84 of *Evangelii Gaudium*, 'We feel that we must disagree with those prophets of doom who are always forecasting disaster, as though the end of the world were at hand. In our times, divine Providence is leading us to a new order of human relations which, by human effort and even beyond all expectations, are directed to the fulfillment of God's superior and inscrutable designs, in which everything, even human setbacks, lead to the great good of the Church.'

As I already mentioned, when I'm going places on my motorbike, especially at night, I rely on my headlamp to light my way. As Ps 119:105 says, 'Your word is a lamp to my feet and a light for my path.' While God's word in scripture will certainly light our way, we also need to be open to the prophetic word of God as truth for the present and light for the future. Recently, I came across a homily that Papal preacher, Fr. Raniero Cantalamessa had preached on John the Baptist. As he neared the end Fr. Cantalamessa quoted the following words from Rev 19:10, 'Jesus' testimony is the spirit of prophecy.' He went on to say that the spirit of prophecy is required to bear effective witness to Christ. Then he asked, is this spirit of prophecy in the Church? Is it cultivated? Or do we believe, implicitly, that we can do without it, depending instead on human efforts?

Having asked those important questions Fr Cantalamessa added, 'In 1992 there was a retreat for priests in Monterrey, Mexico, on the occasion of the 500th anniversary of the first evangelisation of Latin America. There were 1,700 priests and about 70 bishops present. During the homily I spoke about the urgent need that the Church has for prophecy. After Communion, prayer was offered, asking for a new Pentecost, in small groups scattered throughout the great basilica. I remained in the presbytery. At a certain moment a young priest came up to me in silence, knelt down in front of me and with a look I will never forget said to me: 'Bless me, Father, I want to be a prophet for God!' A chill went down my spine because I saw that he was clearly moved by grace.' Then Cantalamessa added, 'With humility we can all make that priest's desire our own, 'I want to be a prophet for God... someone who has fire in his heart, words on his lips, and prophecy in his outlook.'

So with Pope Francis we can pray, 'Lord, may we never lack prophets in your people. All of us who are baptised are prophets. Lord, save your people from the spirit of clericalism and legalism by helping us with the spirit of prophecy.'[6] If, having read this book, you are of the opinion that you have not yet received the charism of prophecy, be encouraged by the following words of Jesus, 'Anyone who receives a prophet because he is a prophet will receive a prophet's reward' (Mt 10:41). Let us identify and listen to the prophets among us, they are God's spokesmen and spokeswomen.

NOTES

1. *Method in Theology* (London: Darton, Longman & Todd,1972), 55.
2. (New York: W. W. Norton & Company, 2016).
3. *Word and Spirit* (Dublin: Columba, 2011), 163.
4. Pat Collins, C.M., *Encountering Jesus: New Evangelisation in Practice* (Luton: New Life, 2017).
5. Quoted by Ralph Martin in *The Final Confrontation* (Ann Arbor: Renewal Ministries, 2015), 7
6. Pope Francis at the Mass celebrated in 'Santa Marta' on the third Monday of Advent 2013.

Some Helpful Books

Adrienne von Speyr, *The Mission of the Prophets*. San Francisco: Ignatius Press, 1996.

Benedict Groeschel. *A Still, Small Voice: A Practical Guide on Reported Revelations*. San Francisco: Ignatius Press, 1993.

Bruce Yocum. *Prophecy: Exercising the Prophetic Gifts of the Spirit in the Church Today* . Ann Arbor: Servant Publications, 1976.

Dave Nevins, *Surrendering to Abundance: Receiving and Giving Spirit-Filled Messages*. CreateSpace Independent Publishing, 2015.

David Aune. *Prophecy in Early Christianity and Mediterranean World*. Grand Rapids: Wm. B. Eerdmans, 1983.

Jack Deere. *The Beginner's Guide to The Gift of Prophecy*. Ventura: Regal, 2001.

James D. G. Dunn. *Jesus and the Spirit*. London: SCM Press, 1975.

Niels, Christian Hvidt. *Christian Prophecy: The Post Biblical Tradition*. Oxford: Oxford University Press, 2007.

Paul Synave, O.P. and Pierre Benoit, O.P., eds, *Prophecy and Inspiration: A Commentary on the Summa Theologica II-II, Questions 171-178*. New York: Desclee, 1961.

Prospero Lambertini. *On the Beatification and Canonization of the Servants of God*. Vol. 3, Heroic Virtue. London: Thomas Richardson and Son, 1852.

R. L. W. Moberly. *Prophecy and Discernment* (Cambridge Studies in Christian Doctrine). Cambridge: Cambridge University Press, 2008.

Roy H. Schoeman. *Salvation is From the Jews: The Role of Judaism in Salvation History from Abraham to the Second Coming.* San Francisco: Ignatius Press. 2003.

Thomas Aquinas. *Summa Theologiae*. Edited by Brian McDermott. London: Methuen, 1989.

Timothy Paul Jones. *Rose Guide to End-Times Prophecy.* Peabody, Mass: Rose Publishing, 2011.

Wayne A. Grundem. *The Gift of Prophecy in 1 Corinthians.* West Broadway: Wipf & Stock, 1999.

Wayne Grundem. *The Gift of Prophecy in the New Testament and Today.* Wheaton: Crossway Books, 2000.

Yves Dupont, *Catholic Prophecy: The Coming Chastisement.* Rockford; Tan, 2009.

Alphabetic Index of Names and Topics

Further copies of this book can be obtained from

Goodnews Books
Upper level
St. John's Church Complex
296 Sundon Park Road
Luton, Beds. LU3 3AL

www.goodnewsbooks.co.uk
orders@goodnewsbooks.co.uk
01582 571011